Get on Track to FCE

Judy Copage
Lucrecia Luque-Mortimer
Mary Stephens
Unit tests by Peter Lucantoni

Longman

Coursebook

Pearson Education Limited
Edinburgh Gate
Harlow
Essex CM20 2JE
England
And Associated Companies throughout the World

www.longman-elt.com

(c) Pearson Education Limited 2002

First published in 2002
Seventh impression 2005

ISBN 0 582 451051

Set in Officina Sans 10.5/11.5 pt

Printed in Spain by Graficas Estella

Authors' Acknowledgements
With grateful thanks to Heather Jones, Kate Mellersh, Debra Emmett, Clare Nielsen-Marsh and all the team at Longman.

Publishers' Acknowledgements
The Publisher wishes to express thanks and appreciation to the following reporters:
Arek Tkacz, Agnieszka Tyszkiewicz-Tora (Poland); Lisa Girling (Spain); Nora Krichmar, Cristina Djivanian (Argentina); Mark Skipper (England); Georgia Pappas School, Helen Koumatou School, Kyriakos Petropuleas School, Stamatis Papadimitriou School, Mrs Anna Leventeris, Ms Zozetta Androulaki, Mr Yiannis Stamatakos; Georgia Zographou (Greece).

We are grateful to the following for permission to use copyright material:
@Bristol for an extract adapted from an @Bristol leaflet; D C Thomson & Co, Limited for an extract adapted from "Do horoscopes rule your life?" published in Shout August / September 1999, © D C Thomson & Co, Limited 1999; EMAP Elan for an extract adapted from "Did you match the right boy to the right room?" published in Bliss August 1999; Encyclopaedia Britannica for an extract adapted from Encyclopaedia Britannica CD 99 – Multimedia Edition, Users' Guide; Friends of the Earth for an extract adapted from "Climate catastrophe!" published in Earth Matters – Kids' Matters Section; Merris Griffiths for an extract adapted from her "Why are soap operas so popular?" published on the website of the University of Aberystwyth www.aber.ac.uk; Guardian Newspapers Limited for extracts adapted from "How to put cars off-limit" by Paul Brown published in The Guardian 6th June 1997, © The Guardian 1997, and "Designer's uniforms perks up schoolyard" by Hadley Freeman published in The Guardian 3rd July 2001, © The Guardian 2001; Longleat Enterprises Limited for an extract adapted from their information leaflets; Museum of London for an extract adapted from the Museum of London website www.museum-london.org.uk; National Magazine Company Limited for an extract adapted from "Food for life" by Catherine Turner and Caroline Brien published in Company February 1999; News International Newspapers Limited for extracts adapted from "Creating a hit" by Dave Coombs published in The Funday Times 30th May 1999, © Times Newspapers Limited 1999, and "Solving the secret of genius" by Richard Woods published in The Sunday Times 6th June 1999, © Times Newspapers Limited 1999; Nexus Media Limited for an extract adapted from "Ice maiden" by Kathryn Leigh published in Health and Fitness January 2000; npower for an extract adapted from "Keep in touch" published in energise Autumn 2000; Penguin Books Limited for an extract adapted from The Way Things Work by David Macauley published by Dorling Kindersley, text © 1988 David Macauley; The Royal Pavilion, Brighton, for an extract adapted from www.aboutbritain.com; Salon Internet, Inc. for an extract adapted from "A talk with Bill Bryson" by Don George which first appeared in Salon.com, at http://Salon.com (an online version remains in the Salon archives); Scholastic Inc. for extracts adapted from "Cut to fit" published in Current no.4 March / April 2001 Mary Glasgow Magazines, and "Build a pizza pyramid" published in Scholastic Choices November / December 2000; and Understanding Global Issues Limited for an extract adapted from "Healthy cities: improving urban life – the Curitiba experience" published in Understanding Global Issues 96/4.

In some instances we have been unable to trace the owners of copyright material and we would appreciate any information that would enable us to do so.

The Publishers would like to thank the following for permission to use photographs:

Andes Press Agency: pp. 23, 65, 69; Ardea : pp. 167; Art Directors & Trip: pp. 7 (2), 21, 23, 31, 32 (2), 46, 49, 52 (3), 53, 57, 65, 70, 91, 93, 96, 97, 103 (4), 105 (2), 121, 123, 126 (2), 141(2), 151, 153 (2), 154, 156, 157 (2), 167 (3), 111; BBC: pp. 109, 159; Big Pictures: pp. 41, 75, 86; Biofotos/Heather Angel: pp. 113; John Birdsall: pp. 13, 29, 31, 97, 125 (3); Anthony Blake Photo Library: pp. 57 (6); Bubbles Picture Library: pp. 31 (2), 123; Bridgeman Art Library: pp. 171; Bristol Science Centre: pp. 32; Britstock: pp. 15, 41, 143; Collections: 41, 167; Corbis: pp. 58; 64, 95, 130, 111, Dineshi: pp. 84; Empics: pp. 16 (2) 17 (2), 49; Greg Evans Picture Library: pp. 7, 23, 25, 28, 41, 55, 57 (2), 65 (2), 70, 7 (2), 117, 125, 151, 155, 172 (2); Mary Evans: pp. 84 (2), 99 (2), 102, 147; Format Photographers: pp. 37; Scott Goldman: pp. 138; Ronald Grant Archive: pp. 161, 162, 164 (2); Robert Harding Picture Library: pp. 17, 23, 36, 65 (2), 83, 93 (2), 96, 123, 133, 143, 156 (2); Hulton Picture Library: pp. 91 (2), 99 (6), 104; Hutchison Picture Library: pp. 43 (2), 70 (2), 94; Image Bank: pp. 159; Impact Photo Library: pp. 7, 31, 41 (2), 117; Katz Picture Library: pp. 12; Lebrecht Collection: pp. 149; Longleat: 33; Moviestore Collection: pp. 41 (2), 159 (4), 160, 163 (2); Museum of London: pp. 33; Oxford Scientific Films: pp. 93, 119, 122, 124 (3), 157, 159; V. Panagioutou: pp. 101; Panos Pictures: pp. 143, 151; Pearson Eduction (James Walker): p54; Pearson Picture Library: pp. 159 (2); Photofusion: pp. 31; Pictor: pp. 23; Powerstock zefa: pp. 7, 9, 31, 57, 59, 92, 117, 119 (2), 134, 146, 167(2); RNIB: pp. 121; Redferns: pp. 75 (5), 78 (2), 159; Retna: pp. 83, 159; Rex Features: pp. 37, 39, 46 (2), 49, 55, 54 (2), 59, 58, 60, 72, 83 (3), 87, 88, 93, 101, 107, 111, 126, 129, 134, 156; Science Photo Library: pp. 107, 175; Sporting Pictures: pp. 15 (5), 18, 19, 21, 49, 83, 159; Still Pictures: pp. 101; Stockmarket: pp. 9, 12 (2), 15, 29, 31(2), 35, 151; Thames TV: pp. 159; The Funday Times: pp. 77; John Walmsley: pp. 167 (4); Janine Wiedel: pp. 7, 9 (4), 24, 25 (3), 41, 45, 49 (2), 66 (2), 67 (2), 80, 91, 125 (3), 145 (4), 153.

Cover photograph kindly supplied by Telegraph Colour Library.

The publishers have made every effort to trace copyright holders. However, if any material has been incorrectly acknowledged, we would be pleased to correct this at the earliest opportunity.

Illustrated by Tony Coles (Plum Illustration); Clive Collins; Mark Duffin; John Haslam; Graham Humphries (The Art Market); Ned Jolliffe; Bonnie Ogden; Michael Ogden; Mark Watkinson (Illustration Ltd).

Designed by Venita Kidwai
Project Managed by Debra Emmet

Contents map

The First Certificate in English

The Cambridge First Certificate in English consists of five papers, each testing a different area of language ability. *Get on Track to FCE* teaches you the skills that are tested in each paper and introduces you to all the task types in the exam. The tasks start at a lower level, but gradually increase in length and difficulty. By the end of the book, you will have reached FCE level. In Units 17-20, you can test the skills you have learned.

Paper	Task description	Task focus
1 Reading • 1 hour 15 minutes • 4 texts, each with a task • 35 questions in total	**Part 1:** matching headings or summary sentences to paragraphs in a text (6 or 7 questions) **Part 2:** choosing between 4 options to answer questions or complete statements (7 or 8 questions) **Part 3:** deciding which sentences or paragraphs should fit into gaps in a text (6 or 7 gaps) **Part 4:** matching a series of prompts (usually questions) to the correct parts of a text (13-15 questions)	**Part 1:** reading for the main points in a text **Part 2:** reading for details in a text **Part 3:** understanding text structure **Part 4:** reading for specific information
2 Writing • 1 hour 30 minutes • 2 parts, each with a writing task or choice of tasks • 120-180 words	**Part 1:** a compulsory writing task with input material, e.g. advertisements, letters, notes etc. **Part 2:** one writing task from a choice of 4 which may include: a letter, an article, a report, a composition, a short story (and a set book question)	**Part 1:** processing given information to produce a formal/informal letter in an appropriate style **Part 2:** writing for a specific reader, using appropriate format and style
3 Use of English • 1 hour 15 minutes • 5 parts, 4 texts and a set of sentences • 65 questions	**Part 1:** choosing which word from 4 options fits in gaps in a text (15 gaps) **Part 2:** filling in gaps in a text with an appropriate word (15 gaps) **Part 3:** using a given word to complete a new sentence so that it means the same as a previous sentence (10 sentences) **Part 4:** identifying which lines of a text contain words that are unnecessary (15 lines) **Part 5:** changing the form of a word to make it fit in a text (10 words)	**Part 1:** Vocabulary **Part 2:** Grammar and vocabulary **Part 3:** Grammar and vocabulary **Part 4:** Grammar **Part 5:** Vocabulary
4 Listening • Approximately 40 minutes • 4 parts • 30 questions	**Part 1:** 8 short extracts, each with a multiple-choice question **Part 2:** 1 longer extract with 10 gap-fill questions (note-taking or sentence completion) **Part 3:** 5 short extracts to match to one of 6 options **Part 4:** 1 longer extract with 7 questions either true/false, yes/no, or multiple choice	**Part 1:** understanding main points, relationships, feeling, attitude, opinion, intention **Part 2:** understanding specific information or deducing meaning **Part 3:** as for Part 1 **Part 4:** understanding attitude and opinion as well as specific information and gist
5 Speaking • Approximately 14 minutes • 4 parts	**Part 1:** interlocutor interviews each candidate (3 minutes) **Part 2:** comparing and contrasting 2 photos (1 minute each candidate, 4 minutes in total) **Part 3:** candidates work together on an interactive task based on a visual prompt (3 minutes) **Part 4:** interlocutor leads a discussion with both candidates (4 minutes)	**Part 1:** giving personal information **Part 2:** giving information and expressing opinions **Part 3:** exchanging information and ideas, justifying opinions, agreeing/disagreeing, suggesting, speculating **Part 4:** developing the topic from Part 3

1 One world

Speaking ▶ Part 1

1 About you

1 Look at the photos of young people in different countries. Say what is happening in each photo.

2 What aspects of daily life do the photos illustrate? Match them to the topics below.

A Home	**E** Leisure time
B Family life	**F** Hobbies
C Studies	**G** Work
D Daily transport	

3 Which situations in the photos are most similar to your own life?

2 Quiz

Complete the quiz about yourself.

WHO ARE YOU?

My name is

The thing I like best about my town is

The person I like best in my family is

My favourite subject at school is

My favourite free-time activities are

The kind of music I like listening to is

In three years' time I will

In 10 years' time I will

3  Interview a partner

1 How did your partner complete the quiz? Ask and answer questions like these to find out what you have in common.

'What do you like best about your town?'

'Who do you like best in your family?'

'What's your favourite school subject?'

2 Complete these sentences about you and your partner. Then tell the class.

> We both like ...
> Neither of us likes ...
> My partner likes ... and so do I.
> My partner doesn't like ... and neither do I.

▶▶ WB p.2

Reading ▶ *Part 1*

Communicating

1 Think about the topic
Look at the title of the text and the photos. How many reasons can you find for learning English?

2 Reading strategy

▶▶ *first sentences*

Read the first sentence of a paragraph carefully. It often summarises the main idea of the paragraph and can help you predict what follows.

1 Read the first sentence only of paragraphs 1–3. What will each paragraph be about? Choose from a)–e).

	Paragraph
a) some good advice about how to learn a language	.....
b) differences between American and British English	.....
c) how many people speak English today	.....
d) how a knowledge of other languages can be useful	.....
e) the history of the Spanish language	.....

2 Read the whole of each paragraph quickly. Were you right?

3 Read for main points
1 Read paragraph 1 again.

1 Where do people speak English a) as a first language? b) as a second language? <u>Underline</u> the countries named.

2 How many people are studying English?

Now choose the best heading for the paragraph.

A English in schools

B How to communicate in English

C English, a global language

2 Read paragraph 2 again.

How many times do the words *language, work, job, career* **appear?** <u>Underline</u> **them. Then choose the best heading for the paragraph.**

A Jobs for young people

B Languages for work

C How to make friends

3 Read paragraph 3 again.

What do the words *First, Second, Third* **introduce?**

Can you think of a good heading for the paragraph?

1

<u>The English language is growing faster than at any time in the last 400 years.</u> At the beginning of the twenty-first century, about 400 million people speak English as a first or **native language**[1], mainly in
5 Britain, the USA, Canada, Ireland, Australia, New Zealand and South Africa. English is also an official 'second' language in over 70 countries, including India, Nigeria and Singapore. In fact, the number of people who speak English as a second language is
10 now greater than the number of native speakers. On top of that, as many as one billion people are learning English at any one time. And there are about 1.5 billion people who can communicate in English for work or leisure. That adds up to around
15 a quarter of the world's population! So should we stop learning other languages and concentrate on English? Definitely not! Real communication between nations means learning each other's languages.

2

<u>In recent years, there has been a huge increase in</u>
20 <u>the number of areas where foreign languages are needed.</u> The workplace is becoming more and more international and many people are now travelling abroad as part of their job. The people who stay at home are more likely to work in a
25 **multi-lingual**[2] environment. So a knowledge of other languages is more important than ever before for your career. Remember the saying: 'You can use your own language to buy things, but if you want to sell, you must use the language of
30 your customers.' As well as being able to speak the foreign language, it's important to know about the culture of the country where the language is spoken. **Cultural awareness**[3] is just as important as linguistic skills. If you plan to work abroad, a
35 good knowledge of the language is also **a springboard to**[4] new and exciting social contacts and friendships.

across the globe

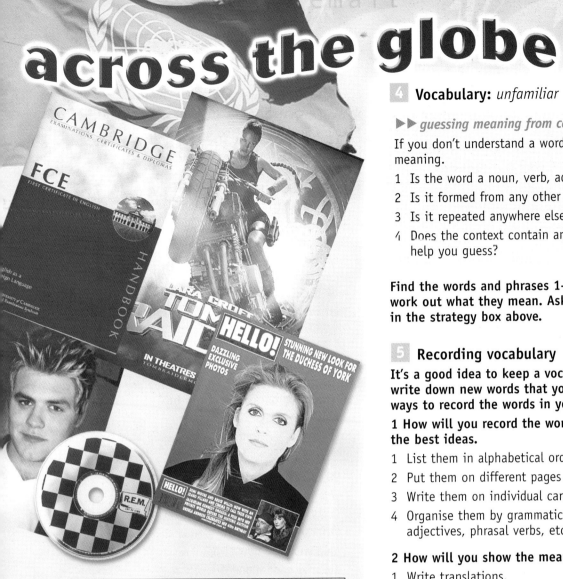

3

To learn a language well, you need to do more than just go to class – there are several strategies
40 you can use to develop your reading, writing, listening and speaking skills:

- First, try not to use your own language in class or translate things into your own language. When you translate, you are **relying on**[5] your
45 native language, not developing your foreign language skills.
- Second, don't worry about making mistakes when you speak. Learning to communicate in a foreign language is a process, and making
50 mistakes is a natural part of that process.
- Third, read as much as possible. Try to guess the meaning of new words from the context as far as possible. If you cannot, look them up in a good monolingual dictionary.
55 - And **last but not least**[6], keep a vocabulary notebook. Write down at least three new phrases each day, including idioms. Try to use these words whenever you can.

4 Vocabulary: *unfamiliar words*

▶▶ *guessing meaning from context*

If you don't understand a word, try to guess the meaning.

1 Is the word a noun, verb, adjective, ...?
2 Is it formed from any other words you know?
3 Is it repeated anywhere else in the text?
4 Does the context contain any information that can help you guess?

Find the words and phrases 1–6 in the texts. Try to work out what they mean. Ask yourself the questions in the strategy box above.

5 Recording vocabulary

It's a good idea to keep a vocabulary notebook and write down new words that you meet. There are different ways to record the words in your notebook:

1 How will you record the words in Exercise 4? Choose the best ideas.

1 List them in alphabetical order.
2 Put them on different pages according to the topic.
3 Write them on individual cards.
4 Organise them by grammatical category (nouns, adjectives, phrasal verbs, etc.).

2 How will you show the meaning? Choose the best ideas.

1 Write translations.
2 Write an example sentence from the text.
3 Write examples that are true for you.
4 Draw a picture.

6 💬 Over to you

Read these two comments by English teenagers. Which do you agree with?

'*I think it is good that we as a human race have more and more in common. We should all speak the same language so it is easier to communicate.*'

'Communication between countries is important. But it is also important to have an identity. Everyone should learn many languages, not just one.'

▶▶ WB p.3

Grammar: *present simple/continuous*
▶ *p.181*

grammar file 4

A Present simple: facts, habits and routines

1 *My dad* **speaks** *Russian fluently.*

2 *I* **usually learn** *three new words* **every day.**

B Present continuous: temporary actions

3 *My brother* **is studying** *Italian* **this year/at the moment.**

C Present simple or continuous?

• **state verbs**

4 *I* **know** *(NOT* ~~am knowing~~*) English well.*

• **with a change of meaning**

5 *I* **think** *French is very difficult.* (my opinion)

6 *I'm* **thinking** *of learning German.* (I'm considering the idea)

! What's wrong?

1 *He does his homework at the moment, so he can't come to the phone.* X

2 *'What are you doing?' 'I'm a student.'* X

3 *That book is belonging to me.* X

4 *I go often to Brazil for my holidays.* X

1 Present simple or continuous?

Read the conversations and fill in the gaps. Use the verbs in brackets.

1 **A:** How good is your English?

   B: Not bad. It *is getting* (get) better slowly.

2 **A:** What kind of job .... (your father/do)?

   B: He .... (work) for a bank. He .... (travel) on business at the moment.

3 **A:** Where .... (you and your family/usually spend) the holidays?

   B: Oh, we .... (always/go) to France.

4 **A:** Which .... (you/prefer), doing sport or playing computer games?

   B: Neither. I .... (usually/listen to) music in my spare time. But my brother .... (love) playing football.

5 **A:** .... (your sister/have) any hobbies?

   B: Yes, she .... (play) the guitar really well. And now she .... (learn) the piano.

2 Questions

Write a question for each of these situations.

1 Your friend is busy. You ask: What/you/do?

   What are you doing?

2 You make a new friend. You ask: Where/you/live?

3 You want your friend's opinion of your favourite singer. You ask: What/you/think of (NAME)?

4 Your friend sounds angry. You ask: Why/you/shout?

5 You want to phone a friend in Britain. You ask: anybody/know/code for Britain?

6 Your friend has lost something. You ask: What/you/look for?

7 Your friend has a brother. You ask: Which school/your brother/go to?

3 Frequency adverbs

Rewrite the sentences below so they are true for you. Use a word or phrase from the box.

always	often	occasionally	rarely	seldom
sometimes	from time to time		now and again	
never	once or twice a week		every day	

1 I get up at six in the morning.

   I always get up at six in the morning.

2 I go to the cinema.

3 I swim in the sea.

4 I help with the housework.

5 I am in a good mood.

6 I do my homework.

7 I speak English.

4 Mixed tenses

Read the postcard and fill in the gaps with the correct form of the verbs in brackets.

Dear Marcus,

I (1) .... (write) you this postcard from Madrid! I (2) .... (have) a fantastic time here. I (3) .... (not feel) homesick at all!

I (4) .... (go) to Spanish classes every day from 8 a.m. to 2 p.m. I (5) .... (study) hard but I (6) .... (still/not/speak) the language very well!

I (7) .... (stay) with a great family. They're very kind to me and they (8) .... (often/take) me out sightseeing.

The eldest boy, Juan, is my age. He (9) .... (have) lots of friends. We (10) .... (often/meet) them after class and we (11) .... (sometimes/go) to the cinema or a disco together. Spanish people (12) .... (certainly/know) how to enjoy themselves!

See you in two weeks,

Love, Paula

▶▶ **WB** p.4

Vocabulary building

▶▶ *using your dictionary*

In this book you will do a lot of exercises to help you build your knowledge of English vocabulary. The **LONGMAN** *Active Study* **DICTIONARY** can help you with these exercises.

Try the exercises on this page. Then look at the extracts from the LONGMAN *Active Study* DICTIONARY on p.177 to check your answers.

1 Words that go together

Fill in the gaps with the correct form of *get* or *have*. Then ask and answer the questions with a partner.

1 What do you and your friends do when you want to .... fun?

2 Did you .... a party last weekend? If not, what did you do?

3 Do you ever .... angry with your best friend? Why?

4 Who do you usually go and talk to if you .... problems and worries?

5 Who looks after you if you .... ill at school?

6 Do you and your family often .... dinner in a restaurant?

7 Do you usually walk to school or do you .... the bus?

8 What do you do with your CDs when you .... tired of them?

9 Do you .... a bath or a shower in the mornings?

10 How often do you go for long walks? Have you ever .... lost?

2 Choosing the right word

Fill in the gaps with the right word.

trip / travel / voyage / journey

1 One day, I'd like to .... round the world.

2 To visit my grandparents, we have to go on a long car ....

3 In the past, people sailed to America by ship, and the .... took six weeks.

4 My dad's gone abroad on a two-day business ....

3 Word formation

Complete these sentences using the appropriate form of *obey*. Be careful! Sometimes you need the negative form.

1 My dog is very .... ; he does everything I tell him. (*adjective*)

2 If you .... the law, you may go to prison! (*verb*)

3 The leader demanded .... from all the boys in his group. (*noun*)

4 The headmaster sent the boy home in disgrace because he'd been so .... (*adjective*)

4 Phrasal verbs

Each of the sentences below contains a phrasal verb formed with *go*. Complete the verbs by filling in the gaps with the appropriate particle(s), e.g. *on*, *out*.

1 I've gone *off* playing computer games; I prefer going *out* with friends now.

2 Oh no! My friend's gone .... my homework book!

3 How long has your sister been going .... her boyfriend?

4 Go ..... ! I want to hear more!

5 When I finish school, I want to go ..... teaching; I'd like to teach English.

6 Do you go ..... very often during the week or do you stay at home?

5 Prepositions/prepositional phrases

Fill in the gaps in the sentences with *on* or *in*. Then rewrite the sentences so they are true for you.

1 I was born ..... August.

2 I grew up ..... a farm.

3 I have been ..... a school trip recently.

4 I live ..... a village.

5 My best friend was born ..... the 30th of July.

6 I always speak ..... a quiet voice.

7 I went ..... holiday for two weeks last year.

8 I'll finish school ..... three years' time.

9 I've got a poster of my favourite band ..... my bedroom wall.

10 When I'm ..... trouble, I go and talk to my best friend.

▶▶ **WB** p.5

Listening ▶ Part 1

1 Listening strategy

▶▶ *listening for a purpose*

Always read the question before you start listening. The question tells you what information to listen for and gives you a purpose for listening.

1 Look at the Listening task. Read questions 1–6. For each question, decide:

a) who is speaking.

b) what is the situation.

2 What do you have to listen for? Match questions 1–6 to the following descriptions a)–d).

a) FACTS or DETAILS   Question(s) .....

b) PLACE/LOCATION   Question(s) .....

c) OPINIONS   Question(s) .....

d) FEELINGS   Question(s) .....

3 Think about words or phrases you can listen for. Match these expressions to each option A or B in questions 1–3. Write A or B on the line.

Question 1

1 act, actor, part, lines   .....

2 sing, play music, song, singer   .....

Question 2

1 teacher, have patience with (someone)   .....

2 beginners, teacher, have a go at   .....

Question 3

1 a thriller, scenery, made on location   .....

2 the cover, a thriller, a novel   .....

4 Now think of words and phrases you might hear for questions 4–6.

2 📼 Listening task

1 Listen to the recording and do the task. You will hear each extract twice.

2 Compare your answers with the class. What phrases made you choose your answer?

3 💬 Over to you

1 Have you been to a film or concert recently? Did you enjoy it? Why/Why not?

2 What did you like best about the place that you went to on holiday this year?

Listening task

You will hear people talking in six different situations. For questions 1–6, choose the best answer A or B.

1 You hear two friends talking in a coffee bar. Where have they been?

   A to a film

   B to a concert

2 You hear a boy talking to a friend on his mobile phone. What past event is he remembering?

   A trying to learn something

   B trying to teach someone something   2

3 Two friends are out shopping. What type of shop are they in?

   A a bookshop

   B a video shop   3

4 You hear two friends talking about going hiking. What is Stephen worried about?

   A having an accident

   B feeling wet and uncomfortable   4

5 You hear a girl talking about the place where she goes on holiday. What does she like best about this place?

   A spending time with her family

   B meeting people of her own age

6 You hear two friends talking about a piece of equipment. What is it?

   A a mobile phone

   B a personal computer

Writing: *brainstorming ideas*

1 Sample writing task

Anna has received her first letter from John, a Canadian student. Read the extract below. How many questions does John ask? <u>Underline</u> them.

Well, that's enough about me. Now it's your turn. What do you do in your free time? Have you got any special hobbies? What's your family like? And what sort of town do you live in?

Please write back soon!

Best wishes,

John

2 💬 Brainstorm ideas

1 Look at the notes Anna made before writing her reply. Then look again at John's questions. Which ideas do you think Anna should include? Tick them.

free time = listening music, disco, cinema

fav. hobbies = dancing, playing guitar

brother at college, sister (age 5) not at school yet

subjects I'm studying at school

live on coast – exciting town – popular – lots to do!

our neighbours & their pets

dad – has own business

my friends – how we met

mum – works at university

my bedroom – how it's decorated

2 Now group the ideas you have ticked under these headings.

<u>My family</u>   <u>Free time/hobbies</u>   <u>My town</u>

3 Read a sample answer

1 Now read Anna's reply.

1 Which of her notes did Anna use? Did you tick the same items?
2 Does Anna group her ideas into paragraphs?

2 Which topic does Anna deal with in each of her paragraphs?

Para. 1 Introduction: Thanks for letter
Para. 2 Topic: ....
Para. 3 Topic: ....
Para. 4 Topic: ....

Dear John,

Thanks for your letter – I really enjoyed reading it. Life in Canada sounds great! I hope I can come out and visit you one day.

I haven't got a big family – just one brother and one sister. My mum's a teacher at the university, and my dad's got his own business. My brother's studying Computer Science at college. My sister's only five and she starts school next month – she's really excited about that!

In my free time, I usually listen to music with my friends (I love rock music) or we sometimes go to the disco. I like the cinema, too. My favourite hobbies are dancing and playing the guitar.

My town is quite big. It's on the coast and I live near the harbour. There are lots of things to do so it's quite exciting. It's popular with tourists and gets very crowded in summer.

Write back soon!

Yours

Anna

4 Writing skills: *expanding notes into sentences*

1 Compare the notes and sentences below.

1 What sort of words do we add when we expand notes into sentences? Underline the words.

2 What other changes are there, for example in punctuation, capital letters, etc.?

NOTES	SENTENCES
1 dad – has own business	1 My dad has got his own business.
2 mum – works at university	2 My mum works at the university.
3 fav. hobbies = dancing, playing guitar	3 My favourite hobbies are dancing and playing the guitar.

2 Complete the rule.

> When you expand notes into sentences, you may need to add:
> a) pronouns.
> b) auxiliary verbs.
> c) ....
> d) ....
> You should also write abbreviated words in full.

3 Turn these notes into full sentences, starting with the word given.

1 hobbies = listening music & rollerblading
  My ....

2 have fantastic collection CDs
  I ....

3 sometimes go karaoke parties with friends
  I ....

4 brother = studying to be doctor
  My ....

5 third year at secondary school, best subject = Maths
  I .... and ....

6 lot of homework – so not much free time!
  I ....

Over to you

5 Writing strategy

Read the notes.

▶▶ *brainstorming ideas*

• Think what you are going to write about and make notes.

• Group your notes according to topic.

• Choose the best ideas from your notes.

6 Writing task

Read this extract from a letter you have just received. Underline the topics Barbara wants you to tell her about.

> So, I've told you all about myself. Now I'd like to know about you! Please tell me about your interests, friends, and school.
>
> I'm really looking forward to hearing from you.
>
> Yours,
>
> Barbara

7 Brainstorm ideas

1 On a piece of paper, write a heading for each of the topics.

A My interests
B ....
C ....

2 Note down as many ideas as you can think of under these headings. Remember to write notes, not whole sentences.

3 Your letter should be about the same length as Anna's on p.13. Decide which ideas to include. Remember that you can't include too many! Tick the most interesting ideas in your notes.

8 Write

Write your letter, using your notes in Exercise 7.

• Use the same introduction and ending as Anna's letter.

• Write three main paragraphs, one for each topic heading above.

• Write between 120–180 words.

9 Check your work

When you have finished, read your letter carefully. Are the grammar, spelling and punctuation correct?

▶▶ **WB** p.6

2 Sport

Speaking ▶ Part 2

1 About you

1 Look at the photos. Which ones show:

a) a team sport? b) an individual sport? c) a winter sport? d) a water sport? e) a track and field event?

2 Which of the sports do you enjoy watching?

3 Do you do any of these sports yourself?

2 Vocabulary

1 Look at the words in the box. Put them into two groups. Then match the words to the sports in the photos.

helmet   goggles   paddle   swimming pool
ball   gloves   court   boxing ring   shorts
net   piste   pole   sports hall   boots
stadium   trainers   swimming cap   pitch

A Place	B Equipment/clothing

2 What qualities do you need for these sports? Choose from the box.
Example:
To play/do ... , you need to be very strong and fit.

to be fast   fit   strong   agile   powerful
to have good concentration   stamina   good balance

3 Which adjectives would you use to describe each sport?

dangerous   exciting   aggressive
competitive   boring   popular

3 🔊 Listen

1 Listen to a student talking about high-jumping and football. Tick the points she mentions.

- where you can do the sport
- how easy/difficult it is
- funding for sportspeople
- equipment
- training

2 Listen again and complete the sentences in the box with ideas from the recording. Do you agree with the opinions?

comparing and contrasting
In this picture there's a ...
I think this sport is pretty hard because ...
In the other picture I can see ...
This sport is probably easier because ...

4 💬 Speaking task: *photos*

Take turns to choose two sports in the photos and compare them. Use the points in Exercise 3.1.

▶▶ WB p.7

Reading ▶ Part 2

1 Think about the topic

1 Look at the photos. What sport are they playing?

2 Look at the words in the box. Find these items in the photos.

> ice rink   ice skates   hockey stick
> puck   goalposts   net   barrier

3 Answer these questions.

1 Is ice hockey popular in your country? Why/Why not?

2 Why do you think people enjoy playing or watching it?

2 Predict

Look at the title and sub-heading of the article.

1 Who is the article about?

2 What questions did the interviewer probably ask?

3 Reading strategy

▶▶ *skimming*

To get a general idea what a text is about:
• read the first paragraph (the introduction) and the last paragraph (the conclusion).
• read the first and last sentences of the other paragraphs.

1 Read the first and last paragraphs of the text. Complete these sentences about Fiona King.

1 Fiona started playing ice hockey at the age of ....

2 She recently became captain of ....

3 Although ice hockey is a difficult sport, Fiona ....

2 Read only the first and last sentences of paragraphs 2–5. What is each paragraph about? Match the paragraphs to the topics.

Topic	Paragraph
a) the kind of training a hockey player does	.....
b) the qualities you need to play ice hockey	.....
c) the problems of practising as a team	.....
d) Fiona's physical appearance and build	.....

3 Now read the whole of each paragraph 2–5. Were you right?

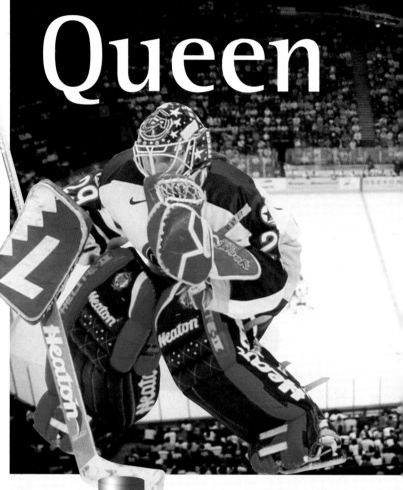

Queen

1 ▶ Ice hockey has been an important part of Fiona King's life ever since she was a child. She started going to figure-skating lessons when she was ten, then joined her local ice-hockey team at the age of twelve. 'I loved figure skating but I wasn't very good at it,' she says. She joined the national ice-hockey team at sixteen and now, at twenty-six, she has just become its captain.

2 ▶ Ice hockey is tough and fast and demands good balance and agility, plus the ability to **concentrate**[1]. 'Top players can skate at 40–50 kilometres per hour and shoot the puck at 160 kilometres per hour,' explains Fiona. 'The team has five players and a goalkeeper on the ice at any one time. Players <u>are constantly coming on and off the ice every few minutes, so you have to be ready to play alongside anyone in the squad</u>.' Fiona has always played a forward position, so she has to be aggressive and ready to attack the goal. 'I wear a helmet with a cage over my face, shoulder pads, leg and elbow pads and gloves, but I still get bruises,' she says.

3 ▶ People look surprised when they meet Fiona face to face and hear that she is a hockey player. They expect her to be taller and look stronger. 'It's true that I'm not very tall, only 1.6 metres. It's a physical game and when we play international teams, we often face very big women,' Fiona says. 'Our average age is 18 and <u>we are quite small, but we are fast and fit, and this</u> **makes up for**[2] our small size.'

of the ice

Kathryn Leigh interviewed ice-hockey captain, Fiona King

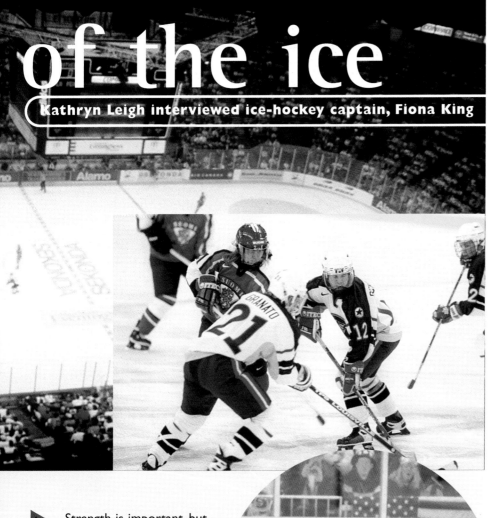

▶ **4** Strength is important, but, above all, ice-hockey players need to **build up**[3] stamina. Fiona is responsible for her own fitness training and <u>tries to do something every day</u>. 'It's very important to practise fast skating because it helps to <u>increase</u> your fitness,' she explains. 'Work in the gym is also essential. I did four sessions last week, about an hour and a half each, with a lot of aerobic exercises and some light weightlifting.'

▶ **5** Training with the full team of 15–20 players isn't easy. The squad meets once or twice a month to work together on skills, such as controlling, passing and shooting the puck. They also get together for week-long training camps before any important tournament. But like most ice-hockey teams, they have problems getting enough time on the ice. They have to use public ice-rinks and they can only practise after the public has gone home. 'Last Friday we started at 11.15 p.m. and finished at 1 a.m.,' she says. 'It's tough. You have to **put in**[4] a lot of hard work <u>to get anything out</u>.'

▶ **6** The <u>difficulties</u> of the sport have <u>never</u> **discouraged**[5] Fiona King. '<u>I've played for my country for ten years</u> and I'll **keep going**[6] <u>as long as I can</u>,' she says. 'It's a fantastic sport. I love it.'

---

4 Read for detail

Now read the whole text again carefully and answer the following questions in your own words.

Paragraph:

1 How old was Fiona when she started playing for her country?
2 Why does she wear protective equipment during the game?
3 In what ways is Fiona different from other players?
4 How does she keep fit?
5 Why does Fiona's team practise late at night?
6 How does Fiona feel about the difficulties of the sport?

5 Vocabulary: *unfamiliar words*

▶▶ *using the context*

If you don't understand a word, read the whole sentence carefully, as well as the sentences before and after the word. Look for explanations that can help you guess the meaning.

Find the words 1–6 in the text. Use the <u>underlined</u> parts to help you work out what they mean. Then match each word to the right definition below.

a) have so much of one quality that it does not matter that you do not have others
b) spend time and effort doing something
c) think carefully about something you are doing
d) continue doing something
e) make someone less likely to do something
f) make something increase or grow

6 💬 Over to you

How does ice hockey compare with your favourite team sport?

▶▶ **WB** p.8

Grammar: *present perfect/past simple*
▶ *p.181*

grammar file 5

A Past simple: actions completed at a definite time

1 *Michael joined his national soccer team **three months ago**.* (we know when)

B Past actions related to the present

• **present perfect simple**

2 *Michael **has played** five matches **this season**.* (the season isn't over)

3 *He **hasn't scored** any goals yet.* (up to the present)

4 *His team **has (already) won** the Cup twice.* (we don't know when exactly)

• **present perfect continuous**

5 *Michael **has been playing** for 50 minutes.* (he's still playing)

6 *The football pitch is wet. It **has been raining**.* (present result)

! *What's wrong?* ―――――――

1 *I have played football yesterday.* ✗

2 *Did you finish that book yet?* ✗

3 *He's been playing three matches this season.* ✗

---

1 Past simple or present perfect simple?

Complete the conversations using the verbs in brackets.

1 **A:** Do you know how to play squash?
   B: No. *I've never played.* (never/play) it.

2 **A:** Are you any good at diving?
   B: Yes, I .... (have) lessons when I was on holiday.

3 **A:** What do you think of the new sports centre?
   B: I've no idea. I .... (not/see) it yet.

4 **A:** Have you ever met a famous sportsperson?
   B: Yes, I .... (meet) the captain of the national team last month.

5 **A:** Is that a new bike?
   B: Yes, my parents .... (buy) it for me yesterday.

6 **A:** Why are you looking so pleased?
   B: I .... (just/hear) that my team .... (win) the Championship.

2 Present perfect simple or continuous?

Complete the conversations using the verbs in brackets.

1 **A:** Sam looks very hot!
   B: That's because he .... (run).

2 **A:** .... (you/ever/play) hockey?
   B: Yes, I .... (play) for about two years now.

3 **A:** Why .... (Dad/not/buy) the tickets for the match yet?
   B: Because he .... (just/find out) the price!

4 **A:** How many games of tennis .... (you/play) so far today?
   B: None. We .... (wait) for a court all morning!

5 **A:** How long .... (you/learn) to ski?
   B: For ages. I .... (have) lots of lessons, but I .... (not/make) much progress so far!

3 💬 Time expressions

Fill in the gaps with the correct word from the list. Some may be used more than once. Then, ask and answer the questions with a partner.

since / never / ever / ago / for / already / yet / still

1 I haven't played a game .... ages. Have you?

2 What's your favourite sport? How long .... did you start playing?

3 I can skate but I haven't tried roller-blading .... What about you?

4 My sister .... hasn't learnt how to swim! Have you?

5 I've been asking Dad to let me go bungee-jumping .... I was 14. Have you .... tried it?

6 I've .... been on a skiing holiday. Have you?

7 I only started playing baseball last year but I've .... won a place in the national team. Have you .... won a sports competition?

4 Extra word

There is one unnecessary word in each sentence below. Cross it out.

1 I have ~~yet~~ tried scuba diving.

2 We have been played table tennis twice this week.

3 Tom learned how to ski since five years ago.

4 The athlete has won a medal in the last Olympics.

5 I've been just listening to the match on the radio.

6 Luke hasn't already found his boots yet.

▶▶ **WB** p.8

Vocabulary building

1 Adjectives + prepositions

1 Look at the examples in the box.

good / bad / hopeless / skilful	at
afraid / capable / envious / fond / proud / scared / tired	of
angry / happy / impatient / satisfied	with

2 🗩 Fill in the gaps with *at, of* or *with*. Then ask and answer the questions with a partner.

1 Are you good ..... sport? If so, which ones are you best ..... ?

2 Are you satisfied ..... the sports facilities in this area? If not, why not?

3 Are there any sports you are bad ..... ? Which are you worst ..... ?

4 Is there any sport or activity that you are afraid ..... doing? Why?

5 Which national sportsman or woman do you feel most proud ..... ? What are his/her most important sporting achievements?

3 Now complete these sentences with an appropriate adjective. Choose from the box in Exercise 1.1.

1 I wouldn't be *capable* of running a marathon.

2 Harry's mum was .... *with* him for playing football in his best clothes.

3 I was .... *of* watching the football match, so I switched off the TV and went to bed.

4 My friends are .... *of* me because I've got a ticket for the Cup Final.

5 Top footballers are extremely .... *at* controlling the ball.

6 Bob's family were very .... *of* him for winning the 100-metre race.

2 Words that go together

1 Put these sports into the correct column. How many more sports can you add?

tennis   swimming   gymnastics   soccer
weightlifting   athletics   jogging   aerobics
ice skating   hockey   running

do	play	go
	tennis	

2 🗩 Now ask and answer questions like these about the sports in Exercise 2.1.

How often do you play tennis?

Have you ever done weightlifting?

3 Choosing the right word

<u>Underline</u> the correct word in each pair. Can you answer the questions?

1 How many players are there in a baseball *group/team*?

2 In which sport(s) do players *make /score* a goal by kicking the ball between the goalposts?

3 In which game(s) do players *hit /kick* the ball with a bat?

4 In which sport(s) do players *wear/carry* knee pads?

5 Name the country which *gained/won* most medals in the 2000 Olympics.

6 Who did France *beat /win* in the 2000 football World Cup?

7 In tennis, how many *games /plays* are there in a set?

8 In which sport(s) do players bow to their *opponents/ enemies* before they start?

4 Lexical cloze

Read the text below and decide which answer A or B best fits each space. There is an example at the beginning (0).

0 A spectator   **B** audience

BASKETBALL

Basketball is a popular **(0)** *.A.* sport in the USA. It is usually played indoors on a rectangular **(1)** .... . In basketball, you have to **(2)** .... the ball with one hand all the time you are running. If you score more goals than your opponents, you **(3)** .... the game.

The Harlem Globetrotters were the first all-black basketball **(4)** .... in the USA. They became world famous because they were all such talented players. They could even **(5)** .... the ball to a team-mate behind them without turning their heads. It looked easy but it took hours of **(6)** .... . They played exhibition **(7)** .... all over the world. They were great entertainers – but they made sure they **(8)** .... their opponents, too!

1 **A** stadium	**B** court
2 **A** drop	**B** bounce
3 **A** win	**B** gain
4 **A** group	**B** team
5 **A** present	**B** pass
6 **A** practice	**B** trial
7 **A** matches	**B** plays
8 **A** won	**B** beat

▶▶ WB p.10

1 Read the notes 1–7 below. Try turning them into questions.

DUNCAN SHORT: FOOTBALLER

1 Year of birth: ....

2 Father's job: ....

3 Age Duncan started playing football: ....

4 Sport he played with his brother: ....

5 Sport he gave up for football: ....

6 Football club he joined at 16: ....

7 Job he's been offered: ....

2 Match these questions to the notes. Are they the same as your questions?

a) Which club did he join when he was 16?

b) What sport did he play with his brother?

c) What job has he been offered?

d) How old was he when he started playing football?

e) What does/did his father do?

f) When was he born?

g) What sport did he give up for football?

Listening ▸ Part 2

1 Before you listen

You are going to hear an interview with a successful footballer.

1 Who is the most famous footballer in your country?

2 What do you know about his life and career?

3 How can gifted young footballers become professionals?

2 Listening strategy

▶▶ *understanding notes*

You may need to complete notes when you listen. To make sure you know what information you have to listen for, you can turn the notes into full questions before you listen.

3 🔊 Listening task

1 Listen to the recording. Complete the notes in Exercise 2. Use only one or two words, or a number, in each space. You can write numbers as figures.

2 Listen again to check your answers.

3 Compare your answers. Use your completed notes to say what you know about Duncan.

Example:

Duncan was born in ...

4 💬 Over to you

Do you agree or disagree with this statement? Give reasons.

'*People take football too seriously.*'

Writing: planning

1 Sample writing task

Jim has just received a letter from an American friend, Kevin. Read the last paragraph of Kevin's letter and <u>underline</u> the questions.

1 How many questions does Kevin ask Jim?

2 What topics should Jim write about in his reply to Kevin?

2 Read a sample answer

1 Read Jim's answer to Kevin's letter. How many paragraphs does Jim's letter have?

2 Match the paragraphs in Jim's letter with the questions in Kevin's letter.

3 Look at paragraph 2 of Jim's letter. One sentence summarises the content of the paragraph. This is the 'topic sentence'. Find it and <u>underline</u> it. Then do the same with paragraphs 3 and 4.

Anyway, that's all my news. But what about you? Why haven't you written? What have you been doing recently? Have you got any plans for the holidays? Write soon and give me all your news!

All the best

Kevin

Dear Kevin,

It was great to get your letter and hear all your news. Sorry I haven't written for ages, but I've been really busy!

First of all, I've been training hard for our school Sports Day. I'm taking part in the swimming competition – the 100-metre butterfly race – so I need to be really fit. I go running every morning before school. Then, after school, I go to the pool and swim for two hours. I just hope I win. Wish me luck!

As well as that, I've started working for my dad on Saturdays. He's got a computer shop, and it gets very busy at the weekends. It's really interesting and I'm learning a lot about computers. I'm also earning money for the holidays!

You asked me about my holiday plans. I'm going to a place called Brighton with my family for two weeks. It's a really great place – it's by the sea and there's lots to do. Why don't you fly over and come with us?

Write again soon and let me know!

Best wishes

Jim

3 Writing skills: *topic sentences*

1 Last week David wrote to Maria asking her some questions. Read the letter she wrote in reply. Ignore the missing sentences.

Dear David,

Thanks a lot for your letter. I'm really sorry I haven't written for so long. I've got exams this summer, so I've had a lot of school work this term.

(1) .... I'm doing quite well, although it's much larger than my old school and I'm always getting lost! The best thing is the indoor sports hall – it's huge, with lots of equipment. I've joined the school volleyball team, and we practise every lunch break.

(2) .... Pietro helped me a lot when I first arrived. Now we often get together after school to help each other with our homework. He's great, and we laugh a lot!

(3) .... My older brother's just got a place in college to study Art, so he's really pleased. The rest of the family are very busy too. They send you lots of love.

That's it for now! Write back soon.

Love

Maria

2 Which questions do you think David asked Maria in his original letter? Match each question with a paragraph in Maria's letter. There are two questions you don't need.

a) How's your family?

b) What is your new house like?

c) How are you getting on at your new school?

d) Why haven't you written for so long?

e) What did you do last summer?

f) Have you made any new friends?

3 For (1)–(3), choose the best topic sentence from the options below.

a) I play volleyball every day.

b) I've got lots of new friends.

c) My family are all doing fine.

d) My other friends are all very busy.

e) You asked me about my new school.

f) I've made friends with a really nice guy called Pietro.

4 Why do you think Maria ordered her paragraphs in this way? Is another order possible?

Over to you

4 Writing strategy

Read the notes.

▶▶ *planning your writing*

• Decide how many separate topics you need to write about.

• Group ideas on each topic together to make a paragraph.

• Write a topic sentence to summarise each paragraph.

• Decide on the best order for your paragraphs.

5 Writing task

Imagine an English friend has written to you asking for your news. Prepare to write your reply.

1 Think about what you have been doing lately. Choose three of the topics below. Note down as many ideas as you can think of. Write notes, not sentences.

School / Studies   Free-time activities
Family news   A special event

2 Copy and complete the paragraph plan below. Decide which order to put your topics in. Then choose your best ideas to put in paragraphs 2, 3 and 4.

3 Write a topic sentence for each paragraph. Look back at the sample on p.21 for help.

Para. 1 Introduction

Para. 2 Topic: ....
Topic sentence: ....
Details: ....

Para. 3 Topic: ....
Topic sentence: ....
Details: ....

Para. 4 Topic: ....
Topic sentence: ....
Details: ....

Closing remark: ....

6 Write

Write your letter, using your plan in Exercise 5.

7 Check your work

When you have finished, read your letter carefully. Are the grammar, spelling and punctuation correct?

▶▶ **WB** p.11

3 Friends and family

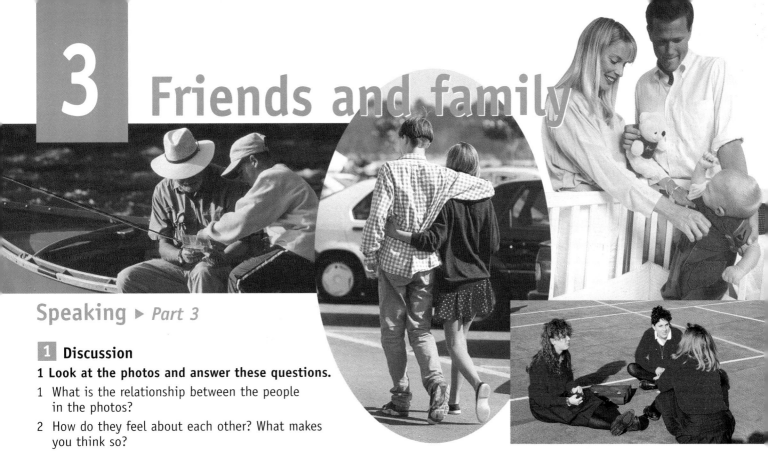

Speaking ▶ *Part 3*

1 Discussion

1 Look at the photos and answer these questions.

1 What is the relationship between the people in the photos?

2 How do they feel about each other? What makes you think so?

2 Say which of the relationships below is most important at:

a) age 5 b) age 16 c) age 25 d) age 50 e) your age.

Relationship with:

- parents
- brothers and sisters
- grandparents
- uncles and aunts
- friends
- boyfriend/girlfriend

2 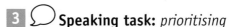 Listen

1 Look at the table below. Which two characteristics are most important for you in a boyfriend or girlfriend? Tick these two items in the 'You' column.

Characteristics people look for in a boy/girlfriend	You	Speaker 1	Speaker 2	Your partner
a) beauty/good looks				
b) intelligence				
c) kindness				
d) good taste in clothes				
e) honesty				
f) sense of humour				
g) imagination				

2 Listen to two friends discussing the same question. Tick their answers in the table. Are they the same as yours or different?

3 Listen again. Complete the sentences in the box.

> *giving/asking for opinions; agreeing*
> **A:** So what's important for you?
> **B:** The most important thing <u>for me</u> is …
> **A:** <u>Yes, you're right</u>. And what do you think? Is it important to be … ?
> **B:** I prefer …, but that might be … or …
> **A:** Yes, that's right. I agree with you.
> **B:** But I also think that … is very important.

4 <u>Underline</u> the expressions they use to give and ask for opinions, and express agreement.

3  Speaking task: *prioritising*

1 Work with a partner and complete the last column in Exercise 2.1. Use expressions from the box in Exercise 2.3.

2 Compare your answers with the class.

▶▶ WB p.12

Reading ▶ Part 3

1 Predict

1 You are going to read a story. Look at the title. What kind of story do you think it is?

a) a thriller b) a love story c) a ghost story

2 Look at the pictures and try to work out what happens in the story.

2 Reading strategy

▶▶ *understanding the sequence of events*

When you read a story, ask yourself these questions:
- Who are the main characters? Why are they there?
- Where does the story happen? When?
- What happens? What is going to happen next? How does the story end?

Underline key words such as names, places and time expressions.

1 Read the story paragraph by paragraph. Underline the parts of the text that answer these questions.

Paragraph 1

1 When does the story start?

2 Who is the main character?

3 Where is he going, and how does he feel?

Paragraph 2

4 What new character is introduced?

5 Why doesn't Jon talk to her?

Paragraph 3

6 What happens next?

Paragraph 4

7 What is the result of the accident?

8 What do Jon and Liz learn about each other when they start talking?

Paragraphs 5, 6

9 What happens next?

Paragraph 7

10 How does the story end?

2 Compare the story with your ideas in Exercise 1. Were you right?

3 Retelling

Retell the story. Start like this:

The story describes how Jon Key met his wife. It all began ...

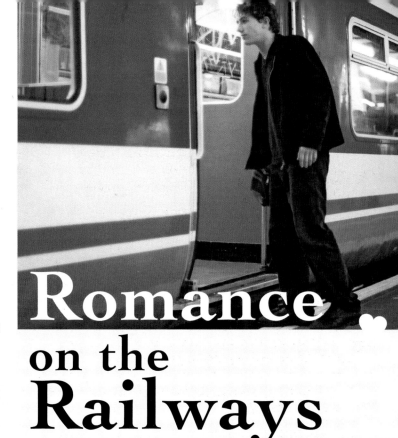

Romance on the Railways

I t all started on a cold Friday morning four years ago. Jon Key had booked a ticket on an early train to Liverpool, where his grandparents lived. **1** [ ] However, his taxi was late and he missed his train. This meant that he had to
5 **hang around**[1] and wait for the next train, which didn't go for another two hours. To make matters worse, Jon had a bad cold and <u>it</u> was making him feel really miserable.

At last his train was announced. He managed to find himself a seat, although <u>it</u> was very crowded. Then, just as the
10 train was **pulling out of**[2] the station, Liz rushed on and took the seat opposite him. **2** [ ] When she had got her breath back, she got up to put her bag on the overhead rack – and stepped on Jon's foot. She apologised, but Jon was feeling too ill to look up. <u>This</u> was unusual for him, as he was
15 a sociable person and usually tried to **strike up**[3] a conversation with other travellers. But right now all he wanted to do was stare out of the window.

Eventually, Jon decided that a hot drink would help him feel better. He went to the dining car and came back with a
20 strong cup of coffee. **3** [ ] As he reached his seat, he stumbled over a bag and, to his horror, spilled half his coffee over Liz's smart white coat. He apologised repeatedly and tried to **mop** <u>it</u> **up**[4], but it left an ugly stain. Jon went red with embarrassment.

25 As he had ruined Liz's coat, Jon could hardly ignore her. **4** [ ] It **turned out**[5] that they lived in the same town – Brighton. They liked the same kind of music and had been to the same open-air concerts. They loved the cinema and

4 Referencing

▶▶ *grammatical reference links*

Writers use various ways to link their ideas together:
Personal pronouns: Jon Key > **He**
Articles: **an** early train > **the** next train
Demonstrative pronouns:
Jon missed his train. > **This** meant …
Note: *this/that* can refer back to a word or a whole sentence.

1 Look at the underlined words in the text. Circle the words or phrases they refer back to.

2 The following sentences have been removed from the text. Decide where they go. Circle the words or phrases the underlined pronouns refer back to.

> **A** <u>This</u> took him ages because the train was so crowded.
>
> **B** <u>They</u> started talking.
>
> **C** <u>It</u> was the last empty place in the carriage.
>
> **D** <u>He</u> was carrying a large sign.
>
> **E** <u>They</u> were having a party for their 50th anniversary that weekend.
>
> **F** <u>He'd</u> put <u>it</u> in his pocket, but it wasn't there any more.

5 Vocabulary: *phrasal verbs*

1 Find the phrasal verbs 1–6 in the text and match them to the correct meaning below.

▶▶ *guessing meaning from context* Unit 1 p.9, Unit 2 p.17

a) to start moving away from

b) to become successful (*informal*)

c) to clean liquid from a surface

d) to stay in one place and wait (*informal*)

e) to happen in a particular way

f) to start / begin

2 How will you record the verbs in your vocabulary notebook?

6 ◯ Over to you

1 In some countries, young people don't choose their husband or wife. Instead, their parents arrange their marriages. What are the benefits of this? What are the disadvantages?

2 How do people normally meet their future partners in your country?

▶▶ **WB** p.12

had seen the same films. <u>It</u> all seemed too good to be true. Jon
30 persuaded Liz to give him her phone number. He promised to phone her next week, when they were both back in Brighton.

The following Monday, Jon decided to phone Liz. But where was the number? **5** ☐ He must have dropped it! He thought of Liz, waiting for his phone call. He had to find her somehow – but what
35 could he do?

A few weeks later, Liz set off for the cinema with a friend. She was feeling really down because she'd heard nothing from Jon. Outside the cinema there was a long queue for tickets, and she and her friend joined <u>it</u>. As
40 they stood there chatting, Liz saw a man walking up and down the queue. **6** ☐ It said: 'Liverpool Liz, where are you? Ring Jon, 02159 46 91 37.' Liz's heart leapt!

When Liz rang Jon, she discovered that he had been looking for her desperately all this time. He had
45 persuaded six of his friends to patrol outside all the cinemas in the town, hoping that she would eventually see his message. Their relationship just **took off**[6] and one year later, Liz and Jon got married.

Grammar: *past tenses* ▶ *p.182*

grammar file 6

A Past simple: sequence of actions

1 *I **left** the house, **walked** down the street and **waited at the bus stop**.*

2 *When the phone rang, I **answered** it immediately.*

B Past continuous: interrupted or simultaneous actions

3 *I **was getting onto** the train when someone called my name.*

4 *We heard the news **while** we **were eating** dinner.*

C Past perfect: action completed before another action

5 ***By the time** we got home, everyone **had gone** to bed.*

6 *The roads were dangerous because it **had been snowing** all day.* (emphasises duration)

! What's wrong?

1 *Ben was living in Poland for three years as a child.* ✗

2 *Sally waited at the bus stop when her bus arrived.* ✗

3 *By the time I reached the airport, the plane already took off.* ✗

4 *Paul had been standing outside the cinema when I arrived.* ✗

1 Past continuous or past simple?

Read the conversations and fill in the gaps. Use the verbs in brackets.

1 **A:** Where .... (you/first/meet) your best friend?

 B: In a coffee bar. I .... (chat) with friends when Marc .... (come) in.

2 **A:** I .... (try) to phone you twice last night but you .... (not/answer). What .... (you/do)?

 B: Oh, I .... (be) out. I .... (go) to the cinema with some friends.

3 **A:** When you were younger, ... (you/get on) well with your brothers and sisters?

 B: No! We .... (fight) all the time!

4 **A:** .... (you/have) a good time at the disco last weekend?

 B: Not really. I .... (slip) while I .... (dance) and .... (fall) over. It was really embarrassing!

2 Past simple or past perfect (continuous)?

Fill in the gaps, using the words in brackets.

1 By the time I got to the party, everyone else .... (already/arrive).

2 We went to the beach and then we .... (have) a barbecue.

3 We were exhausted by the end of the evening because we .... (dance) for hours.

4 When my friend cut his hand, I .... (take) him to see the doctor.

3 Mixed tenses

Read the text and fill in the gaps. Use the verbs in brackets or add a time word or linker.

TWINS REUNITED!

Jim and Dave are identical twins. When they were ten months old, different families (1) .... (adopt) them. Jim went to the USA, but Dave stayed in Britain.

Jim only (2) .... (discover) that he had a twin brother a year ago. He (3) .... (look) through some papers (4) .... he found an old photo. The photo (5) .... (show) himself and Dave as babies. When Jim asked his parents about it, they (6) .... (tell) him the truth. Jim started to look for his missing twin.

Last week, Dave (7) .... (watch) TV when the phone rang. It was Jim! Dave was thrilled. He (8) .... (search) for Jim (9) .... years – without success. The twins are astonished at how alike they are. They are both detectives. They both got married (10) .... they were training for the police force. Both their wives are nurses. And both families have two children – twins of course!

4 Sentence completion

Combine each pair of sentences to make a new sentence starting with the words given.

1 The concert started at 8 p.m. I got to the theatre at 8.15 p.m.
 By the time I got *to the theatre, the concert had started.*

2 Laura was excited. This was her first flight.
 Laura was excited because she ....

3 Paula arrived. We immediately set off for the cinema.
 We ....

4 I waited for 30 minutes. Then Ben's train arrived.
 By the time Ben's train ....

5 Maria saw Dave. She hugged him.
 As soon as ....

6 Alan played football. He hurt his leg.
 Alan hurt his leg while ....

▶▶ **WB** p.13

Vocabulary building

1 Words that go together

1 Fill in the gaps with the correct verb from the list.

go / fall / celebrate / get / have

- ☐ a) You .... on a date.
- ☐ b) You .... engaged.
- ☐ c) You .... your wedding anniversary.
- ☐ d) You .... divorced.
- ☐ e) You .... on your honeymoon.
- ☐ f) You .... children.
- ☐ g) You .... in love.
- ☐ h) You .... a row.
- ☐ i) You .... back together again.
- ☐ j) You .... married.

2 In which order do these things normally take place? Number the boxes.

3 Will the order change in the future, do you think?

2 Physical appearance

1 Match the sets of adjectives 1–5 to the appropriate part of the body.

1 straight, curly, wavy, short, long   a) nose

2 hazel, sparkling, bright blue   b) hair

3 pale, olive, tanned   c) eyebrows

4 turned-up, snub, big   d) eyes

5 bushy, heavy   e) skin, complexion

2 Match the sets of adjectives 1–4 to their opposites.

1 attractive, pretty   a) blond

2 slim, skinny   b) plain, unattractive

3 tall   c) plump, fat

4 brunette, dark brown   d) short, small

3 Word formation: *compound adjectives*

Compound adjectives have two parts which are joined with a hyphen. Complete the compound adjectives below with the word endings from the list. Use your dictionary to help you.

-aged / -headed / ~~-tempered~~ / -going / -fashioned / -sighted / -haired / -handed / -working / -looking

Someone who ...

1 is easily annoyed is bad *-tempered* .

2 uses his or her left hand to do most things is left-............. .

3 isn't modern is old-............. .

4 has grey hair is grey-............. .

5 is not strict and not easily upset or worried is easy-............. .

6 is unable to see far without glasses is short-............. .

7 thinks they are better than other people is big-............. .

8 has an attractive face is good-............. .

9 is between 40 and 60 years old is middle-........... .

10 works hard is hard-............. .

4 Word formation: *adjectives from nouns*

1 Make adjectives from these nouns by adding a suffix. Put them in the correct column below according to the ending. What spelling changes do you have to make?

1 fun   2 beauty   3 action   4 horror   5 cheer   6 artist   7 sport   8 music

-al	-ful	-ible	-(t)ic	-ive	-y

2 Use the noun in CAPITALS at the end of each sentence to form an adjective that fits in the gap.

1 I adore sentimental love stories. I'm very .... ROMANCE

2 My younger sister is very .... ; I think she's going to be a writer. IMAGINATION

3 My older brother can be quite .... – one minute he's laughing, the next he's in a bad temper. MOOD

4 My cousin used to be rather silly but he's more .... these days. SENSE

5 My uncle often helps me with my homework; he's really kind and .... THOUGHT

6 My aunt is very .... – she always knows how to fix things. PRACTICE

3 Add the adjectives to the correct column in Exercise 4.1

5 ⬤ Over to you

Describe your friends and family.

Example:

My cousin is tall and slim. He's got short, brown hair, blue eyes and he's always very tanned. He's very funny. He makes jokes all the time.

▶▶ WB p.14

Listening ▶ *Part 3*

1 Before you listen

You are going to hear five people talking about what they value most in their best friend. Before you listen, think about what you might hear:

What do <u>you</u> value the most in your best friend?

2 Listening strategy

▶▶ *identifying the main points*

When you listen to someone talking, try to distinguish between:

a) the main point that the speaker is making.

b) the examples or details that they give to support their point.

1 Read the extract below.

1 <u>Underline</u> the main point the speaker is making.

2 How many examples does she give to support her point?
a) one b) two c) three

3 Circle the phrases the speaker uses to introduce the examples.

'Carol's a great friend, and I like lots of things about her! What do I value the most? Mmm, I remember when I had a problem with my boyfriend, I didn't know if I wanted to break up or not, and she told me to stop seeing him for a month. That really helped! And also when I find things difficult at school ... For example, the other day I was writing a composition for homework and I didn't know what to write. So Carol said, take a break, you'll have more ideas after that! She was right! When I don't know what to do, she always gives me good advice.'

2 🖭 Now listen to Clara and Peter. Note down what they each value most about their friends.

Clara: ....

Peter: ....

3 🖭 Listen again. How do Clara and Peter introduce the examples they give to support their point? Tick the phrases they use.

introducing examples

I remember when ...

For example, ...

Take last week, ...

Let me tell you what happened ...

3 🖭 Listening task

1 You will hear three other people talking about their best friends. Choose from the list A–D the main point each speaker makes. There is one extra letter which you do not need to use.

Listening task

A My best friend tells me the truth even if it hurts.

B My best friend has helped me to become self-confident.

C My best friend helps me with my school work.

D My best friend likes the same kind of activities I like.

Speaker 1 ☐ **1**

Speaker 2 ☐ **2**

Speaker 3 ☐ **3**

2 Listen again and check your answers.

4 💬 Over to you

Do you prefer spending your free time with one friend or with a group of friends? Explain your answer.

Writing: *developing a paragraph*

Paragraph A

Ben, my oldest brother, is great – in fact, he's more like a friend than a brother. If I have a problem, for example, I always go and talk to him. He always listens and gives me good advice. He hardly ever loses his temper with me, even when I do really stupid things. On one occasion, for instance, I spilled Coke all over his new girlfriend's white dress. She was really angry but he calmed her down and told me not to worry. Ben looks after me very well. He often takes me out with his friends to the cinema or sometimes to the disco. He's the best brother anyone could have!

1 Compare two paragraphs

1 Read paragraphs A and B. <u>Underline</u> the topic sentence in each paragraph.

2 Complete the statements.

a) Paragraph ..... repeats the same point and does not give specific examples.

b) Paragraph ..... contains details which illustrate and explain the topic sentence.

2 Paragraph structure

1 Read paragraph A again. Circle the expressions we can use to give examples or illustrate a point. Does the writer illustrate all the points he makes?

2 Below is part of the plan the writer made for Paragraph A. Can you finish it?

Paragraph B

My oldest sister, Clare, is really annoying. She drives me crazy. She's sometimes generous. She can be good fun. She is really irritating, though. My sister is extremely untidy. She's really nosy, too! She is so hard to live with.

Topic sentence: *Ben, my eldest brother, is great – in fact, he's more like a friend than a brother.*

Detail 1: *Helps me with problems*

Example/illustration:
– Listens and gives good advice

Detail 2: ....

Example/illustration:.......................

....

Detail 3:..

Example/illustration:........................

....

3 What is the function of the final sentence in paragraph A?

3 Writing skills: *improving a paragraph*

1 You are going to improve paragraph B. Look at the sentences below.

1 Which sentences illustrate the topic sentence? Tick them.

2 Which sentences are not about the topic (not about 'my sister's faults')? Cross them out.

3 Which sentence(s) just repeat the same ideas? Cross them out.

> a) She is really thoughtless and keeps borrowing my things and breaking them.
> b) She's irritating.
> c) She likes animals, especially dogs.
> d) She's very untidy.
> e) She's hard to live with because she's so annoying.
> f) She's so nosy!
> g) She leaves things on the floor and then shouts at you if you stand on them.
> h) She looks after me in school.
> i) Yesterday, for example, she broke the strings of my guitar.
> j) When I'm on the phone, for example, she listens to my conversations!

2 Now write the paragraph out in full, putting the sentences in the best order.

Over to you

4 **Writing strategy**
Read the notes.

▶▶ *how to develop a paragraph*
- Write a topic sentence summarising the topic of the paragraph.
- Give examples or explanations to illustrate your main point.
- Do not include details that are not about the topic.

5 **Writing task**
You are going to write a description of your best friend.

1 Answer these questions.

1 What's your best friend's name?
2 How long have you known him/her?
3 How and where did you meet?

Now copy and complete the topic sentence and details in paragraph 1 of the plan opposite.

2 Decide which topics you are going to write about in paragraph 2. Tick a topic sentence from the list below.

Do the same for paragraph 3. Write the topic sentences in your plan.

a) *You never get bored when you're with* (NAME).

b) (NAME) *is very kind and generous.*

c) (NAME) *is really funny.*

d) (NAME) *always helps me when I'm in trouble.*

3 For paragraphs 2 and 3, think of examples or explanations to illustrate your topic sentences. Note them in your plan.

Para. 1 (Introduction)
Topic sentence: *My best friend,* (NAME) *, is one of the nicest people I know.*
Details: Have known her/him for .... years. We met in/at ....
when/because/while ....
Para. 2
Topic sentence: ....
Details + examples: ....
Para. 3
Topic sentence: ....
Details + examples: ....
Para. 4 (Conclusion)

4 One of the conclusions below is not suitable. Why?

A

When we first met, I had no idea that (NAME) and I would become best friends. But I'm really glad we did. I just hope that we will always stay friends.

B

I'm very glad that (NAME) *and I met.*
He/She is the best friend anyone could have.

C

(NAME) is one of the nicest people I know.

6 **Write**
Write your description, using your plan in Exercise 5.

7 **Check your work**
When you have finished, read your work carefully. Are the grammar, spelling and punctuation correct?

▶▶ **WB** p.16

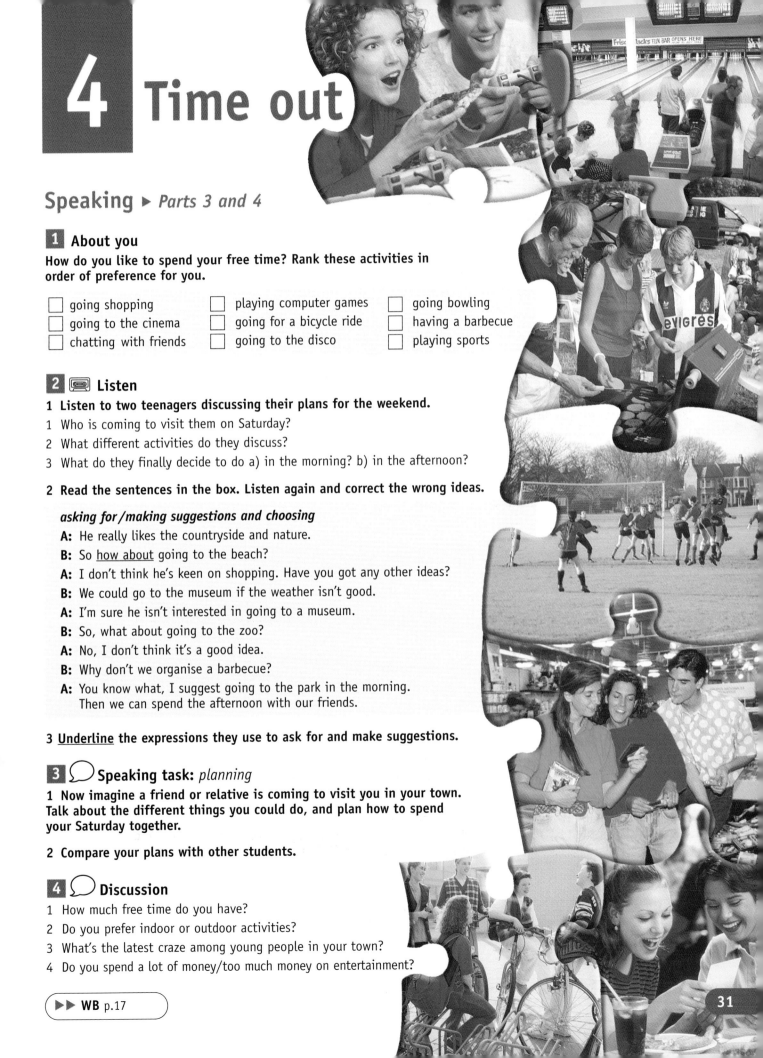

4 Time out

Speaking ▶ *Parts 3 and 4*

1 About you

How do you like to spend your free time? Rank these activities in order of preference for you.

- ☐ going shopping
- ☐ going to the cinema
- ☐ chatting with friends
- ☐ playing computer games
- ☐ going for a bicycle ride
- ☐ going to the disco
- ☐ going bowling
- ☐ having a barbecue
- ☐ playing sports

2 🎦 Listen

1 Listen to two teenagers discussing their plans for the weekend.

1 Who is coming to visit them on Saturday?

2 What different activities do they discuss?

3 What do they finally decide to do a) in the morning? b) in the afternoon?

2 Read the sentences in the box. Listen again and correct the wrong ideas.

asking for/making suggestions and choosing

A: He really likes the countryside and nature.

B: So <u>how about</u> going to the beach?

A: I don't think he's keen on shopping. Have you got any other ideas?

B: We could go to the museum if the weather isn't good.

A: I'm sure he isn't interested in going to a museum.

B: So, what about going to the zoo?

A: No, I don't think it's a good idea.

B: Why don't we organise a barbecue?

A: You know what, I suggest going to the park in the morning. Then we can spend the afternoon with our friends.

3 <u>Underline</u> the expressions they use to ask for and make suggestions.

3 💬 Speaking task: *planning*

1 Now imagine a friend or relative is coming to visit you in your town. Talk about the different things you could do, and plan how to spend your Saturday together.

2 Compare your plans with other students.

4 💬 Discussion

1 How much free time do you have?

2 Do you prefer indoor or outdoor activities?

3 What's the latest craze among young people in your town?

4 Do you spend a lot of money/too much money on entertainment?

▶▶ WB p.17

Reading ▶ Part 4

1 Think about the topic

Imagine you are studying at a language school in Britain. The programme includes excursions to places of interest. Your teacher has given you some information about four different places. Look at the headings and the photos opposite.

1 What kind of place can you see in the photos?
2 Have you heard of any of them?
3 Which one looks most interesting to you?

2 Reading strategy

▶▶ *scanning for specific information*

When you only want specific information:

- don't waste time reading every word.
- run your eyes over the text quickly, looking for key words and phrases to help you find the part you need.

1 You want to find out the following information about each place in the texts. What kind of words do you need to look for?

1 <u>Where</u> is it <u>located</u>?
names of places, words like south, west ...
2 <u>How much</u> does it cost <u>to go in</u>?
3 Can you get anything to <u>eat or drink</u> there?
4 <u>When</u> is it <u>open</u>?

2 Copy and complete the table below. (Leave a blank if there is no information in the text.)

	A	B	C	D
Location				
Cost				
Food/Drink				
Opening times				

Great destinations for

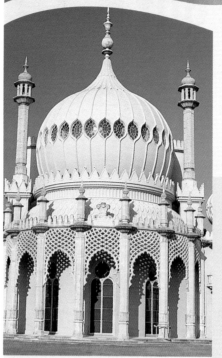

Open all year, 10 a.m. – 6 p.m.

Adults £4.90, students £3.55, children £3.00

A THE ROYAL PAVILION

Experience the **magical** world of the Royal Pavilion in the seaside town of Brighton. This famous royal residence was built for King George IV in the early nineteenth century and has been home to three British kings. On the outside, it looks like an Indian palace, while the interior is decorated in Chinese style.

A recent £10 million restoration scheme has recreated the original decorations and furniture. Enter a fantasy world filled with mythical creatures and **astonishing** colours. Admire the pure gold ceiling of the Music Room. Visit the Great Kitchen, with its **superb** collection of cooking utensils, and the magnificent Banqueting Hall, where the King entertained his guests.

Refreshments are available in the Royal Tearooms. In the Pavilion gift shop you can choose from a variety of unique souvenirs.

B Explore@Bristol

Located in Bristol's historic harbour district, Explore@Bristol is a **terrific** new science centre for the 21st century. Discover how the world works using the latest hands-on techniques and multi-media experiences.

Your **amazing** brain is responsible for who you are and what you can do. Find out how the human brain and body tick.

Test your personal staying power in **Move it**, and investigate a range of **ingenious** inventions. Pump, pedal, push and pull, lift yourself right off the ground, and follow your dream to fly.

Enter the eye of a tornado in the **Curiosity zone**! Find out about forces and patterns in the world around us from the weather to the science of sound.

Communicate using the latest digital technologies in **Get connected**. Challenge the computer in a game of virtual volleyball.

Step into the **Orange Imaginarium**, a 100-seat stainless steel sphere, for the latest star shows through the Universe and journeys into the future.

Open every day from 10 a.m. to 6 p.m.
Special rates available for groups and school parties.

a great day out

C LONGLEAT HOUSE & SAFARI PARK

Voted 'Best Animal Attraction in Britain', Longleat House and Safari Park in the heart of England's West Country offers a great day out for all the family.

Longleat House is home to the 7th Marquess of Bath. Dating back to the 16th century, it is full of treasures, with **stunning** ceilings and tapestries and **fine** furniture. Learn all about the **fascinating** history of this beautiful home from knowledgeable guides.

The world-famous Safari Park was the first outside Africa to be opened to the public. See for yourself lions, tigers and other **fabulous** wild animals roaming free in natural surroundings. The Safari Park offers a FREE commentary tape or CD to all Coach Groups.

Other attractions include a Safari Boat trip, Pets' Corner, Longleat Railway and much, much more.

There's a wide range of shops and places to eat, including Noah's Ark Gift Shops, the Cellar Café and Fast Food kiosks.

For opening times, prices and group bookings, contact Customer Services on 01985 844328 or visit our website on www.longleat.co.uk.

D

MUSEUM OF LONDON

FOR A FASCINATING INSIGHT into London's history, visit the world's largest urban history museum on the site of the old City Wall.

Millions of people of many races and beliefs have lived and worked in London over the centuries and have contributed to its unique character. Find out who they were and why they came to London.

Like every great city, London has its dark side. In the 'Macabre London' Gallery, you can hear some of the **scary** stories connected with the city.

Today, traffic in the capital flows more slowly than it did in the age of horse-drawn carriages. The Transport Gallery gives a taste of Londoners' transport since Roman times.

Throughout its history, London has been a centre of entertainment. Find out what drew the crowds over the centuries.

The Museum also organises many events and workshops. Weekend workshops might involve making coins or shoes, or working with the archaeologists.

Opening times: Mon.–Sat. 10 a.m.–5.50 p.m., Sun. 12–5.50 p.m.
Admission: Adults £5, children under 16 free

3 Multiple-matching task

Now answer the questions below. Write A, B, C or D in the boxes. Two questions have more than one answer, so you will need to look for similar information in more than one text.

Before you scan the texts, decide what kind of words you will look for. Use the underlined phrases in each question to help you decide. The first one has been done for you as an example.

In which place	
can visitors get <u>recorded information</u>?	**0** C
can you find out how people <u>travelled</u> around <u>in the past</u>?	**1**
can you see how people used to <u>prepare food</u>?	**2**
can you try to <u>beat a computer at sport</u>?	**3**
will someone <u>show you round</u>?	**4**
can you learn more about <u>outer space</u>?	**5**
can you get practical experience by <u>doing things yourself</u>?	**6** **7**
can you buy <u>gifts to remind you of your visit</u>?	**8** **9**

4 Vocabulary: *adjectives*

1 Find the following adjectives in the texts. What nouns do they describe? Write them in your notebook. There may be more than one noun.

1 magical	7 ingenious
2 astonishing	8 stunning
3 superb	9 fine
4 unique	10 fascinating
5 terrific	11 fabulous
6 amazing	12 scary

2 All the adjectives have a positive meaning except one. Which one?

3 What other nouns can go with these adjectives? Use your dictionary to find more.

5 💬 Over to you

1 Decide with a partner which one of the four places in the texts you would like to visit.

2 Tell the class what you have decided. Give reasons.

▶▶ WB p.17

Grammar: *-ing forms and infinitives (1)*
▶ *pp.183–184*

grammar files 9,10

A -ing forms
- **after certain verbs:**
1 I **love / enjoy / can't stand** *skating*.
- **after phrasal verbs and prepositions:**
2 I'm **thinking of** *going* to the beach this weekend.
- **after some fixed expressions:**
3 That new film **is worth** *seeing*.

B verb + to-infinitive
4 I **want / would like to visit** the USA.

C verb + object + to-infinitive
5 My parents don't **want me to go out** in the week.

D -ing form or to-infinitive?
6 I love **dancing / to dance**. (no change of meaning)
7 a) We **stopped** *watching* the game and went home!
     (we did not continue this)
   b) We **stopped to watch** the game. (we stopped in order to do something else)

! What's wrong?

1 *I enjoy to play computer games.* X
2 *I'm looking forward to see you.* X
3 *My friend wants that I go shopping with her.* X

1 🗩 -ing form or infinitive?

Put the verbs in brackets into the correct form. Then ask and answer the questions with a partner.

1 Do you like ...*meeting*. (meet) new people? Why / Why not?
2 Is there anything you can't stand ..*doing*... (do)? Why not?
3 Which country do you want .....*to*..... (visit) most? Why?
4 What kinds of films do you prefer ....*to*..... (watch)? Why?
5 Are you planning ..*doing*.... (do) anything interesting this weekend? What?
6 Do you expect ...*to*...... (go) to university?
7 Do you sometimes get fed up with .... (learn) English?

2 -ing form or to-infinitive?

Fill in the gaps with an appropriate verb in the correct form.

1 **A:** Did you remember .... the tickets for the concert?
   B: Yes, I bought them this morning.
2 **A:** You promised you'd come to the park with me!
   B: Did I? I don't remember .... that!
3 **A:** Your brother is very noisy, isn't he?
   B: Yes! I'll tell him to stop .... that music so loudly.
4 **A:** Why are you so late?
   B: I'm sorry. We had to stop .... some petrol.
5 **A:** I tried .... you last night but I couldn't get through.
   B: Yes, my mobile was switched off. I was revising.
6 **A:** The video isn't working. Do you think it's broken?
   B: Why don't you try .... it on, you silly thing!

3 Jumbled sentences

Put the words into the correct order to make sentences. Which sentences are true for you? Write T (True) or F (False) next to each one.

1 forward school I'm leaving to looking
   I'm looking forward to leaving school.
2 weekends I like at go to swimming
3 prefers father watching my TV to washing up
4 to well English my me parents want speak
5 never can time do remember to my I homework on
6 to taught aunt me swim my

4 Transformations

Complete the second sentence so that it has a similar meaning to the first sentence, using the word given. Do not change the word given. Use between two and five words including the word given.

1 Sandra can never remember what she's said. **keeps**
   Sandra .... what she's said.
2 It would be great if you could come to the party. **want**
   I really .... to the party.
3 I must buy Tom a present – don't let me forget. **remind**
   Please .... a present for Tom.
4 You should save your money! **stop**
   You must .... money!
5 'I'll be home before midnight,' Tom said. **expected**
   Tom .... before midnight.
6 Don't bother ringing Ryan because he's not home. **use**
   It's .... Ryan because he's not home.

▶▶ **WB** p.18

Vocabulary building

1 Word formation: -ed/-ing adjectives

1 Compare the sentences below. Which adjective:

a) describes how someone feels about the film?

b) describes the film?

1 The film was really **boring**.

2 I was really **bored** by the film.

2 Use the word in CAPITALS at the end of each sentence to form an adjective that fits in the gap.

1 Are there any really .... things to do in your town? **INTEREST**

2 Do you enjoy activities like skateboarding or do you think they're .... ? **BORE**

3 Would you be .... if someone offered to take you to an art exhibition? **EXCITE**

4 Do you get .... if your parents ask you to help out in your free time? **ANNOY**

5 Would you like to go bungee jumping or do you think it would be too ....? **FRIGHTEN**

6 Do you like playing computer games or are you .... of them? **TIRE**

3 ⃝ Ask and answer the questions with a partner.

2 Verb + preposition + -ing

1 Fill in the gaps with in, of or for. What form of the verb is used after all the prepositions?

1 The boys *apologised* ..... breaking the window.

2 He *succeeded* ..... persuading his parents to pay for guitar lessons.

3 I'm *thinking* ..... taking up a new hobby.

2 Finish these sentences so they are true for you. Put the verb in the -ing form.

1 I have always dreamed of *taking part in the national skateboard championships* .

2 I'm thinking of .... next year.

3 I like spending money on ....

4 I hope I will succeed in .... before I'm 30.

5 My parents sometimes criticise me for ....

6 I'm determined that nobody will stop me from
....

3 Underline the preposition that follows each verb.

▶▶ *tip!*

When you record words in your vocabulary book, include the prepositions that go with them, e.g.

praise someone for (doing) something

◀◀

3 Phrasal verbs

1 Match each phrasal verb 1–4 to its meaning.

1 give sth. up	a) start (doing) an activity
2 go in for sth.	b) stop (doing) sth.
3 go off sth.	c) stop liking sth.
4 take sth. up	d) take part in sth.

2 Read what John says about how he spends his free time. Fill in the gaps with a phrasal verb from the list above.

I'm really into rollerblading! I (1) .... it .... two or three years ago and now I'm quite an expert. I had to spend a lot of money on skates and all the other gear in the beginning – but it's not an expensive hobby, really. My mother isn't very happy, though. Secretly, she's hoping that I'll get bored and (2) .... it. She thinks rollerblading is a waste of time! She says I ought to (3) .... it .... and (4) .... something more useful. I think she really wants me to (5) .... the violin or the piano! Can you imagine anything more boring?

4 ⃝ Over to you

Talk about a hobby you have now or have had in the past. Use phrasal verbs from Exercise 3 and expressions from the box below.

be into sth.	be mad about sth.
be good at sth.	be an expert (on) sth.
spend time/money on sth.	be a waste of time
get tired of/bored with sth.	
The trouble is, ...	

▶▶ **WB** p.19

Listening ▶ Part 4

1 Before you listen

You are going to hear two friends talking about leisure activities during the summer holidays.

1 Look at the Listening task and read statements 1–6. What kind of leisure activities do they talk about?

2 Discuss each statement 1–6. What's your opinion?
Example:

1 *Some organised activities are interesting. For example, ...*

2 🔊 Listening strategy

As you listen, you have to decide which of the opinions 1–6 are TRUE and which are FALSE according to what the speakers say.

▶▶ *identifying opinions*

When people give their opinions, they often use expressions like:

I think / I don't think ... In my opinion, ...
For me, ... I'm not sure ...
I'm afraid (that) ...

Listen carefully for these introductory phrases. They tell you that an opinion follows.

1 Listen to the first part of the recording once. Who says this, Paula or Robert?

a) '**I don't think** that sounds like much of a holiday.'

b) '**For me,** if you've got something interesting to do, then you do feel relaxed.'

c) '**I'm afraid** a course like that sounds too much like going back to school to me.'

2 Now write T (TRUE) or F (FALSE) in the boxes next to statements 1–3.

3 🔊 Listening task

1 Now listen to the rest of the recording. Decide which of the statements 4–6 are TRUE or FALSE. Write T or F in the boxes.

2 Compare your answers. What did each person say?

4 🔊 Listen to check

Listen to the whole recording again and check your answers.

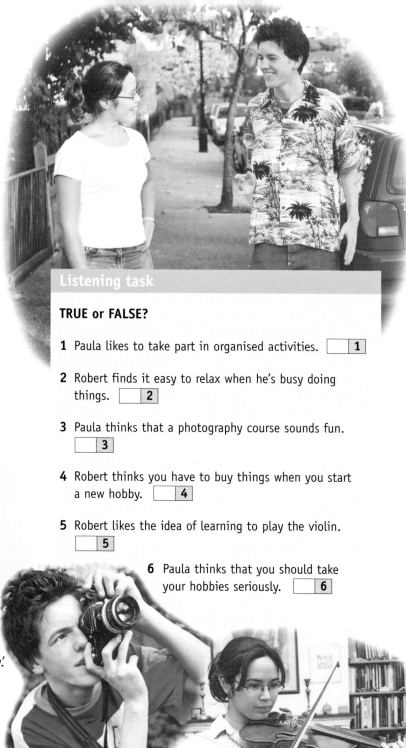

Listening task

TRUE or FALSE?

1 Paula likes to take part in organised activities. ☐ **1**

2 Robert finds it easy to relax when he's busy doing things. ☐ **2**

3 Paula thinks that a photography course sounds fun. ☐ **3**

4 Robert thinks you have to buy things when you start a new hobby. ☐ **4**

5 Robert likes the idea of learning to play the violin. ☐ **5**

6 Paula thinks that you should take your hobbies seriously. ☐ **6**

5  Over to you

1 How do you usually spend your time in the summer holidays?

2 Have you ever signed up for a course like photography during the holidays?

Writing: *linking your ideas*

1 **Linking expressions:** *sequence*

1 Read the composition opposite, which a student wrote about his home town. The paragraphs are mixed up. Number them in the correct order.

2 Which expressions helped you to decide the right order? <u>Underline</u> them.

3 Look at the linking expressions below. You can use them to link points or whole paragraphs to each other. Put them under the right heading.

Linking expressions

In addition, …
Finally, …
First of all, …
Another thing (to mention) is …
Last but not least, …
Also, …
In conclusion, …
In the first place, …
To sum up, …
As well as this, …
To start with, …

(Introduction)

First point:

To start with, /………/………

Next points:

Also, /………/………/………

Final point:

Finally, /………

Conclusion:

In conclusion, /………

☐ To sum up, I think I'm very lucky to live in my town. You can enjoy life <u>here</u> even if you are poor.

☐ Finally, there are plenty of tennis and basketball courts in the town. And you don't need to worry about equipment – you can just borrow rackets and balls if you don't want to buy <u>them</u>! You don't have to pay to use the courts either.

☐ It's great living in my home town because there's so much to do. You can have lots of fun <u>here</u> without spending much money at all. And if you're a student, it's even better!

☐ Also, students in my town can get a special student card. With one of <u>these</u>, they can get discounts on cinema and theatre tickets. They can also get into a gym or sports club more cheaply.

☐ To start with, there are lots of cafés in the town where you can go to meet your friends. These cafés are great. You don't just drink coffee <u>there</u> – you can watch films on a huge screen too and even play computer games. There are also lots of parks and squares in the town where you can go rollerblading or skateboarding or just sit in the sun and chat.

2 **Grammatical reference links**

Look at the <u>underlined</u> words in the sample composition. Circle the words or phrases they refer back to.

3 Writing skills: *grammatical links*

1 Read this paragraph and fill in the gaps with one suitable word.

My village is very peaceful. Some people who live (1) .... think it's boring. But I don't agree with (2) .... I think (3) .... is fantastic. (4) .... village is in a valley. It's surrounded by high mountains and every winter (5) .... is snow. I love this time because it means that (6) .... can go skiing and snowboarding. Spring is beautiful here because (7) .... is the time when all the wild flowers come out. And in summer there's the river. We can swim in (8) .... if we are careful, and we can have picnics and barbecues there as well.

2 Read this short text. What's wrong with it?

My town is situated on the coast, and there is always something to do in my town.

You can do windsurfing in my town. The best time to do windsurfing is April to September. It's a great way to spend the day.

You can go scuba diving if you join one of the local clubs. Scuba diving is very popular with tourists. The sea is very clear and you can see some fantastic sea creatures.

There are lots of pizza places and burger bars. After a day on the beach, you can go to pizza places and burger bars with your friends.

3 Improve the text in Exercise 3.2.

1 Use a linking expression at the beginning of paragraphs 2–4.
2 Replace repeated words with reference words.

Over to you

4 Writing strategy
Read the notes.

▶▶ *linking your ideas*

- Use a new paragraph for each main idea.
- Use linking expressions to connect your paragraphs.
- Use reference words to avoid repetition.

5 Writing task

1 Your teacher has asked you to write a description of a place you like very much. Use the questions below to help you plan what to write. Make notes. Use words and phrases, not sentences.

1 What is the name of the place? Where is it exactly? What sort of place is it: a town? a city? a beach resort? other?
2 What interesting/exciting things can you do there?
3 Why else do you like it?
4 What's the best time to go there? Why?
5 Is it a good place for young people to go? Why?
6 What else can you say about it?

Name of place:

Type of place:

Things to do there:

Reason I like it:

Best time to go:

Why it's a good place for young people:

Other points:

2 Choose the best ideas from your notes, and make a plan like the one below. You will need at least four paragraphs but you can write more if you like.

Para. 1 (Introduction)

Para. 2 Topic: ....
Topic sentence: ....
Details: ....
Para. 3 Topic: ....
Topic sentence: ....
Details: ....
Para. 4 (Conclusion)

6 Write
Now write your description. Follow the ▶▶ *Writing strategy*.

7 Check your work
When you have finished, read your composition carefully. Are the grammar, spelling and punctuation correct?

▶▶ WB p.21

Progress test 1

1 Lexical cloze

For questions **1-8**, read the text below and decide which answer **A**, **B** or **C** best fits each space. There is an example at the beginning **(0)**.

Example:

0 A everywhere   **B** all   **C** around

SCHOOL DAYS ARE OVER

At the end of the school year, teenagers **(0)** .*B*. over the world start their long vacation. For many of them, this is a good time to stop **(1)** .*A*. about school and start thinking seriously about the future. For some, the only possibility is to look for **(2)** ..... ; for others, there is the prospect of continuing their education. This means they have to choose what subjects to specialise **(3)** ..... when they return to school after the holidays.

But before they consider the choices open to them, many teenagers **(4)** ..... a break. Now is the time to relax and to forget **(5)** ..... the difficulties that may lie ahead. Some go **(6)** ..... holiday with friends; others prefer a study holiday or summer camp. This is an opportunity for them to improve their English and **(7)** ..... new friends. They can also take **(8)** ..... in organised activities such as sports and sightseeing.

1 **A** bothering   **B** concerning   **C** worrying
2 **A** work   **B** job   **C** task
3 **A** at   **B** in   **C** with
4 **A** use   **B** go   **C** take
5 **A** of   **B** about   **C** for
6 **A** on   **B** off   **C** to
7 **A** know   **B** learn   **C** make
8 **A** place   **B** part   **C** up

2 Open cloze

For questions **9–16**, read the text below and think of the word which best fits each space. Use only one word in each space. There is an example at the beginning **(0)**.

THE OLYMPIC GAMES

The original Olympic Games were held once **(0)** .*every*.. four years in Olympia, Greece. The earliest games ever recorded took place nearly three thousand years **(9)** .... In the late nineteenth century **(10)** .... Frenchman called Baron de Courbertin managed to persuade some sportsmen to start the games again, and the first modern Olympics were held **(11)** .... 1896 in Athens. They have taken place every four years **(12)** .... then, except for the periods during the two world wars. Since 1924, Winter Olympic Games have been held in a different venue **(13)** .... the main summer event. As a result, the numbering of the Summer and Winter Olympics **(14)** .... different: the Sydney Olympics in 2000 was number 27, and the winter event in Salt Lake City was number 18. The number of countries which send athletes **(15)** .... increased from thirteen at the first modern Olympics **(16)** .... nearly 200 in the twenty-first century.

3 Key word transformations

For questions **17–22**, complete the second sentence so that it has a similar meaning to the first sentence, using the word given. **Do not change the word given.** You must use between two and five words, including the word given. There is an example at the beginning **(0)**.

Example:

0 You mustn't spend so much money.
stop

You must *stop spending* .... so much money.

17 I hate iceskating.
stand

I .... iceskating.

18 Football is popular and so is basketball.
are

Both .... popular.

19 We have been playing since five o'clock.
at

We .... five o'clock.

20 Because I was tired, I went to bed early.
so

I was tired .... bed early.

21 I'm considering learning Italian next year.
thinking

I'm .... Italian next year.

22 As I was getting dressed, the phone rang.
when

I .... the phone rang.

4 Error correction

For questions **23–30**, read the text below and look carefully at each line. Some of the lines are correct, and some have a word which should not be there. If a line is correct, put a tick (✓) next to it. If a line has a word which should not be there, underline the word. There are two examples at the beginning **(0 and 00)**.

TENNIS KIT

0 All you need to play tennis is a racket, a ball and a friend ✓
00 <u>for</u> to play with. At the start, you can wear your school kit,
23 but if you <u>are</u> want to be serious, you'll need to spend
24 some money on proper equipment. Choosing correct shoes
25 is important because <u>the</u> running, changing direction and
26 braking <u>they</u> all put a lot of pressure on your feet. Make
27 sure you buy a good pair of tennis shoes, and always replace
28 them when they have worn out <u>of</u>. Choose clothes that are
29 made from light, natural <u>and</u> materials like cotton. Other
30 things you will <u>be</u> need are socks, a tracksuit and a bag to
carry your equipment in.

5 Word formation

For questions **31–36**, read the text below. Use the word given in capitals underneath the text to form a word that fits in the space in the text. There is an example at the beginning **(0)**.

GOOD FRIENDS

What's the **(0)** *difference* between a friend and a good friend? Some people say that a good friend has to be **(31)** .... Others answer that **(32)** .... is the most important thing. And what about looks? Does your friend need to be **(33)** .... in order to be your best friend? In my opinion, **(34)** .... is the key to making people good friends. I always think that a **(35)** .... attitude to life and a **(36)** .... character are the most important factors.

0 DIFFER
31 INTEREST
32 INTELLIGENT
33 ATTRACT
34 PERSONAL
35 CHEER
36 THOUGHT

5 Ambitions

Speaking ▶ Part 2

1 About you

1 Do you know what you want to do after you leave school?
2 Which jobs in the photos would you enjoy doing?
3 What job do you think you will be doing in 10 years?

2 Vocabulary

1 Look at the photos again. What does each person do in their job?

Example:

A doctor looks after sick people and helps them to get better.

2 What qualities do you need for these jobs? Match the jobs to the definitions. More than one job may fit.

1 A/An .... has to be self-confident and determined to succeed – as well as good-looking.
2 A/An .... has to be dedicated, single-minded and competitive.
3 A/An .... needs to be imaginative and enjoy entertaining people.
4 A/An .... has to be ambitious and a good leader.
5 A/An .... needs to be energetic, flexible and good at communicating.
6 A/An .... must be sympathetic, caring and patient.
7 A/An .... must be organised, reliable and careful.
8 A/An .... has to be logical, practical and good at figures.

3 Discuss.

1 Which adjectives describe you best?
2 Which job would you be best at?

3 🔊 Listen

1 Listen to a student talking about two of the jobs in the photos.

1 Which jobs does he talk about?
2 Which job does he think is
   a) more interesting? b) more important? c) harder?
3 Which job would he rather do?

2 Listen again. How does the speaker support his opinions? Match the explanations to the jobs.

a) He can travel around to different places.
b) He has to stay in the same place all day.
c) He can speak to many important people.
d) He has to listen to people, and be positive and sympathetic.
e) He can learn a lot about things and what is happening in the world.
f) It's a very important job.

4 💬 Speaking task: *photos*

Take turns to choose two jobs in the photos. Compare and contrast them, and say which job you would rather do. Give reasons to support your opinion.

5 💬 Discussion

1 What are the most popular jobs among young people in your country?
2 How important is it to like your job?

▶▶ WB p.24

41

Reading ▶ *Part 1*

1 Think about the topic

You are going to read an article about horoscopes.

1 Do you read your horoscope? Why/Why not?

2 Why do you think so many people are interested in their horoscope?

2 Read for general understanding

1 Look at the title and sub-heading of the article and skim the text.

1 Which paragraphs are about Sally? Which are about Katy?

2 Which girl believes in horoscopes?

2 Read the text once. Are these statements true or false?
Section:

0 Sally always reads her horoscope before making a big decision.

1 Sally will only date a boy with the same star sign as herself.

2 Sally has decided to study Maths and Science after reading her horoscope.

3 Katy thinks her aunt takes horoscopes too seriously.

4 Katy is hoping to meet someone new.

5 When she needs advice, Katy talks to her parents and friends.

3 Reading strategy

▶▶ *understanding the main idea*

A paragraph has one main idea. All the details in the paragraph relate to the main idea. This is often summarised in a topic sentence.

1 Read the topic sentences in the box below. Then read the text again paragraph by paragraph. Which topic sentence summarises the main idea? There are two sentences which you don't need. The first one has been done as an example (0).

A She prefers to plan important decisions by other methods.

B She also believes that our stars tell us what kind of person we are.

C According to her star sign, she is good at creative subjects.

D Other people think horoscopes are a waste of time and money.

E It is hard to say if the information in horoscopes is correct.

F Some people pay a lot of money to astrologers.

G She is using the stars to help her plan her career.

H Some people use their horoscopes as a guide for everything they do.

2 What was wrong with the extra sentences? Tick a) or b).

a) They are about details and don't summarise the main idea.

b) They are not true.

Do horoscopes
Horos

Two of our readers, Sally and Katy, have very different views on stargazing!

SPECIAL REPORT

0 .... **H** .... Sally, a student, reads her horoscope every day. She keeps a notebook and writes down the main points each day and then she checks them at
5 the end of the day. Some of her horoscopes have come true in the past, so she is **convinced**[1] that they help her to avoid unpleasant events. She does a lot of careful research whenever she's going to do
10 something really important.

1 .... As a Virgo, she is supposed to be hard-working and a perfectionist. She also knows the characteristics of all the other star signs.
15 Some star signs are **compatible**[2] but others don't get on at all. For example, a Pisces and a Scorpio are supposed to make perfect partners because they're both sensitive and idealistic. A Taurus and a Leo, however, make
20 a disastrous combination because a Taurus is home-loving and a Leo loves parties. Sally once decided not to go out with someone because his star sign didn't go with hers.

rule your life?
copes

►► WB p.25

4 Vocabulary: *unfamiliar words*

►► *using linking words*

Look out for linking words that introduce a result, reason or contrast, e.g. *so, but, although*. They can help you work out the meaning of words you don't know.

Find the words 1–6 in the text. Read the whole sentence and use the <u>underlined</u> linking words to help you work out what they mean. Choose the correct meaning a) or b).

1 a) certain   b) worried
2 a) able to get on   b) not able to get on
3 a) agrees they are right b) refuses to change her opinion
4 a) find them funny   b) can't think of anything else
5 a) not clear or definite b) clear and definite
6 a) a true prediction   b) something that happens by chance

5 Over to you

1 Who do you agree with? Give reasons.

a) Sally b) Katy c) neither Sally nor Katy

2 Think of the biggest decision you have made in the last year. Who or what influenced you?

2 .... She was thinking
25 about training to be a nurse after leaving school, but luckily she checked her horoscope. It gave quite a different answer. Because she is a Virgo, she has decided to concentrate on languages and creative subjects, instead of studying Science
30 and Maths. <u>Although</u> her teachers have told her that astrology should not guide such important decisions, Sally remains **stubborn**[3]. She says that astrology has helped her in her private life, so there is no reason to forget about it in school.

35 **3** .... 'I don't take them seriously,' says Katy, Sally's friend. 'They're OK if you treat them as a bit of harmless fun,' she says, '<u>but</u> I know some people are **obsessed**[4] by them and read them all the time.' One of her
40 aunts goes to an astrologer every month for her own personal horoscope. 'I don't know why she bothers,' says Katy. 'I think astrologers just make everything up and then charge a lot of money for their predictions. My aunt believes
45 everything she is told and her astrologer takes advantage of that.'

4 .... According to Katy, horoscopes are written in <u>such</u> **vague**[5] language <u>that</u> everyone can interpret them in their own way. 'If your horoscope says that someone new will come 50 into your life, you may think something romantic is going to happen, if that's what you are hoping for. But it could be almost anything – a new neighbour, or even someone you don't like,' says Katy. 'And if you do meet someone, how do you know if it's just 55 a **coincidence**[6] <u>or</u> a prediction come true?'

5 .... 'I usually talk things over with my mum. Then I'll consult my closest friends as well,' says Katy. 'For example, part of my language course next year involves a trip abroad. 60 I'm going to be away from home for two months. At first I felt a bit nervous about it, but now that I've discussed it with my parents and friends, I feel much better, and I've decided to do the course. I certainly didn't think about my star sign before 65 making my decision!'

But whatever you think, horoscopes have been around for centuries and the number of stargazers just keeps on growing.

Grammar: *the future (1)*
▶ *p.182*

grammar file 8

A *going to* + infinitive

1 *I'm going to study* medicine. (intention)

2 *Look at the time! We're going to be late!* (prediction from present evidence)

B Present continuous

3 *I'm meeting* Paul tonight. (fixed arrangement)

C Present simple

4 *The film starts at 7 p.m. tonight.* (scheduled event)

D *will/shall* + infinitive

5 *My sister will be 12 next month.* (future fact)

6 *It will be hot and sunny tomorrow.* (a prediction)

7 *Are you going for a walk? I'll come with you.* (unplanned decision)

8 *I'll write to you every day!* (a promise)

9 *Shall I find out more about that job for you?* (an offer)

E Future time clauses

10 *I'll probably get a job after/when I finish school.*

! What's wrong?

1 *I can't meet you later because I go to the dentist's.* ✗

2 *He's going to work for his father after he'll leave school.* ✗

3 *I won't probably see him this evening.* ✗

1 *will/shall* or *be going to*?

Fill in the gaps with *will/shall* or *be going to*.

1 Listen to the thunder. There .... be a storm.

2 I feel sick. I don't think I .... go to the disco.

3 I promise I .... return your book tomorrow.

4 My brother .... study medicine at university. He's finally decided.

5 .... I bring some CDs to the party on Saturday?

6 My friends and I .... form a band – we've got it all planned.

2 Present simple or present continuous?

Use the prompts to make questions or statements. You may need to add some words.

1 you/do/anything tonight? Have you got any plans?
Are you doing anything tonight?

2 We/go/to the beach/after/we/finish/school/tomorrow.

3 Come on! The train/leave/9 p.m.

4 Please ring me/as soon as/you/get/home/tonight.

5 Sorry, but I can't babysit tonight. I/play/volleyball.

6 I/have/a party/Saturday. Can you come?

7 Jane/see/new boyfriend/tomorrow.

3 Mixed tenses

Complete the conversations using the verbs in brackets.

1 **A:** .... (you/go out) this evening?

   B: Yes, I .... (go) to my French class.

2 **A:** Have you decided what .... (you/do) after you leave school?

   B: I'm not sure. Maybe I .... (study) engineering.

3 **A:** .... (I/come round) to your house on Friday?

   B: No, I .... (probably/not/be) home until late.

   A: Okay! I .... (see) you next week instead.

4 **A:** What would you like to do today? .... (we/go) to the beach?

   B: No, I've just heard the weather forecast. It .... (rain).

4 Error correction

1 Read the text below and answer these questions.

1 What kind of summer jobs does it mention?

2 Why is a summer job abroad a good idea?

2 Read the text again and look carefully at each line 1–8. Two lines are correct. Tick them. The other lines each have a word which should not be there. <u>Underline</u> it. There are two examples at the beginning (0 and 00).

WORKING ABROAD

 0 Are you going to college after you <u>will</u> leave school? Have

00 you considered working abroad in the holidays? Interested? ✓

 1 You will find definitely some great jobs on the Internet.

 2 There are many reasons for taking a holiday job. You will be earn

 3 some money – and it's fun! Maria and Tony are planning to work

 4 in Spain next summer. Tony's going to go pick fruit. He is

 5 hoping to improve his Spanish, but he won't probably have

 6 time to study! Maria thinks she'll get perhaps a job

 7 working with children, in a holiday camp. Tony and Maria

 8 and thousands of other young people will to experience life in another country this summer. Why not join them?

▶▶ **WB** p.25

Vocabulary building

1 Word formation: *making words negative*

1 Make the words 1–6 negative by adding a prefix or suffix from this list:

dis- / im- / il- / in- / un- / -less

1 fit	3 obedient	5 care
2 possible	4 flexible	6 logical

2 Make the words in CAPITALS at the end of each sentence negative to fit in the gap.

1 Teaching isn't the right job for you. You're a bit too .... PATIENT

2 I don't think Lucia would be a good tourist guide. She's very .... ORGANISED

3 Erica wouldn't be a good office worker. She's too .... DEPENDENT

4 I'm not sure you'd be a good engineer. You're too .... PRACTICAL

5 Being a secretary wouldn't be right for Paula. Her typing is .... HOPE

6 Gary wouldn't be a good writer. He's too .... IMAGINATIVE

3 💬 What jobs would be wrong for you? Why? Tell a partner and see if he/she agrees.

2 Prepositions

1 Fill in the gaps with the correct preposition:

at / for / as / in / on

1 My cousin is working ..... a trainee nurse in the local hospital.

2 I can only phone my father ..... work in an emergency.

3 I don't intend to work ..... an office when I leave school.

4 My uncle works ..... a big company. He's working ..... a very important project at the moment.

5 One of my cousins is self-employed – he works ..... himself.

6 My father often goes abroad ..... business trips.

7 My sister gets very nervous when she has to go ..... an interview.

8 My brother is ..... college studying Maths.

2 Which of the sentences are true for you or your relatives? Tick them. Reword the others to make them true.

Example:

1 *My cousin is still at school.*

3 Lexical cloze

1 Read the text below. What is Lucy's problem?

2 Read the text again and decide which answer A, B or C best fits each space. There is an example at the beginning (0).

0	**A** career	**B** course	**C** work

WHICH CAREER?

When people asked Lucy about her future **(0)** ..A.., she always shrugged her shoulders. She had no idea what she wanted to do. So, when her teacher told the class they had to do work **(1)** .... next term, she panicked. She looked at the list of jobs and the application **(2)** .... the teacher had given her to **(3)** .... . She didn't think she wanted a **(4)** .... with any of the companies on the list. Her parents were lawyers and hoped she would choose law as her **(5)** .... too. But Lucy wanted to do something different, something unusual. She wasn't interested in **(6)** .... a big salary. She didn't want a job where she had to worry about **(7)** .... to a top position or getting a good **(8)** .... when she retired. She read the list of jobs again: medicine, accountancy, secretarial ... Lucy sighed. 'What would I really like to do?' she asked herself.

1	**A** practice	**B** experience	**C** trial
2	**A** paper	**B** page	**C** form
3	**A** fill in	**B** write down	**C** note down
4	**A** work	**B** job	**C** employment
5	**A** profession	**B** course	**C** area
6	**A** earning	**B** winning	**C** gaining
7	**A** movement	**B** retirement	**C** promotion
8	**A** payment	**B** pension	**C** reward

4 💬 Over to you

1 What sort of career would your parents like you to follow? Is it suitable for you? Why/Why not?

2 Would you like to do work experience with a local company? Which one?

3 When you start work, how important will a large salary be for you?

▶▶ **WB** p.27

Listening ▶ *Part 1*

1 Before you listen

▶▶ *listening for a purpose* Unit 1 p.12

Look at the Listening task. Read questions 1–6 and underline the words that tell you:

a) what the situation is

b) what you need to listen for.

2 🖭 Listening strategy

▶▶ *listening for linking words*

Speakers often give reasons to support their points. Sometimes they contradict themselves and say something different. To understand what they really mean, listen for:

- linking words that introduce reasons, e.g. *so*
- linking words that introduce an opposite idea, e.g. *but, although*.

1 Look at the clues provided for questions 1–3, which show you what linking words to listen for. Then listen to the first part of the recording and choose the best answer A or B. You will hear each extract twice.

2 Compare your answers with the class.

3 🖭 Listening task

Now listen to Questions 4–6 and choose the best answer, A or B.

4 💬 Over to you

1 Would you like to have a summer job in a department store? Why/Why not?

2 Would you like to go rock climbing or trekking? Why/Why not?

Listening task

You will hear people talking in six different situations. For questions 1–6, choose the best answer A or B.

1 You hear a <u>successful singer</u> talking about her <u>childhood ambitions</u>.
Who was the <u>biggest influence</u> on her?
A Madonna
B her family ⬚ 1
Clue: *'But really ...'*

2 You hear a boy talking about moving to a new town. When will he move house?
A in May
B in April ⬚ 2
Clue: *'My father has to start his new job in ..., so ...'*

3 You hear a girl talking about her summer job in a department store.
What department is she going to work in?
A the sports department
B the food department ⬚ 3
Clue: *'I really wanted to ... but ...'*

4 You hear a young man talking about his next holiday. How will he spend his time?
A rock climbing
B trekking ⬚ 4

5 You hear a student talking about her studies after school.
What course is she going to take?
A Electronics
B History ⬚ 5

6 You hear a horoscope prediction on the radio.
What is going to happen to Geminis this month, according to the horoscope?
A They are going to win some money.
B They are going to find love. ⬚ 6

Writing: *formal letter*

1 Choose the right style

1 Read the extracts from three letters. For each extract, answer these questions:

1 Why is the person writing the letter?

2 Who is going to read the letter?

3 How well does the writer know the person he/she is writing to?

2 Now match the extracts to the following styles.

a) informal, chatty   .....

b) very formal, polite   .....

c) neutral   .....

2 Formal and informal language

Complete the table with examples from the extracts A–C.

	Formal / Neutral	Informal
Greetings	Dear Sir or Madam	....
	Dear	
Endings	....	Love,
	....	
Useful Phrases	I am writing to ask about	....
	....	Please write soon!
Vocabulary	....	job
	very good	....
Contractions / full forms	I am	I'm
	....	....
Punctuation	No dash (–)	....
	....	exclamation mark (!)

3 Writing strategy

Complete the notes.

▶▶ *choosing the right style*

- Use informal style when you write to people ....

- Use formal or neutral style when you write to people ....

- <u>Don't</u> mix formal and informal styles in the same letter!

Letter A

Dear Sir or Madam,

I saw your advertisement in last Friday's 'Evening News'. I would like to apply for the position of tourist guide.

I have just left school, and I am hoping to go to college in September to study English. I am available for work all this summer.

I believe I am suitable for the post because

I look forward to hearing from you.

Yours faithfully,

Robert Evans
Robert Evans

Letter B

Dear Francesco,

It was great to get your letter and to hear all your news. I can't believe your brother is getting married this year. I hope he's going to invite me to the wedding!

Now I'm looking for a summer job

I've got to stop now. Please write soon.

Love
Julia

Letter C

Dear Mrs. Morris,

I am writing to ask about the private guitar lessons that you have advertised in the local paper. Could you tell me how much they cost, and where the lessons will take place? I can attend classes most evenings after 6 p.m.

Yours sincerely,
Antonia Sanchez

4 Sample writing task

Read the task.

1 What job is being advertised?

2 If you apply for this job, what information should you include in your letter? <u>Underline</u> the key points.

3 Who will read the letter?

4 Should your letter be a) formal b) informal?

Writing task

You have read the following job advertisement in your local paper.

Summer jobs for students

PART-TIME TOUR GUIDES WANTED

A number of British school groups (aged 12–16) are coming to visit our town this summer.

We are looking for energetic young people who can speak English to show them around.

Interested? If so, write and tell us who you are, why you think you are suitable and when you will be available.

**Apply to:
John Adams, Manager
First Choice School Tours
P.O. Box 2312**

Write a letter of application in 120–180 words.

5 Read a sample letter

Read the letter of application below. Then complete it by rewriting sentences a)–g) in a more formal way and putting them in the correct gaps 1–7.

a) Best wishes

b) Dear John

c) I want to try and get the job

d) I'm just the person you're looking for because ...

e) I saw your ad. somewhere and ...

f) Please write soon.

g) I'm free and ready to start work ...

---

(1) ....

(2) .... in yesterday's Evening News. (3) .... of tour guide.

I am 16 years old, and I am at secondary school. I have been studying English for four years, and I speak it quite well. I am hoping to study English at university in the future.

(4) .... I have always been interested in our city, and I know the best places for tourists to visit. I would also like to work with people of my own age. In addition, I have done some part-time work with the local tourist information office.

(5) .... in July and August, and I am free to work during the week and at weekends.

(6) ....

(7) ....

Over to you

6 Writing task

Now write a letter of application for the job on the right. You can make the information up – it doesn't have to be true. Follow the ▸▸ *Writing strategy*.

7 Check your work

Have you used formal style throughout? Are the grammar, spelling and punctuation correct?

Students!

Are you looking for some extra money? Can you speak a foreign language?

We need part-time waiters/waitresses for our busy restaurant. Many of our customers are foreign tourists.

If you think you could do this work, please apply in writing to the address below, telling us something about yourself, why you would like to work here, and which days/times you are available.

**The Manager
The Golden Rose Restaurant
London W12 6WS**

▸▸ **WB** p.28

6 Communication

Speaking ▶ Part 2

1 Vocabulary

1 Look at the photos. Which of the people:

1 is smiling or grinning?
2 is hugging someone?
3 is throwing his/her arms in the air?
4 is waving at somebody?
5 is frowning?
6 is raising his/her eyebrows?
7 has their head in their hands?

2 How are the people feeling? Match the emotions in the box to the people.

happy	worried	pleased	annoyed
proud	jealous	frightened	disappointed
angry	upset	relieved	surprised
impatient	bored	in a good/bad mood	

2 🎞 Listen

1 Listen to a student talking about one of the photos.

1 Which picture is she describing?
2 What explanation does she give for the way the people are feeling?

2 Look at the sentences in the box. Listen to the first part again and circle the correct option in each pair.

describing and speculating
In this picture there are *two people/some young people*.
They are *holding/waving* some pieces of paper.
The boy in the *foreground/background* is grinning.
He looks very *upset/pleased*.
I think he has received *good/bad* news.
The girl *on the right/left* is reading carefully.
I can see from her face she is rather *happy/disappointed*.
Maybe she has *passed/failed* her exams.

3 💬 Speaking task: *photos*

Student A: Choose two photos. Compare and contrast them. Say how you think the people are feeling and why.

Student B: Guess which photos your partner is talking about. Say if you agree or disagree with your partner's explanation.

4 💬 Discussion

1 Have you ever been in any of these situations?
2 How did you feel?

▶▶ WB p.29

49

Reading ▶ Part 2

1 Predict

1 Look at the title and sub-heading of the article, and read the first paragraph only.

1 Why is it useful to understand body language?

2 Who first discovered that our bodies can 'talk'?

3 How did he make this discovery?

2 Can you match the pictures a)– e) to these unconscious messages?

1 'I'm lying.'   *a*

2 'I'm listening carefully.'   *e*

3 'I don't want to listen.'   *b*

4 'I'm honest and reliable.'   *d*

5 'I don't agree with you.'   *c*

3 Read the rest of the text once quickly to find out if your answers to Exercise 1.2 were right.

2 Reading strategy

▶▶ *understanding details*

When you want to understand detailed information in a text, slow down and read carefully. You may need to read parts of the text more than once.

Read the text again and decide if the following statements are true or false according to the text. <u>Underline</u> the parts of the text that help you decide.

Paragraph:

1 Most of our thoughts and feelings are communicated through words. *F*

2 It's easy to hide our true feelings from others. *F*

3 If someone looks away from you during a conversation, they could be lying. *T*

4 Our body language may contradict what we actually say out loud. *T*

5 If you want to gain someone's trust, don't copy their body language. *F*

6 Every culture uses body language. *T*

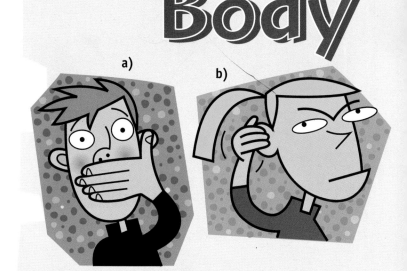

Body

a)   b)

Have you ever wished you could read someone's mind? Well, you can, just by picking up the unconscious messages their body gives you.

Did you know that 93 per cent of our communication with others is non-verbal? What we actually say makes up only seven per cent of the picture! That's what US scientist Ray
5 Birdwhistell found out when he began to study body language back in the 1950s. He filmed conversations and then played them back in slow motion to examine gestures, expressions and posture. When he noticed the same movements
10 happening again and again, he realised that the body can talk too!

We use our bodies to send messages all the time. We nod instead of saying 'Yes', shrug our shoulders to mean 'I don't know', or raise our eyebrows to
15 show surprise. But even when we don't want other people to know how we're feeling, our body language can give us away. It's not difficult to find out what someone is really thinking – and they won't even know it! The way we sit or stand, the
20 expression on our face can reveal far more than words. But many of us miss these important signals, because we don't know what to look out for. Here are some useful tips!

How can you tell if a friend is fibbing to you?
25 They'll often start blushing. They're embarrassed because they know they're not telling the truth. They'll probably look away while they're talking as well. That's because our eyes can reveal what we're thinking, even if we're saying the opposite out loud.
30 Boys tend to look at the ground when they're lying, while girls look at the ceiling. If they put a hand over their mouth, it's another signal they're lying. It's as if they're trying to cover up the lie.

Language

c)

d)

e)

   Imagine you're asking your teacher for a few
35 more days to finish your homework. As you talk,
she starts rubbing her ear. This is a signal that she
doesn't want to hear what you're saying – so
forget it! Remember putting both hands over your
ears as a child to block out your parents' words?
40 Someone who folds their arms tightly across their
chest is sending a similar signal. We use folded
arms as a defensive barrier to protect ourselves
when we feel nervous or think someone is
criticising us. So, if you're making a point in a
45 discussion, and the others fold their arms, you'd
better give up! They're shutting your ideas out and
you won't convince them – even if they say they
agree with you.

   Have you begun to understand how body
50 language works? Now you can use it to your own
advantage. Follow these tips, and you could
become the most popular student in the school!
You've met someone who you'd like to get to know
better. Look them in the eye – it shows you're
55 sincere. When they're talking, lean slightly forward
towards them and tilt your head on one side. This
gives the message 'I'm interested and I'm paying
attention.' Imitate their gestures. If they cross their
legs, do the same. But be careful! Don't be too
60 obvious or they'll think you're making fun of them.

   Even though body language is common to
everyone, there are still some cultural differences.
To avoid any communication problems, it's a good
idea to learn these if you want to travel abroad and
65 make friends with people from another culture.

3 💬 Check answers

Compare your answers to Exercise 2. Use these clues
if you have different answers.

Clues:

1 What does *non-verbal* mean?
2 What does *to give someone away* mean?
3 This paragraph lists three ways of checking if
   someone is telling a lie. What is the second one?
4 Look at the last sentence of the paragraph.
5 This paragraph gives tips on how to use body
   language *to your advantage*.
6 What does *common to everyone* mean?

4 Vocabulary: *phrasal verbs*

1 Fill in the gaps with the correct particle *out* or *up*.

1 Our gestures, expressions and posture *make* 93
   per cent of our communication.
2 It was an American scientist who first *found* ..... that
   our bodies can talk.
3 If you know what signals to *look* ..... for, you can read
   someone's mind.
4 When they are lying, people often put their hand over
   their mouth as if to *cover* ..... the lie.
5 Putting your hands over your ears helps to *block* .....
   other people's voices.
6 If someone folds his arms in a discussion, it means he
   doesn't agree with you. It's better to *give* ..... rather
   than go on talking.

**2 Match the phrasal verbs above to the correct
meaning below.**

a) discovered
b) stop you hearing
c) combine to form
d) stop trying
e) hide
f) try to notice

5 💬 Over to you

Compare these body language facts with your country.

In Britain,

1 nodding your head means *Yes*, shaking your head
   means *No*.
2 people who know each other stand about 1.22 metres
   apart when talking.
3 friends say *Hi* when they meet, but don't normally
   shake hands or kiss.
4 it is rude to stare at someone.

▶▶ **WB** p.30

Grammar: *conditionals* ▶ *p.184*

grammar file 11

A Zero conditional: general truths

- *if* + present + present /imperative

1 *If* you **nod** your head, it **means** 'yes'.

2 *If* you **want** to show you are listening, **tilt** your head on one side.

3 *If* someone **blushes** while talking, they **may be telling** a lie.

B First conditional: likely future events

- *if* + present + *will* /*may* /*might* /*can*

4 *If* my parents **buy** me a computer, I'**ll be** very pleased.

5 *If* you have a computer, you'**ll be able to** send emails to your friends. (ability)

C if or unless?

6 **Unless** you answer my letters, I'll stop writing to you. (If you don't answer my letters, I'll stop writing ...)

> **! What's wrong?**
>
> 1 If I'll win the prize, my parents will be very pleased. ✗
> 2 You won't pass your exams unless you'll study harder! ✗

1 Zero conditional

Fill in the gaps with a verb from the list in the correct form.

study / use / shrug /give / want /not care /be / understand

1 If you .... to know how someone is feeling, *study* his or her body language.

2 If someone *shrug* his shoulders, this shows he *not care* .

3 If you .... always the last to be picked for a game of football, you may .... off the wrong signals.

4 If you .... what your body language is saying, you can *use* .... it to your own advantage.

2 Zero or first conditional?

Put the verbs in brackets into the correct form.

1 If you *use* .. (use) computers in school, you probably *will know* (know) about the Internet.

2 Unless you *learn* .. (learn) to use the Internet, you *won't be able* (not be able to) send emails.

3 If you *have* (have) a computer at home, you *can use* (can/use) it to make new friends.

4 If you *join* .. (join) an emailing list, you *will be able to* (be able to) chat with people all over the world.

grammar file 11

Second conditional: unlikely or hypothetical situations

- *if* + past + *would* /*could* /*might*

1 *If* I **saw** my boyfriend with another girl, I **would feel** jealous.

2 *If* I **was**/**were** rich I **might be** happier – but I don't think so.

> **! What's the difference?**
>
> 1 If I **win** the competition, I'**ll be** really happy.
> 2 If I **won** the competition, I'**d be** amazed.

3 Second conditional

Use the prompts to make questions. Then ask and answer the questions with a partner.

1 What/you/do/if/you/win/a lot of money?

2 If/you/not/have television/you/miss it?

3 If/someone/offer you/a choice of a Discman or mobile phone/which/you/choose?

4 How/you/react/if/your/friend/tell you/a lie?

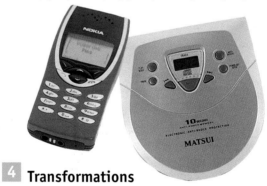

4 Transformations

Complete the second sentence so that it has a similar meaning to the first sentence, using the word given. Do not change the word given. Use between two and five words.

1 Paulo hasn't rung me so I'm feeling down. **better**
   I'll .... me.

2 Smiling is a sign of happiness. **if**
   Most people .... happy.

3 I'm very shy so I blush a lot. **self-confident**
   If .... , I wouldn't blush so much.

4 I won't listen if you shout. **unless**
   I won't listen .... more quietly.

5 Sarah comes home late so her parents get upset. **earlier**
   If Sarah .... , her parents wouldn't get upset.

6 I've got no money so I can't buy my friend a present. **some**
   If I .... , buy my friend a present.

▶▶ **WB** p.30

Vocabulary building

1 Word formation: *adverbs from adjectives*

1 Make adverbs from these adjectives. What spelling changes must you make? Which adverbs are irregular?

1 quick	3 hopeful	5 tragic	7 hard
2 easy	4 terrible	6 fast	8 good

2 Some adverbs have two forms, depending on the meaning. What's the difference?

1 a) I work very **hard**.

  b) I can **hardly** believe the news.

2 a) Don't ring too **late**!

  b) I've been to the cinema a lot **lately**.

3 Adjective or adverb? Underline the correct option.

1 John sighed *angry/angrily* as he waited for his friend.

2 Stella was *careful/carefully* not to hurt her friend's feelings.

3 'You look *sad/sadly*,' Clare told Tom.

4 Alice smiled *happy/happily* when she got her results.

5 Monica could *hard/hardly* stop herself from crying.

6 'Good, you've studied *hard/hardly*,' the teacher said.

7 'What have you been up to *late/lately*?' Kate asked.

8 'You're *late/lately* again!' the teacher said *cross/crossly*.

2 Adverbs that modify adjectives

1 Match each adjective 1–8 with a word that has a similar meaning from a)–h). Then tick the adjective in each pair with the stronger meaning.

1 furious	a) thrilled
2 bad	b) surprised
3 astonished	c) fantastic
4 happy	d) angry
5 good	e) sad
6 miserable	f) horrified
7 scared	g) awful
8 shocked	h) terrified

2 Look at the adverbs below. We use the adverbs in box B with strong adjectives. We use the adverbs in box A with most other adjectives.

A	B
rather/a bit (+ *negative adjs.*) very/really/extremely	absolutely/utterly

Examples:

1 I'm **absolutely** furious with my friend.

2 I'm **rather/a bit/very** annoyed with my friend.

3 I'm **really/very/extremely** happy.

3 ⬭ **Ask and answer these questions.**

How would you feel:

- if you were alone in a dark street at midnight? *Absolutely terrified.*

- if you won £1 million in the national lottery?

- if you passed an exam that you thought you would fail?

- if you lost your best friend's favourite CD?

- if your boyfriend/girlfriend didn't turn up for a date?

- if your brother/sister took something of yours without asking you first?

3 Word formation: *nouns from adjectives/verbs*

Make nouns from these adjectives and verbs. Put them in the correct column below according to the ending. What changes do you have to make?

1 astonish	3 jealous	5 accurate
2 independent	4 happy	6 annoy

-ance	-ce	-cy	-ment	-ness	-y

4 Word-formation task

1 Read the text below. Use the word in CAPITALS underneath to form a noun, adjective or adverb that fits in the space. One space needs a negative form. There is an example at the beginning (0).

LEARNING A LANGUAGE

If you want to learn English well, you need quite a lot of **(0)** *patience* . Trying to pronounce unfamiliar words causes some people a lot of **(1)** .... One of my friends is **(2)** .... able to speak a word without turning bright red! But if you think you're **(3)** .... and will never learn anything, don't worry. Keep practising, and you'll **(4)** .... find that everything is getting easier.

If you want to improve your **(5)** .... , why not go somewhere where they speak English? Travel is easier these days and you'll **(6)** .... find a cheap flight. After a few days, you'll have a lot more **(7)** .... in the language. In fact, you'll be amazed how much **(8)** .... you have made in a very short time.

0 PATIENT	**3** HOPE	**6** PROBABLE
1 EMBARRASS	**4** SUDDEN	**7** CONFIDENT
2 HARD	**5** FLUENT	**8** IMPROVE

2 Add the nouns to the correct column in Exercise 3.1.

▶▶ **WB** p.31

Listening ▶ *Part 4*

1 Think about the topic

Look at the photos.

1 What methods of communication do the photos show?

2 Which methods do you use most/least often?

3 Which method is most suitable for:

a) passing on urgent news?

b) making arrangements?

c) keeping in contact with friends in other countries?

d) keeping in contact with your parents?

2 Before you listen

1 Look at the Listening task.

1 What are you going to hear?

2 What do you have to do?

2 Read statements 1–6.

1 Which statements do you agree with?

2 Which statements would your parents agree with?

3 Can you think of any more advantages and disadvantages?

3 Listening strategy

▶▶ *identifying agreement and disagreement*

When you listen to a discussion, you often need to understand if the speakers agree or disagree with each other. Listen out for expressions that indicate agreement or disagreement.

1 Look at the expressions in the box below. Which indicate agreement? disagreement? Write A or D next to each one.

So do I.	Neither do I.	I think so too.	No, I don't.
No, I prefer to ... not.	Not me.	Yes, but ...	Definitely
	You're (absolutely) right.	I suppose you're right.	

2 ▣ Listen to the first part of the conversation between the parents.

1 Which expression(s) in the box did you hear?

2 Do the speakers agree or disagree about statement 1?

Listening task

You will hear two adults talking about the advantages and disadvantages of children having mobile phones. Decide whether they AGREE or DISAGREE about each of the statements. Write A or D in the boxes.

1 Mobile phones are useful in an emergency. ⬜ 1

2 It's important for teenagers to be in regular contact with their friends. ⬜ 2

3 Parents should limit how much their children use mobile phones. ⬜ 3

4 Children need to be aware of the cost of using mobile phones. ⬜ 4

5 Using mobile phones too much could be dangerous for children's health. ⬜ 5

6 It's better for children to keep their mobile phone switched on at all times. ⬜ 6

4 ▣ Listening task

1 Listen to the rest of the recording. As you listen the first time, tick the expressions of agreement and disagreement that you hear.

2 Listen again and complete the task.

3 Compare your answers with the class.

5 💬 Over to you

Read this statement. Are you for or against?

'Mobile phones should be banned from schools!'

Writing: *informal transactional letter*
▶ Part 1

1 Sample writing task

Read the task.

1 Who is the letter from?

2 What is she going to do?

3 What choices has she got?

4 What advice would you give her?

5 Should you use a formal or informal style when you reply?

Writing task

Your friend Carla wants to do a summer course and has written to ask you for your advice. Read her letter and the two extracts from some brochures she has sent you. Then write a letter to Carla giving her your advice in about 120–180 words.

The long summer holiday starts soon, and guess what? I've decided to come to your country. I'm going to take one of the 'holiday courses' advertised in the brochures I've sent you. The problem is, I can't decide whether to choose the Art course, which means staying in the capital, or the Adventure course which is based in the mountains. Which do you think I should choose?

Hope to hear from you soon.

Love, Carla

NATIONAL GALLERY – Summer Programme

Art appreciation for beginners

Would you like to learn about the world's greatest artists and see their work with your own eyes? Small friendly classes. No previous knowledge required. Hotel accommodation provided in central London.

Ten-day courses in July, August and September (see separate list).

Adventure courses in the UK

Enjoy the thrills of white-water rafting and abseiling in the Scottish mountains.

Small groups led by very experienced tutors.

Accommodation in our local youth centre.

Two-week courses June, July and August (see separate list).

---

2 Read a sample letter

1 Read the letter that Carla's friend wrote. Complete the letter by filling in the gaps. Choose from the following phrases.

a) Thanks a lot for your letter.

b) From my point of view,

c) Sorry for not writing before.

d) As for me,

e) On the other hand, I think you should

f) I'd better stop now

g) I'll drop you a line

h) However, I think you ought to

i) You asked me what I thought about

j) I must tell you about

Dear Carla,

(1) .... I got it yesterday, and I'm writing back immediately.

(2) .... the courses you want to do. The Art Appreciation course could be really interesting – especially as you're so keen on painting! It would also be great to be in London because there's so much to do there.

(3) .... do an Adventure course. You'd have a lot more fun, in my opinion. I think it's a good idea to come in August because the weather will be warmest then.

(4) .... , I haven't got much news to give you. I haven't thought about my holidays yet – but I think I'll ask Dad if I can go abroad too! Well, (5) .... and post this letter. Do write back soon and let me know what you decide. Please give my regards to your family.

All the best,

Paul

2 Read the letter again. Has Paul answered Carla's question?

3 Is his advice the same as yours or different?

Over to you

3 Writing strategy
Complete the notes.

▶▶ *formal and informal letters*
When you write a letter:
- use .... style when you write to friends.
- use exclamation marks (!) and dashes (–) in .... letters but not in .... letters.
- use contractions (*I'm, He's*) in .... letters but not in .... letters.

4 Writing task
1 Read the task. <u>Underline</u> the questions you need to answer in the letter.

Writing task

You are studying at a college in Britain. You have received a letter from a friend who would like to do a language course in Britain. Your friend has sent you an advertisement for a language school. Read the letter and the advertisement and write a reply, giving your advice in 120–180 words.

So, anyway, I've sent you the advert from the school I want to go to. What do you think? Should I do a three-month course or the one-month intensive course? Do you think it's better to live in a student house, or with a local family? When's the best time of year to visit Britain?

Woodfield University
≈ SCHOOL OF ENGLISH ≈

Language courses throughout the year.

Three-month courses: 10 hours a week.
Intensive one-month courses: 25 hours a week.

Accommodation:

with host family or in student house on university campus.

2 You have made some notes to help you reply. Read the notes below and match them to your friend's questions.

host family = best: learn about way of life, speak English all the time! (though student house good fun)

You'll speak better if stay longer (learn fast in one month but not enough time to practise).

Best time = summer, July–August (weather better)

5 Plan your letter
Make a paragraph plan using the notes in Exercise 4.2.

Para. 1
Introduction: Thanks for letter
Para. 2
Topic: Ideas/advice about 1-month intensive course
Para. 3
Topic: Ideas/advice about 3-month course
Para. 4
Topic: Best time to come + best accommodation
Para. 5
Closing remarks

6 Write
Now write your letter. Follow the ▶▶ *Writing strategy*. Use some of the informal language you have seen in this unit.

7 Check your work
Are the grammar, spelling and punctuation correct?

▶▶ WB p.33

7 Your health

Speaking ▶ Parts 3 and 4

1 Vocabulary
How many different kinds of foods can you think of for these categories?

Food that is good for you

Food that is bad for you

2 💬 Quiz
1 Do The Eating Test with a partner.

2 Turn to p.178 to find out what your answers say about your personality.

The Eating Test

1 What do you usually have for breakfast?
- (A) Cereal and milk.
- (B) Eggs and toast.
- (C) Nothing.
- (D) Other: ....

2 If you could have anything you wanted, what would you have for breakfast?
- (A) Scrambled eggs.
- (B) A piece of cake.
- (C) A slice of pizza.
- (D) Other: ....

3 It's lunchtime. You:
- (A) eat the food you have brought from home.
- (B) go to the school cafeteria and buy some chocolate.
- (C) skip a meal because you are worried about your weight.
- (D) Other: ....

4 In a dream, you are in the world's best restaurant. You order:
- (A) steak and chips.
- (B) everything on the menu. (It's a dream, right?)
- (C) a big salad with everything in it.
- (D) Other: ....

5 You are stranded alone on a desert island. What are the foods you need to have with you?
- (A) Meat
- (B) Ice cream, chocolate and cake
- (C) Fruit and vegetables
- (D) Other: ....

3 📼 Listen
1 Students in an English school have been given the chance to run their school cafeteria for a day. Listen to two students planning the menu for the midday meal.

1 Which kinds of food do they think would be
   a) healthy? b) popular with students?

2 What do they finally decide to offer?

2 Listen again and complete the extracts with words from the recording.

asking for/giving suggestions/alternatives
- **A:** What kind of food should we offer?
- **B:** We have to think about ... , so we should have ...
- **A:** But don't you think we should choose popular things like ... ?
- **B:** Maybe we could have something ... and ... , so why don't we choose ...?
- **A:** Do you think we should offer something for dessert, maybe some ... ?

coming to a conclusion
- **B:** I think that's a good combination.
- **A:** So, we've decided. We'll have ... , right?

3 <u>Underline</u> the expressions they use to ask for and give suggestions.

4 💬 Speaking task: *planning*
Plan the menu <u>you</u> would like to have if you had the chance to run the school cafeteria.

5 💬 Discussion
1 Have eating habits changed in your country?
2 What dishes are the most popular?
3 What traditional dish is your favourite?

▶▶ WB p.34

Reading ▶ *Part 3*

1 Predict

1 Look at the title and the introduction to the article. Answer the questions truthfully.

2 What tips about eating habits do you think the article will give?

3 Skim the text to check your ideas.

2 Read the text

Read the text carefully and answer these questions according to the information in the text.

Paragraph:

1 Why should we eat lots of different types of food?

2 What happens when we eat our food too fast?

3 When we want a snack, why is it better to eat fruit rather than sweets?

4 Why should we avoid eating pasta before exercising?

5 Why is it a good idea to eat pasta after exercising?

3 Reading strategy

▶▶ *related words*

Writers often use synonyms and parallel expressions to link their ideas together. If you can identify related words, you will understand the text better.

1 Read the underlined phrase in paragraph 1, line 6. What words in the previous sentence does it refer back to? Circle them.

2 The following sentences have been removed from the text. Look at the gaps in the text and decide where they fit. Look for expressions in the sentence before or after the gap that mean the same as the underlined phrases.

A Foods like these will give you high energy levels.

B That 'happy feeling' is usually followed by a 'mood crash'.

C This signal is important because it will let you know when you are full.

D But this is a temptation you should resist!

E These suggestions may not appeal to you if you hate lettuce or can't stand hot food.

FOOD,

- **Do you eat the same thing every day?**
- **Do you eat your meals in a hurry?**
- **Do you eat lots of fast food?**
- **Are you addicted to sweets and chocolate?**

If you answered YES to any of those questions, then it's time to pay more attention to what you eat and how it affects you, according to nutrition expert Jane Clarke. Read these tips from her new book, *Body Foods for Life!*

TIP 1

If you eat **junk food**[1] day after day – like hamburgers and pizzas – you won't feel satisfied (and you won't be as healthy)! Our nose and mouth are extremely sensitive to the
5 flavour, the smell and even the temperature of the food we eat. We need to stimulate <u>all these senses</u> by eating a wide variety of really tasty foods. So, start experimenting! Instead of your usual boring junk food, why don't you try a
10 crisp mixed salad, with a blue cheese dressing? Or a spicy vegetable soup with fresh bread? **1** ☐ Whatever you choose, the important thing is to try something different and give your taste buds a treat.

TIP 2

15 Always make time to sit down and eat your meals at the table instead of gobbling them down on your way from A to B. This way, you won't eat so much. Even the way you chew your food is important. If you eat in a hurry
20 and don't chew your food properly, you often end up eating more than you really need. Your mouth has lots of nerve endings that send a message to your brain. **2** ☐ If you eat your food too fast, your brain misses the signal, so
25 it doesn't realise that you've eaten anything. As a result, you'll want to carry on eating.

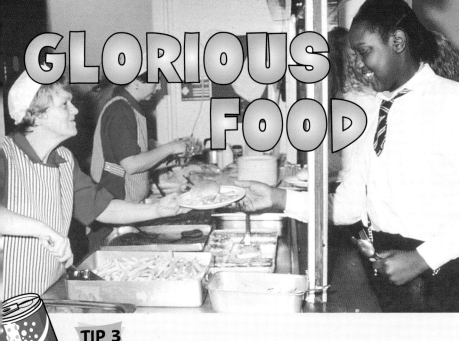

GLORIOUS FOOD

TIP 3

Cut out **sugary snacks**[2] like biscuits, sweets and cake – they're bad for your mind and your body! Your body absorbs sugar very quickly, so eating sugary foods can give you an immediate sense of energy and well-being. But it doesn't last long, unfortunately. **3** So why eat foods that will make you feel high and then low? Just give them up! Instead, have a piece of fresh fruit when you need to increase your energy level quickly. You'll feel much better. Jane Clarke also advises eating more foods that contain protein, like fish, chicken and eggs, and strongly recommends **pulses**[3], such as beans and peas. **Protein-rich foods**[4] are satisfying and nutritious and can give you the same 'happy' feeling as sugar.

TIP 4

Take more exercise! When you start exercising, you'll need to eat the right food at the right time to help you keep going. Jane Clarke warns: 'We're often tempted to fill up on **foods that are full of carbohydrates**[5], such as pasta, bread and rice.' **4** The problem is that these foods make you relax, which is fine if you only eat a little bit. However, if you eat too much, you'll end up feeling sleepy. And this is definitely not a good idea if you're going for a jog!

TIP 5

When you exercise, you need to be wide awake and alert. The best plan is to eat lots of protein along with **fibre-rich**[6] fruit, vegetables or salad. **5** And when you've finished your workout, eat carbohydrates to get back the energy which your body used up during exercise.

4 Vocabulary: *classifying*

Find the words and phrases 1– 6 in the text and answer the questions.

1 What examples does the writer give of these types of foods?
2 What phrases does the writer often use to introduce these examples?
3 Can you add any more examples to each category of food?

5 Vocabulary: *phrasal verbs*

1 Fill in the gaps using phrasal verbs from the text in the correct form. The meaning is given in brackets.

1 It's not a good idea to .... your food. (= *eat very fast*)
2 Eating a lot of sugar is bad for you, so you should .... sweets and chocolate. (= *not include it in your diet*)
3 You'll feel a lot healthier if you .... junk food. (= *stop eating*)
4 Bread and rice .... you .... , so don't eat them before doing exercise. (= *make you feel full*)
5 Foods that contain protein give you energy, so you can .... exercising for longer. (= *continue*)
6 When you exercise, your body .... a lot of energy. (= *consume*)

2 Which four particles do the phrasal verbs above contain?

▶▶ *tip!*

One way of recording phrasal verbs in your vocabulary notebook is under the particle, e.g. *up*.

◀◀

6 💬 Over to you

Has this article changed your attitude to what you eat? Why/Why not?

▶▶ WB p.34

Grammar: *relative clauses* ▶ *p.188*

grammar file 20

A Defining relative clauses: essential information

• **relative pronouns as subject**

1 *I don't like food **which/that** is very spicy.*

2 *People **who/that** exercise a lot should eat protein.*

3 *I know a boy **whose** father is a chef.*

4 *We've found a place **where** they serve great food!*

• **relative pronouns as object**

5 *The coffee **(which/that)** they sell in the cafeteria is awful.*

B Non-defining relative clauses:

• **to add extra information**

6 *Chocolate, **which I love**, gives me spots!*

7 *My brother eats fried food, **which is bad for him**!*

• **to refer to the previous clause**

8 *I'm a vegetarian, **which** means I don't eat meat or fish.*

! What's wrong?

1 *The meal which we had it last night was really good.* ✗

2 *There's the café, that I told you about.* ✗

---

1 Relative pronouns

Fill in the gaps with a relative pronoun. Put brackets ( ) round the pronouns that can be omitted. Do you agree or disagree with the statements?

1 I know lots of people .... are vegetarian.

2 Children .... parents encourage them to eat fruit and vegetables are likely to be healthy.

3 Fast food restaurants .... sell take-away food have become very popular.

4 I like the sort of meals .... you can eat on your lap in front of the TV.

5 I know a place .... you can get fantastic food!

2 Defining relative clauses

Combine the sentences using a defining relative clause. Put brackets round the pronouns that can be omitted.

1 I know the girl. She won that cookery competition on TV.
   I know the girl *who won that cookery competition on TV* .

2 I was looking for a knife. I found it in the drawer.
   I found the ....

3 The boy invited me round for a coffee. I met him last week.

4 I have a friend. His parents own a big restaurant.

3 Non-defining relative clauses

Combine the sentences. Remember to use commas.

1 The first Hard Rock Café attracted a great deal of interest. It opened in London in 1971.
   The first Hard Rock Café, which opened in London in 1971, attracted a great deal of interest.

2 It was owned by two Americans called Isaac Tigrett and Peter Morton. They were big rock music fans.

3 They decorated the café with rock memorabilia such as classic guitars, albums and photos. They had been collecting it for years.

4 The menu was very popular with customers. It included classic American dishes.

4 Error correction

1 Read the text below. What kind of diet should an athlete eat? Why?

2 Read the text again and look carefully at each line 1–8. Two lines are correct. Tick them. The other lines each have a word which should not be there. <u>Underline</u> it. There are two examples at the beginning (0 and 00).

AN ATHLETE'S DIET

 0 In the past, athletes didn't worry about food. But today anyone <u>which</u>
00 who is serious about sport must eat carefully. The reason is clear. ✓
 1 Those athletes that they control their diet usually win in competitions!
 2 Glen Davies, that who is an Olympic champion, revealed the secrets of
 3 his diet last week. He eats food which contains iron because it is good
 4 for the blood. People without iron suffer from anaemia. Glen who is
 5 slim and muscular but he eats a huge amount of food. His main meals,
 6 the which contain lots of protein and carbohydrates, are not enough
 7 for his needs. The food that he likes to snack on it includes bread,
 8 bananas and chocolate! His diet, which he is very strict about, that
   has helped him to become a world champion.

▶▶ **WB** p. 35

Vocabulary building

1 Survey

1 Ask and answer these questions with a partner. Compare your answers with the rest of the class. Who is the healthiest person in the class?

HEALTHY LIVING SURVEY

Tick the right answer for you.

1 How much **exercise** do you get every day?
   ❑ a lot ❑ some ❑ a little ❑ very little ❑ none

2 How much **sport** do you do?
   ❑ a lot ❑ some ❑ a little ❑ hardly any ❑ none

3 How many **hours** do you watch TV every day?
   ❑ none ❑ one ❑ two ❑ three ❑ five ❑ more

4 How many **times** have you eaten junk food this week?
   ❑ none ❑ two ❑ five ❑ seven ❑ more

5 How much **sugar** do you take in your coffee/tea?
   ❑ a lot ❑ a little ❑ none

6 How much **fruit** do you eat every day?
   ❑ a lot ❑ a little ❑ none

7 How many fresh green **vegetables** do you eat?
   ❑ two helpings a day ❑ more than two
   ❑ less than two

8 How much **chocolate** have you eaten today?
   ❑ a lot ❑ some ❑ a little ❑ very little ❑ none

9 How many sugary **drinks** do you have a day?
   ❑ a lot ❑ a few ❑ none

10 How much **sleep** do you get on average?
   ❑ eight hours ❑ less than eight hours
   ❑ more than eight hours

2 Read the survey again.

1 Which nouns in **bold** are a) countable b) uncountable?

2 What words can go with each type of noun, e.g. *much*, *many*, *few*, *little*?

3 What's the difference?

1 I take *a little/very little* salt with my meals.

2 There are *a few/very few* peaches in the bowl.

2 Countable and uncountable nouns

Some nouns can be countable or uncountable, depending on the context. Choose the correct option. Explain your choice.

1 a) Hurry up! We haven't got *much time/many time*!

   b) *How many times/How much time* a week do you eat pasta?

2 a) Can we have *two coffee/two coffees* with our burgers, please?

   b) If you're going to the supermarket, can you get *some coffee/some coffees*, please?

3 a) *How many exercises/How much exercise* did the teacher give us for homework?

   b) He is overweight because he doesn't do *much exercise/many exercises*.

4 a) Would you like *some chicken/some chickens* for dinner tonight?

   b) My neighbour keeps *some chicken/some chickens* in his back garden.

3 Open cloze

1 Look at the title of the text below. What is a *crash diet*? Is it a good idea? Read the text to find out.

2 Read the text again and think of the word that best fits each space. Use only one word in each space. Most of the words you need are quantifiers and particles of phrasal verbs. There is an example at the beginning (0).

A CRASH DIET

Do you think you're too fat? Would you like to lose a (0) *few* kilos? Have you considered going (1) .... a crash diet and eating nothing (2) .... a week? Forget it! That sort of diet just doesn't work. Take my sister Jessica, for example. A while ago, she decided she was too fat. '(3) .... of my clothes fit me any more!' she complained. 'I'll never get (4) .... boyfriend looking like this.' So for the next few days, Jessica dieted. She ate hardly (5) .... cakes or biscuits – in fact she ate very (6) .... food at all! She even cut (7) .... chocolate, which was her favourite snack. She was very bad-tempered, and spent a lot (8) .... time quarrelling and looking miserable.

After a (9) .... weeks, Jessica had lost three kilos. She was thrilled. 'Great! I can have some biscuits today,' she told us. The next day she ate quite a lot of chocolate. After that, she gobbled (10) .... everything in sight. And after a week, Jessica had put on all the weight she had lost!

▶▶ WB p.37

Listening ▶ Part 3

1 Before you listen

1 You are going to hear four people talking about how they keep fit. Look at the photos, which show different ways of keeping fit.

1 Which do you think is
   a) the most effective way to keep fit? Why?
   b) the most enjoyable way to keep fit? Why?

2 What do you do to keep fit?

2 Read the instructions for the Listening task.
What do you have to do?

2 Listening strategy

▶▶ *predicting what you will hear*

Try to think of words and phrases that each speaker might use to talk about an aspect of the topic.

1 Read the statements A–E in the Listening task. Which are about a) the benefits b) the drawbacks of this type of exercise?

2 Which of the phrases below would you associate with each option A–E?

1 everyday activities   ..C..
2 so much better   .....
3 hard to fit it all in   .....
4 bad for you   .....
5 in a good mood   .....

3 🔊 Listening task

1 Listen to the recording and do the Listening task.

2 Compare your answers with the class. Then listen again to check.

4 💬 Over to you

1 Which of the speakers has chosen the most unusual method of exercising?
2 Would you like to try it?

Listening task

You will hear four different people talking about how they keep fit. For questions 1–4, choose from the list A–E what each speaker says. Use the letters only once. There is one extra sentence which you do not need to use.

This kind of exercise

A sometimes interferes with my other activities.   Speaker 1   [1]

B has made me healthier than I used to be.   Speaker 2   [2]

C goes well with my regular routine.   Speaker 3   [3]

D makes me feel very happy.

E is only healthy if you can do it well.   Speaker 4   [4]

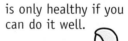

Writing: *report* ▶ *Part 2*

1 Sample writing task

1 Read the task.

1 Who is going to read the report?

2 What is the purpose of the report? What does the reader want to know?

2 What should you look for when you visit the restaurant? Tick the most important points from the list below.

- size
- prices
- where it is
- manager's name
- kind of food
- opening times
- how you can pay
- atmosphere
- what food you ate
- colour of the walls

2 Read a sample report

1 Read the report opposite and write these headings in the appropriate place.

Introduction

Food

Conclusion

Facilities and Entertainment

General information

2 Answer these questions.

1 Which points has the writer included from the list in Exercise 1.2? Did you tick the same points?

2 What is the writer's opinion of the restaurant? Where does he give it?

3 Has he given enough information to support his opinion?

3 Discuss the style.

Is the style formal or informal? Underline examples.

3 Format and style

Look again at the sample report. Which of 1–10 on the right are features of reports? Tick them. Cross out the others.

Writing task

You are working part-time at a tourist centre. The manager has sent you this note.

I'm preparing a tourist handbook for young people coming to this area on holiday. I want to include a section about where to eat. A new restaurant has just opened in the town centre. It's called 'The Stable'. Could you visit it for me, try the food and write a report on it? Let me know if you think it's suitable for young people.

John Hammon

Write your report in 120–180 words.

To: John Hammon
From: Greg Makris
Date: 3 September
Subject: 'The Stable' restaurant

(1) ....

The purpose of this report is to describe the new restaurant, 'The Stable'.

(2) ....

The restaurant is a short walk from the bus station. It is open seven days a week from 7 p.m. – midnight. Prices are very reasonable, so young people can easily afford to eat there. The atmosphere is lively and friendly.

(3) ....

The food is home-made and very fresh. There is a range of dishes to suit everyone, from steak to pasta. The desserts are excellent, particularly the chef's speciality. A vegetarian menu is also available.

(4) ....

There is a garden where you can eat outside in the summer. There is live music every Friday and Saturday night, which is popular with young people.

(5) ....

I would certainly recommend this restaurant to students. It is convenient and good value and is well worth visiting.

A report:

1 is written for a particular purpose usually related to a work situation.

2 begins and ends like a letter: *Dear Sir / Yours faithfully*.

3 uses headings at the top: **To, From, Date, Subject**.

4 states the purpose for writing in the introduction.

5 has paragraphs with topic sentences.

6 has sections with headings to make it easy to read.

7 may contain recommendations.

8 is written in a formal style.

9 presents the information in short, clear sentences.

10 does not include personal details or opinions except in the conclusion.

4 Writing skills: *formal language*

You should use quite formal language in a report. Make these remarks more formal.

1 You wouldn't believe how many dishes they serve!
They serve a wide range of dishes.
2 The facilities are absolutely terrific!
3 The restaurant is really, really huge!
4 You can listen to the most fabulous music!
5 The décor is absolutely awful!
6 The waiters are nicer than you can possibly imagine.
7 Don't buy food and drinks in the cinema whatever you do – they cost the earth!

Over to you

5 Writing strategy

Complete the notes.

▶▶ *writing reports*

When you write a report, you should:
• state the purpose of the report in the ....
• divide the report into .... and use clear ....
to help the reader find the information they need.
• use .... language.
• present the information clearly and concisely, and use .... sentences.
• state your opinion or recommendations in the ....

6° Writing task

Read the task and <u>underline</u>:

1 who will read the report.
2 the purpose of the report.

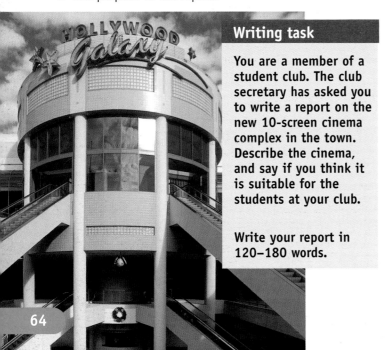

Writing task

You are a member of a student club. The club secretary has asked you to write a report on the new 10-screen cinema complex in the town. Describe the cinema, and say if you think it is suitable for the students at your club.

Write your report in 120–180 words.

7 Plan your report

1 Tick the points you will include in your report. Put a cross next to those that are not suitable. Add ideas of your own, too! But remember, your reader is a busy person, and only wants the most important information.

• where it is
• how to get there
• what kinds of films are shown there
• what facilities there are e.g. cafeteria, shops, video games, etc.
• how much the tickets are
• who you went with
• times of film shows
• what the film theatres are like
• how comfortable the seats are
• the film that you saw
• opening times
• whether there are discounts for young people

2 Put the points you ticked under the appropriate heading.

Introduction
General information
Film shows
Other facilities
Conclusion

3 Now note down what you can say about each point.
Example:
The cinema complex is in the centre of town, next to the train station.

4 Complete these headings.

To:
From:
Subject:
Date:

5 Look back at the introduction to the sample report on p.63. How will you introduce this report?

8 Write

Now write your report. Follow the ▶▶ *Writing strategy*.

9 Check your work

Have you used the correct format and style? Are the grammar, spelling and punctuation correct?

 WB p.38

8 House and home

Speaking ▶ Part 2

1 Vocabulary

Look at the photos of different places to live.

1 What can you see in each photo?

2 What do you think it's like to live in those places?

types of home: semi-detached/detached house block of flats bungalow cottage villa

features: balcony patio garden fence hedge garage verandah

location: in the country/the town centre/the suburbs by/close to the river on the outskirts of town

adjectives: fun boring exciting dull

2 🔊 Listen

1 Listen to a student comparing and contrasting two of the photos.

1 Which two photos does he talk about?

2 Tick the advantages and cross the disadvantages he mentions of living in each place.

- plenty to do
- isolated
- public transport
- shops, cafés and other amenities
- entertainment
- no privacy
- quiet and peaceful
- noisy
- need a car to go anywhere
- neighbours
- no time to relax

2 Complete the sentences in the box with ideas from the recording.

talking about advantages and disadvantages

In a city there are a lot of disadvantages for me. You can … and also … But on the other hand, …

The biggest problem with living in the city is …

In a village there are more advantages because …

You can … in a village.

The countryside is … . That's the biggest advantage.

3 Underline the expressions the speaker uses to talk about advantages and disadvantages.

4 Do you agree with the speaker? Use the points in Exercise 2.1 and the expressions in the box above to express your own ideas.

3 💬 Speaking task: *photos*

Take turns to choose two photos. Compare and contrast them and talk about the advantages and disadvantages of living there.

4 💬 About you

1 What do you like most about where you live?

2 What would you like to change if you could?

3 If you could live anywhere, where would it be?

▶▶ WB p.39

Reading ▶ Part 4

1 Predict

1 Read the title and sub-heading of the article and look at the photos of the four boys.

1 Can you guess what kind of person each boy is? Choose from these adjectives.

disorganised   creative   quiet   sporty   idealistic

2 What do you think each boy's room is like? Is it tidy or messy? How is it decorated?

2 Now read each text very quickly and check your predictions.

2 Reading strategy

▶▶ *scanning for parallel expressions*

When you want to find specific information quickly, think about other ways in which the same ideas could be expressed in the text. Scan the text for these parallel expressions.

1 Read statements 0–5 in the box below and think of different ways to express the underlined ideas.
Example:

untidy – *messy; things lying around*

what kind of person – *personality*

2 Now scan the texts and match statements 1–5 to the right boy. Write A, B, C or D in the boxes. Use the underlined phrases in the texts to help you.

Which boy says this?		
My room is usually <u>untidy</u>.	**0**	B
My room shows <u>what kind of person</u> I am.	**1**	
There are <u>times</u> when I <u>don't like my room</u>.	**2**	
For me, it's <u>vital</u> to have <u>a place away from others</u>.	**3**	
I find my room is a good place <u>to relax in</u>.	**4**	
I wouldn't mind <u>cleaning my room myself</u>.	**5**	

My private

We asked some teenage boys to 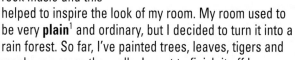 and say why they like them.

A *Jason Furrows, 16, has turned his bedroom into a Brazilian rain forest.*

'I've been fascinated by Brazil since the 1994 World Cup. When they won, I decided to find out more about the country and the people. I've never been to Brazil but I would like to save up and go when I'm older. I also love Latin rock music and this helped to inspire the look of my room. My room used to be very **plain**[1] and ordinary, but I decided to turn it into a rain forest. So far, I've painted trees, leaves, tigers and monkeys across the walls. I want to finish it off by painting the ceiling sky-blue. <u>My room reflects my personality</u>, because the things in it are the most important things in my life: Brazil and music. My friends think my room's quite cool but I'm sure others think it's a bit **weird**[2]. I'm quite proud of it, though. It's my dream room – I wouldn't change anything about it.'

B *Simon Ashley, 21, has a typical student bedroom on a university campus.*

'I've lived in this house for ten months and I'm happy with my room. <u>It looks quite disorganised</u>, probably because I'm terrible at organising my lecture notes and putting them into files. I usually put them in piles on the floor – in fact, I'm not even sure what colour my carpet is any more. I have to spend a lot of time in my room working, especially when I'm revising for exams. <u>The floor's usually covered with piles of paper, dirty clothes and empty coffee cups</u>. Sometimes I wish I was tidier, but I've made a real effort to make it nice. There are various ornaments and bits and pieces I've collected from my travels to Nepal and Africa. These things mean a lot to me, but not much to anyone else. <u>My bedroom's essential to me, because you must have your own space</u> when you're sharing a house with other students. It's a quiet, safe place away from the **hectic**[3] life of the university.'

space

describe their rooms,

C **_Brian Baldwin, 16, has created a room dedicated to his favourite football team._**

50

'Football's an important part
55 of my life, and I spend most
of my time either playing or
watching it. I've been a fan of
Tottenham Hotspur since my
granddad got me interested
when I was eight. I chose to
60 decorate my room like this a couple of years ago, so now
I've got Tottenham Hotspur wallpaper, curtains, lampshade,
clock, and bedcovers. I've also put up photos and posters
of the players all over the walls. I sometimes think it's all a
bit too much, but <u>I really like my room most of the time –</u>
65 <u>except when Tottenham lose.</u> I spend quite a lot of time in
there, and it's good to have a bit of privacy. I've got cable
TV, so if my mum and dad are watching something, I can
just go and watch TV in my room. I'm reasonably **neat**[4] and
<u>I'd tidy my own room</u>, but my mum always does it for me
70 because she hates it being messy.'

D **_Mohamed Nasir, 17, is keen on astronomy, and his room reflects his interest._**

75 'About six months ago, my parents said I could redecorate
my room just how I wanted it. I've been crazy about
astronomy for as long as I can remember, so I painted the
ceiling dark blue and the walls light blue, and stuck
luminous stars on the ceiling. When you switch off the
80 light, you can see the stars shining. I've also stuck posters
of astronauts and maps of the stars on the walls. My
room's at the top of the house, and I get a really good view
of the sky from the window.
I've set up my telescope there,
85 so that I can study the stars
whenever I want. I find looking
at the stars much more
interesting than watching TV
with my parents, so I spend a
90 lot of time in the evenings up
there. It's really peaceful and
relaxing – <u>I think my room is a</u>
<u>great place to</u> **chill out**[5] after
95 school.'

3 Multiple-matching task

Now match the rest of the statements 6–12 to the
right boy. <u>Underline</u> the key words in the questions.
Look for parallel expressions in the texts.

I'm quite a tidy person.	**6**
I think my room is perfect for me.	**7**
I prefer being in my room to watching TV.	**8**
I'm not a very well-organised person.	**9**
People have different opinions about my room.	**10**
My room was decorated very simply before.	**11**
I've tried hard to make my room attractive.	**12**

4 Vocabulary: _unfamiliar words_

►► *synonyms and antonyms*

Sometimes you can work out the meaning of a word
because another word that has a similar or opposite
meaning also appears in the text.

**Find the words 1–5 in the text. Look for a word in
the same sentence that has a similar or opposite
meaning. What do the words mean?**

5 Over to you

1 Which statements in the multiple-matching task
are true about you?

2 If you could redecorate your room exactly as you
want it, what would you do first?

- paint the walls a different colour?
- put up new posters or pictures?
- replace the curtains?
- rearrange the furniture?
- throw out a lot of your old possessions?
What else would you do?

►► WB p.39

Grammar: *wishes (present and future)*
▶ *p.185*

grammar file 12

A *wish* + past: present situations that we regret

1 *I **wish** we **lived** in the country.* (but we don't)

2 *I **wish** it **wasn't/weren't** raining.* (but it is)

3 *I **wish** I **was/were** rich.* (but I'm not)

4 *I **wish** I **could** swim.* (but I can't)

B *wish* + would

• **situations that could change in the future**

5 *I **wish** Dad **would** let me drive his car.* (but he probably won't)

6 *I **wish** it **would** stop raining.* (but it might not)

• **criticising people**

7 *I **wish** Mum **would** knock before coming into my room.* (she doesn't)

8 *I **wish** you **wouldn't** borrow my things all the time!* (it's irritating)

Note: For emphasis, we can use *if only* instead of *wish*.

! What's wrong?

1 *I wish I would speak English more fluently.* X

2 *I wish my bedroom would be bigger.* X

3 *I wish my friends stopped teasing me.* X

---

1 *wish* + past simple

1 Read the statements and imagine you are the person speaking. Then make two sentences to say what you wish and why.

1 My bedroom is very small.

I wish my bedroom was bigger. If I had a bigger bedroom, I could invite all my friends round.

2 I live in a very small town.

3 We haven't got a garden.

4 There isn't a swimming pool near here.

5 I don't own a computer.

2 ⭕ **Is there anything in your life that you wish was different? Tell a partner.**

2 *wish* + would

1 Complete the sentences in a logical way.

1 My boyfriend watches TV all the time.

I wish my boyfriend wouldn't watch so much TV!

2 My sister uses my things without asking me.

I wish she .... first!

3 My parents make me get up very early.

I wish they .... stay in bed.

4 My brother plays the same CD all the time.

I wish he .... something different!

5 My uncle keeps teasing me about my clothes.

I wish he .... doing it.

6 My mum makes me do my homework every night.

I wish she .... it.

7 My parents don't let me put up any posters on my bedroom walls.

I wish they .... a few!

8 I can't go out until my friend rings.

I wish my friend .... !

2 ⭕ **Is there anything that you wish people you know would or wouldn't do?**

3 Transformations

Complete the second sentence so that it has a similar meaning to the first sentence, using the word given. Do not change the word given. Use between two and five words.

1 I don't like living in a flat. **house**

I wish .... instead of a flat.

2 My brother always forgets to take his front door key. **would**

I wish my brother .... his front door key.

3 I have to share a bedroom with my sister. **own**

I wish .... bedroom.

4 I don't have a TV in my bedroom, but I'd like one. **only**

If .... TV in my bedroom.

5 My brother always makes a noise when I'm studying. **quiet**

I wish my brother .... when I'm studying.

6 Peter has to stay at home tonight. **out**

Peter wishes he .... tonight.

▶▶ **WB** p.40

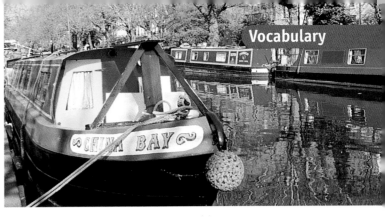

Vocabulary building

1 Prepositions

Fill in the gaps with the correct preposition *in*, *on* or *at*. Then ask and answer the questions with a partner.

1 Do you live in the town centre or ..... the outskirts?

2 What kind of house do you live ..... ?

3 Would you rather live ..... a big city or ..... the country? Why?

4 Do you go out ..... weekday evenings or do you stay ..... home?

5 Have you got lots of posters ..... the walls of your bedroom? What sort?

6 Do any of your friends live ..... your street?

2 Words that go together: *make or do?*

1 Put the items below into the correct column.

a cup of coffee / the washing-up / a noise / an effort / the shopping / dinner / some dusting / your bed / the cleaning / some gardening / the housework

make	do
a cup of coffee	

2 When was the last time you did any of the above? Tell a partner.

3 Phrasal verbs

1 Fill in the gaps in the sentences using a phrasal verb in the correct form.

put up (x3)	pull down	take down	do up
tidy up	wash up	put away	

1 My mum makes me .... my room every weekend – she doesn't like it when it's in a mess.

2 After a meal, it's my job to .... the dishes and .... them ....

3 If I .... posters of rock stars in the kitchen, my dad would make me .... them ....

4 My parents don't mind .... my friends .... for the night if it gets too late.

5 I think they should .... the old houses in my neighbourhood and .... new apartment buildings. There's no point in trying to .... them ....

2 Which sentences above are true for you?

4 Lexical cloze

1 Read the text below.

1 How is this home different from other homes?

2 What are the advantages and disadvantages of living there?

2 Read the text again and decide which answer A, B or C best fits each space. There is an example at the beginning (0).

0 **A** in   **B** at   **C** for

A HOME WITH A DIFFERENCE

When Rebecca Martin takes friends home **(0)** .C. the first time, they usually get a shock. Why? Because Rebecca doesn't live in a house or apartment **(1)** .... most people do. Instead, she and her parents live on a boat on the river.

When you step inside the boat, you have to watch your head because the **(2)** .... is very low. There is very little **(3)** .... on the boat but it is all really cleverly designed. There are five rooms – a living room, a kitchen, a tiny bathroom with a shower and a **(4)** .... , and two bedrooms. There are two sofas in the living room, **(5)** .... can be pulled out and turned into beds at nighttime. This means Rebecca can **(6)** .... friends up overnight from time to time.

Rebecca is not naturally tidy but she has to make a real effort to put her things **(7)** .... on the boat. The good thing is that there are no neighbours next door, so Rebecca can **(8)** .... as much noise as she likes!

1	**A** as	**B** same	**C** similar
2	**A** roof	**B** top	**C** ceiling
3	**A** place	**B** space	**C** area
4	**A** washbasin	**B** sink	**C** bowl
5	**A** who	**B** where	**C** which
6	**A** put	**B** sleep	**C** take
7	**A** off	**B** away	**C** down
8	**A** do	**B** make	**C** produce

▶▶ WB p.42

Listening ▸ *Part 2*

1 Before you listen

You are going to listen to a radio programme about Japan.

1 How much do you know about Japan?

2 Look at the photos. What do they tell you about how Japanese people live?

2 Listening strategy

▸▸ *predicting the information you need*

Before you listen, try to predict what kind of information you need to listen for.

1 Look at the Listening task.

1 What is the topic of the radio programme?

2 What points will the speaker talk about?

2 Ask yourself questions like this.
Question:

1 What kind of material can mats be made of?

2 What types of seating might fit here?

3 How many square metres is <u>my</u> home?

4 What do people usually sleep on?

5 Where can people store bedding?

Now, you continue for questions 6–10.

3 🔲 Listening task

1 Listen to the recording and complete the notes using no more than three words or a number in each space.

2 Compare your answers with a partner.

3 Listen again and check your answers.

Listening task

You will hear part of a radio programme about traditional Japanese homes. For questions 1–10, complete the notes.

TRADITIONAL JAPANESE HOMES

Floor covering: *'Tatami' mats made of* [1]

Seating: [2] *placed on the mats.*

Size of average home: [3] *square metres.*

Sleeping arrangements: [4] *called a futon.*

Bedding: *stored in* [5] *during the day.*

Walls and doors: *covered with* [6]

Heating: *often located under* [7] *called a 'kotatsu'.*

Family life: *strong sense of* [8] *and* [9]

Entertaining: *usually takes place in* [10]

4 💬 Over to you

How do Japanese homes compare with homes in your country now and in the past?

Writing: *article* ▶ *Part 2*

1 Sample writing task

Read the task.

1 Where will this article be published?

2 Who will read it?

3 Think about the kinds of articles you enjoy reading. What makes a good article? What do you think the Editor will look for when choosing the best article for the school magazine?

Writing task

You see this advertisement on the school noticeboard. Write your article in 120–180 words.

CALLING ALL STUDENTS

Would you like your writing to be published?

Our school magazine needs articles.

Write an article describing your favourite room.

Send your article to the Editor.

The best article will be published in our next issue.

---

2 Compare two sample answers

Look at the list of features of a good article. Then read the two articles below. Tick the features that each article contains. Which article is better?

A good article:	Article A	Article B
1 has a title to catch the reader's attention.		✓
2 has a lively introduction that makes the reader want to read on.		
3 is divided into paragraphs that deal with a different aspect of the subject.		
4 has a conclusion that finishes off the article.		
5 includes specific details to add interest.		
6 is written in a style appropriate to the reader (formal or fairly informal).		
7 contains interesting vocabulary.		
8 uses a variety of sentence patterns.		

Article A

My favourite room is my bedroom and I like it very much.

When you go in, the first thing you notice is a big poster on the wall. It's of my favourite singer. Then you can see that I've got a lovely view from my bedroom window. My desk is in front of the window, and it's nice to have such a great view while I am studying. In my room you can see all the things that I like. I've got a lot of books and I have all my favourite photographs on top of my bookshelf. There's a TV and a computer, because I like computer games and videos. You can also see a collection of postcards from all the places I've been on holiday.

So that's why my bedroom is my favourite room.

Article B

THE HEART OF THE HOUSE

Do you prefer to be in a quiet room alone, or do you like a noisy family room? For me, the noisiest place is the most friendly, and so my favourite room is the kitchen.

It's a large room, and my family spend a lot of their time there. In the middle of the room there is a big wooden table where we all meet to have our meals. At other times my brother and I do our homework there, or just sit and chat.

The kitchen reflects our busy lives. It is always messy, because we don't have time to tidy up. There are notes all over the fridge, reminding us to do things. Near the washing machine there are bags of sports clothes that we need to wash for the next football match or swimming lesson.

Although it's a busy and untidy place, I love this room. It's the centre of our house, and you can always find someone there to talk to. I wouldn't change it for anything!

Over to you

3 Writing strategy

Complete the notes.

▶▶ *writing articles*

When you write an article, you should:

- give your article an eye-catching ....
- write an interesting ...., maybe starting with a question.
- divide the article into separate ....
- write a .... that finishes off the article in an interesting way.

4 Writing task

1 Read the task and <u>underline</u>:

1 the topic you must write about.

2 who will read the article.

2 What style should you use?

> ### Writing task
>
> **You have been asked to write an article for your school magazine on the following question:**
>
> *What would your dream home be like?*
>
> **Write your article in 120–180 words.**

3 Look at the photos. Do any of them represent your dream home?

4 Describe your dream home to a partner.

1 Where would it be?

2 What would it look like from the outside/from the inside?

3 How would it be decorated?

4 What special features would it have?

5 Plan your article

1 Tick the points you could include in your article. Add ideas of your own.

- kind of house
- location
- members of my family
- size/number of rooms
- special features (balcony, garden, etc.)
- furniture
- my friends' houses
- decor (modern? traditional?)

2 Decide which points you can group together in the same paragraphs.

3 Make a plan like the one in Unit 4 p.38. Note down details of what you are going to write for paragraphs 2 and 3 (and 4, if necessary).

6 Writing skills: *introductions and conclusions*

1 Look at the introductions to two articles below. Which one:

- is not very original?
- makes the reader want to read on?
- is not the right length?
- starts with a question to make the reader think about the topic?

A *I sometimes think about my dream home and hope I can find it.*

B *If you could live anywhere, what sort of home would you choose? We all have our fantasies, but I think my dream home would amaze you.*

2 Now think of a good introduction for your article and note it down.

3 Think of a good conclusion. Note it down.

7 Write

Write your article. Follow the ▶▶ *Writing strategy*. Remember to write a topic sentence for each paragraph. Check all the details are relevant to the topic.

8 Check your work

Would your article interest your readers? Are the grammar, spelling and punctuation correct?

▶▶ **WB** p.43

Progress test 2

1 Lexical cloze

For questions **1–10**, read the text below and decide which answer **A, B** or **C** best fits each space. There is an example at the beginning **(0)**.

Example:

0 **A** of **B** a **C** for

BUILD A PIZZA!

A slice **(0)** *A* pizza can give you **(1)** ... the nutrients you need from the five basic food groups. These five groups **(2)** ... the foods which we need to eat to stay **(3)** ... . Eating well is especially important during your teenage years **(4)** ... your body experiences its biggest growth increase since birth.

Healthy food does not have to be boring, and pizza **(5)** ... you the chance to create an exciting **(6)** ... using a combination of food from the five groups. Group 1, which includes milk **(7)** ... cheese, provides you with calcium. You get protein and 'B' vitamins from group 2, which is the meat and nuts group. Vegetables are in group 3, and fruit is in group 4. The **(8)** ... group includes bread and pasta.

If you have pizza **(9)** ... dinner, use your imagination and you will eat something from all five food groups! Your pizza won't give you the total daily amount you need from each group, but you will certainly be on your **(10)** ... to eating more healthily.

	A	**B**	**C**
1	some	all	many
2	contain	hold	own
3	good	fine	healthy
4	because	although	however
5	gives	makes	does
6	plate	food	meal
7	or	and	also
8	least	last	end
9	to	for	at
10	road	route	way

2 Open cloze

For questions **11–20**, read the text below and think of the word which best fits each space. Use only one word in each space. There is an example at the beginning **(0)**.

KEEP IN TOUCH

The world **(0)** ..*of*.. mobile communications is changing fast. Three years ago, hardly anyone **(11)** .... the UK sent text messages using a mobile phone. Now, we send more **(12)** .... 20 million every day. Not even the Internet revolution happened this quickly. WAP technology allows you **(13)** .... access the Internet from your mobile, and it's the fastest **(14)** .... most convenient way to get online. You can look up TV schedules, buy CDs, find out what's on **(15)** .... the cinema or check your emails where and when you like. You can have **(16)** .... of fun with a mobile phone, too. On some phones, you can download unusual ring tones from websites. You can **(17)** .... set individual ring tones for different callers, so your phone could play a special song when your best friend calls. With a WAP phone, you can link **(18)** .... with other WAP owners and play games such **(19)** .... 'hangman'. WAP phones are not expensive and it is predicted that **(20)** .... will get better and cheaper very quickly. Now that's progress!

3 Key word transformations

For questions **21–26**, complete the second sentence so that it has a similar meaning to the first sentence, using the word given. **Do not change the word given.** You must use between two and five words, including the word given. There is an example at the beginning **(0)**.

Example:

0 You mustn't spend so much money. **stop**
   You must ....*stop spending*................. so much money.

21 Unless we hurry we're going to be late. **if**
   We're going to be late .... hurry.

22 Unfortunately I can't go to America on holiday. **wish**
   I .... to America on holiday.

23 Maria has to get up very early for school. **later**
   Maria wishes .... for school.

24 I don't like eating in crowded restaurants. **which**
   I don't like eating .... crowded.

25 Susan has eaten very little chocolate recently. **hardly**
   Susan .... recently.

26 You're not patient enough to be a teacher. **too**
   You're .... to be a teacher.

73

4 Error correction

For questions **27–36**, read the text below and look carefully at each
line. Some of the lines are correct, and some have a word which should
not be there. If a line is correct, put a tick (✓) next to it. If a line has
a word which should not be there, <u>underline</u> the word. There are two
examples at the beginning **(0 and 00)**.

LIFE IN A CASTLE

  0 We may think that life in a medieval castle was luxurious, but in fact it was ✓

00 not very easy, even for people who <u>they</u> were wealthy. Unlike today,

27 they didn't have any of central heating. There was just an open fireplace,

28 which wasn't very efficient. The lord of the castle and his family also had

29 heavy blankets and feather mattresses to keep out the cold when in the

30 winter. Servants and soldiers only had thin bedclothes. Even when the

31 weather was good, the castle was remained cool inside, so people spent

32 as much time as possible outdoors in the sunshine. Unlike today, work

33 began at sunrise, when one of the castle guards blew his trumpet and to

34 wake everybody up. Modern alarm clocks have taken out the place of

35 the trumpet! Breakfast it consisted of bread and a drink, and was very

36 different from the type of meal what we are used to eating nowadays.

5 Word formation

For questions **37–44**, read the text below. Use the word given in capitals
underneath the text to form a word that fits in the space in the text. There is an
example at the beginning **(0)**.

WHOSE AMBITION?

My ambition has always been to become a **(0)** *professional* footballer, but I found
out not long ago that I am not nearly good enough to be **(37)** .... – in
fact I'm completely **(38)** .... I really wish I could play in a local team, but
I'm **(39)** .... to say that it seems to be an impossible dream for me to play
football. **(40)** .... , I am just not fit enough, and because of my very
(41) .... school studies, I cannot give up the time needed to reach the
(42) .... high level of fitness that is required by teams nowadays. Now I'm
(43) .... going to study medicine instead because my parents have always
wanted me to become a doctor. That's their **(44)** .... !

  0 PROFESSION
37 SUCCESS
38 HOPE
39 DISAPPOINT
40 FORTUNATE
41 DEMAND
42 EXTREME
43 PROBABLE
44 AMBITIOUS

9 Music

Speaking ▶ Part 2

1 Vocabulary

1 Look at the photos. Which photo shows:

a) a classical orchestra?   b) a jazz band?
c) a Country and Western singer?   d) a pop concert?
e) a salsa band?   f) a rap group?

2 Look at the words in the box. Group them under these headings:

Equipment   Instruments   Performers   Clothing

> suit   microphone   conductor   violin   cowboy hat
> electric/acoustic guitar   loudspeakers   lead singer

Now find the items in the photos. Add some more.

2 💬 About you

Ask and answer these questions.

1   What kind of music do you like best?
2   Which of these is most important to you?
   • you can dance to the music
   • the image of the singer/band/orchestra
   • your friends like it
3   How do you prefer to listen to music?
   • on CD/mini-disk   • at a live concert
   • on the radio   • in a club
   • on MTV

3 📼 Listen

1 Listen to a student talking about two of the photos.

1   Which photos does she compare and contrast?
2   Which of these points does she mention? Tick them.
   • the instruments   • the equipment
   • the clothes   • the audience
3   Which concert would she prefer to go to?

2 Listen again. What reasons does she give for her preferences? Complete the sentences in the box.

> *expressing preferences*
>
> I'm not so keen on ... . For me, it's ... because ...
> I prefer the kind of music that ...
> I'd much rather go to a ... than a ... because ...
> The kind of music that I like most is ...

4 💬 Speaking task: *photos*

Take turns to choose two photos. Use the ideas and expressions in Exercise 3.

Student A: Compare and contrast two of the photos, and say which concert you would enjoy going to.

Student B: Compare and contrast two more photos, and say what type of music you prefer.

5 💬 Discussion

What kind of music is most popular among young people in your country?

▶▶ WB p.46

Reading ▶ Part 1

1 Think about the topic

Look at the title and sub-heading of the article, and the photos.

1 What is the article about?

2 What do you know about how a pop album is made?

3 What do the photos tell you about the process?

2 Reading strategy

▶▶ *using headings to predict content*

Magazine and newspaper articles often use headings:

- to attract the reader's attention.
- to show the reader what each section is about.
- to make the article look more interesting.

Read the headings to get an idea of the paragraph topics in the text.

1 The following headings have been removed from the article. There is one heading for each paragraph in the text. Can you guess what each paragraph is about?

A An early start to the day	**E** It's not as hard as it seems
B Putting the final product together	**F** Last-minute changes
	G A well-deserved break
C Making sure it sounds right	
D A band with many talents	

2 Skim the text and try to match the headings to the paragraphs.

3 Identify the main points

1 Read the text again paragraph by paragraph and answer these questions. Underline the parts of the text that tell you the answer. The first one has been done as an example.

Paragraph:

1 When do the boys in a1 arrive at the studio?

2 What do they have to do before they record today's song?

3 What skills does each member of the band have?

4 According to the producer, is his job as difficult as it sounds?

5 Why does special equipment have to be used while recording?

6 Why do the boys have to stop and rest?

7 What does the producer have to do to make the completed song?

2 Now check your answers in Exercise 2. Which headings paraphrase or summarise the parts you have underlined?

Examples:

Para. 1 The part *while most people are still eating their breakfast* tells us that the band start *early*.

Para. 2 Which heading has a word that means the same as *alterations* and *adjustments*?

Creating a HIT ALBUM!

Boy band a1's first single was a smash hit. Our reporter visited the boys, Ben, Paul, Mark and Christian in the recording studio to find out how they set about creating a hit album.

1

A day in the recording studio is usually a long one. The boys arrive for work at the studio in South London while most people are still
5 eating their breakfast! The building doesn't look impressive from the outside, but a1 are following in the footsteps of many famous pop stars who've recorded hit songs here.

2

10 Before they begin recording, the boys need to make some final alterations to the song they're recording today. The boys know the words by heart, so they don't need a
15 song sheet when they are recording. But Paul likes to make a note of the adjustments they make to the lyrics, just in case one of them forgets something later in the day. 'It takes
20 us about half a day to write a song,' explains Mark. 'And then about two days to record.'

3

Unlike most boy bands, the lads in a1 can do much more than just sing.
25 Says Paul: 'We've written 80 per cent of the album ourselves and the other band members have all played instruments as well. Christian plays piano and guitar, Ben plays piano
30 and Mark plays drums and piano. I can't play any instruments,' he grins, 'but I plan how we're going to dance on stage when we give live performances. I enjoy doing that kind
35 of thing.'

4

Before the band start recording the vocals, the producer Mark Taylor takes his seat in the control room and makes adjustments to the many buttons on the vast recording console. Ben is the first in the sound booth and Mark plays the song's backing track to him
40 through his headphones. 'Ben is listening to an unfinished version of the track,' says Mark. 'We keep the track as simple as possible. Then we build the music around the voices after we have recorded them,' he explains. 'I know this sounds really complicated, but really it's not at all,' he adds.

5

45 It's vital to make sure the sound quality of the recording is perfect. To avoid any background noise while recording, the vocal booth must be completely soundproof. In
50 order to speak to the boys, Mark uses a talkback microphone on the recording console and his voice comes through their headphones. The microphones that the lads use
55 have a large disc in front of them, which is called a pop shield. When you sing loudly, puffs of breath come out of your mouth. The pop shield prevents these puffs of
60 breath from hitting the microphone and making a popping sound.

6

Although each song only lasts about four minutes, it takes two days to record the vocals because
65 each track is recorded in small parts. Mark makes the boys repeat every one until it is just right. All the pieces are then put together later. Before long, a1 are ready to
70 stop for lunch. It's tiring working in the studio, but luckily there's a big kitchen in the building and the boys make straight for the fridge!

7

'We save the vocal recordings onto the hard disc of a
75 computer in the control room,' explains Mark. 'Later we record additional instruments onto the computer. When all the different parts are ready, I produce the final completed song.' Mark needs about ten days to do this after the boys have finished the vocals. 'For me, it
80 means working all hours of the day and night,' Mark adds. The completed song leaves the studio on a DAT (Digital Audio Tape). This
85 tiny, high quality tape is used to duplicate the thousands and thousands of CDs that you can buy in the shops.

4 **Vocabulary:** *give, make, take*
Fill in the gaps with *give*, *make* or *take* in the correct form. Then find the answers to the questions in the text.

1 Why do you think the boys .... changes to a song before they record it?
2 Why does Paul like to .... a note of the changes?
3 How long does it .... a) to write a song? b) to record it?
4 What do the boys do when they .... a live performance, besides sing?
5 How do they .... sure that the sound quality is perfect?
6 What kind of sound does your voice .... if it hits the microphone?
7 When they stop for lunch, where do the boys .... for?

5 💬 **Over to you**
What are your favourite pop songs in your language? How do they compare with pop songs in English?

▶▶ **WB** p.46

Grammar: *indirect questions*
▶ p.185

grammar file 14

A   Asking for information

- **Wh- question words**

1 *What time **does** the concert **start**?*
▶ ***Can you tell me*** *what time the concert **starts**?*
2 *Which group **did** John Lennon **sing** with?*
▶ ***I'd like to know*** *which group John Lennon **sang** with.*

- **Yes/No questions**

3 *Are Girlzone going to play tonight?*
▶ ***Could you tell me if/whether*** *Girlzone **are** going to play tonight?*

B Asking for instructions

4 *How **do** I **get** to the theatre?*
▶ *Could you tell me **how to get to** the theatre?/**how I get to** the theatre?*

Note: The infinitive phrase is more common.

! What's wrong?

1 *Do you know what time does the concert begin?* ✗
2 *Can you tell me what time is it?* ✗
3 *Could you tell me where do I buy tickets?* ✗

1   Forming indirect questions

1 Rewrite the direct questions starting with the words given.

1 'When is the show going to begin?'
'Could you tell me .... ?'

2 'Has the band made a new single?'
'Do you know .... ?'

3 'Who chose the name of the band?'
'I wonder ....'

4 'Are there any tickets left?'
'We'd like to know ....'

2 Complete the questions using infinitive phrases.

1 'How do I operate the video?'
'Could you tell me how ....?'

2 'Where do we go to get tickets?'
'Can you advise us where ....?'

3 'Who do we speak to if we want information?'
'Can you tell .... ?'

4 'Who can I ask about programmes?'
'I'd like ....'

2   Interview

Complete the interview below by turning questions 1–8 into indirect questions.

1 How did you all meet?
2 When did you record your first single?
3 Do you get nervous on stage?
4 Do you argue a lot?
5 How do your girlfriends feel about your fans?
6 Do you have any tips for future rockstars?
7 When is your next single coming out?
8 What's the title?

A: Today, we have the band *Bestboys* here in the studio. I've got lots of questions to ask them! First, I'd like to know (1) ....

B: Well, our manager wanted to form a new group – and he chose us!

A: And can you remind us (2) .... ?

B: Yeah, it was six months ago!

A: Right. Now, one of your fans wants to know (3)...................... .

B: Always! But we relax after the first song.

A: I see. Well, I'd like to know (4) ....

B: Not really. If we get angry, we walk away and cool down.

A: Good idea! And now, can you tell us (5) .... ?

B: Well, it's difficult sometimes. But they get used to it!

A: Now, I wonder if (6)... .

B: Yeah, do it! It's a great life!

A: Well guys, have you any idea (7) .... ?

B: Soon!

A: And can you tell us (8) .... ?

B: No. That's top secret!

3   Error correction

1 Read the text below.

1 What concert is referred to in the title?
2 Who wanted a ticket and how did he get one?

2 Look carefully at each line 1–10. Three lines are correct. Tick them. The other lines each have a word which should not be there. Underline it. There are two examples at the beginning (0 and 00).

A TICKET FOR THE CONCERT

0 I was walking along the street yesterday when a boy came up to ✓
00 me. 'Do you know if Topgirls are <u>they</u> playing in town tonight?'
1 he asked. I said 'Yes.' 'Oh, great!' he said. 'Can you tell to me how
2 to get to the theatre? I said I was going there myself and he could
3 walk with me. 'Have you any idea how much do the tickets
4 cost?' he asked as we have hurried along. I said they were £30 each.
5 'But they have probably all gone by now,' I warned him. The boy
6 looked at disappointed. 'Maybe someone has returned their ticket,'
7 he said. 'Do you know what time does the box office opens?' I
8 didn't think he had any hope of getting a seat. Then a girl she
9 stopped us outside the theatre. 'Do you know how may I can sell
10 this ticket?' she asked. 'My friend can't come tonight.' My companion
grinned. Clearly, it was his lucky night.

▶▶ **WB** p.47

Vocabulary building

1 Word formation: *compound nouns*

1 Match a word in box A with a word in box B to make compound nouns. Three compound nouns are written as one word.

A

head	sound	compact	jazz	record
concert	solo	song		

B

band	artist	producer	writer	track
phones	disc	hall		

2 ⏺ Fill in the gaps with words from the list. Then ask and answer the questions with a partner.

lead / rock / disc / track / recording / record

1 What's your favourite *hit* .... of all time?

2 Have you got a favourite .... *jockey*? Who is it?

3 Which is your favourite band at the moment? Who is the .... *singer*?

4 Have you ever been to an open-air .... *concert*? Where? When?

5 Have you ever been to a .... *studio*? Would you like to?

6 Do you know who wrote the *sound*........ for the last James Bond film?

2 Choosing the right word

Read the dialogue and <u>underline</u> the correct word in each pair.

A: Was the concert good last night?

B: It was fantastic! We had (1) *seats/chairs* in the front (2) *file/row*! When the band came onto the (3) *platform/stage* and began to play, the whole (4) *spectators/audience* started (5) *screaming/crying*. So did I!

A: Did they play their latest hit single?

B: Yes! Everyone (6) *cheered/booed* when they began. And we all (7) *applauded/clapped* our hands in time with the music.

A: Did they sing my favourite song, *Loving you*?

B: Which one is that? Can you sing a bit for me?

A: Well, I can hum the (8) *tune/beat* but I can't remember the (9) *words/vocals*.

B: Oh, I know! Yes, they sang the main verses, and we joined in with the (10) *lyrics/chorus*.

3 Phrasal verbs

Replace the words in *italics* with a phrasal verb from the box in the correct form.

bring sth. out	split up	make sth. up
put sth. off	sell out	turn up

1 We went to hear my favourite band but they didn't *arrive*!

2 I wanted to go to the musical but the tickets were all *finished*.

3 If I can't remember the lyrics to a song I just *invent them*!

4 Oh no! My favourite band have announced that they're going to *separate*!

5 They've *postponed* the concert because the drummer is ill.

6 Robbie Williams has just *produced and begun to sell* a new CD.

4 Open cloze

1 Read the text below. Would you like to see the show it describes?

2 Read the text again and think of the word that best fits each space. Use only one word in each space. Most of the words you need are prepositions or parts of phrasal verbs. There is an example at the beginning (0).

A MUSICAL EVENING

The musical *The Lion King* is (0) ..*on*.. next week. Tickets (1) .... selling out quickly so you need to book (2) .... advance. Don't just turn (3) .... at the box office on the day or you may be disappointed. This production is sensational!

All the singers and dancers in *The Lion King* are dressed (4) .... animals. The costumes are incredible! At the start of the show, the 'animals' come in through the audience, (5) .... is very dramatic! Then the curtain goes up and the audience gets their first view of the stage. It looks just (6) .... the African jungle, with grass and bushes everywhere. And the music is amazing! It starts with the sound (7) .... African drums – then changes to heavy-metal music! There are some great tunes, too. Incidentally, they have just brought (8) .... a CD with hits from the show, which you can buy (9) .... the interval.

The first-night audience certainly enjoyed the show. (10) .... the end of the evening, they cheered and clapped (11) .... at least ten minutes. If you like musicals, this (12) .... one show you shouldn't miss!

5 ⏺ Over to you

Have you ever been to a rock concert, a musical, or any other musical event? Describe it to the class.

▶▶ **WB** p.48

Listening
▶ *Part 2*

1 Before you listen
You are going to hear an interview with a disc jockey.

1 What does a DJ do?
2 What skills does he need?
3 How does someone become a DJ?
4 Would you like to be a DJ?

2 Predict
▶▶ *predicting the information you need* Unit 8 p.70
Look at the Listening task and read sentences 1–9. Decide what kind of information you need to fill in the gaps. For example:
Question:
1 another type of job?
2 a sum of money
3 some kind of skill
4 an adjective?
Now you continue.

3 Listening strategy

▶▶ *listening for parallel ideas*
The words you need to write in the gaps appear in the recording, but the sentences may be expressed differently. Before you listen, think about other ways of expressing the main idea. This will help you to recognise the relevant part of the recording.

Read sentences 1–9 again. How could the <u>underlined</u> parts be expressed by Bill Jason? Match them to these extracts from the recording.

a) you're almost like a ..*1*..
b) link a sequence of tracks up .....
c) you're always on the look-out for .....
d) what do you like best .....
e) the technical side of things .....
f) doing his job right .....
g) learn these skills .....
h) keeps his eyes on .....
i) how much does a DJ make? .....

4 🔲 Listening task
1 Listen to the recording once. Complete the sentences using no more than three words or a number in each space. Remember to listen for meaning.

2 Listen again and check and complete your answers.

Listening task

You will hear an interview with disc jockey Bill Jason. For questions 1–9, complete the sentences.

Today, a DJ can <u>be compared with</u> a [____1____]

A good DJ can <u>earn up to</u> [____2____] for one performance.

In order to <u>join different songs up together</u>, a DJ must have a good [____3____]

<u>At the technical level</u>, a DJ's job is quite [____4____]

There are now [____5____] where people can <u>train</u> to be DJs.

A really good DJ loves music and <u>is always looking for</u> [____6____]

You can recognise good DJs because they always <u>look at</u> [____7____] while they are working.

When a DJ is <u>doing his job well</u>, he [____8____] as much as the audience.

For Bill, <u>the best thing</u> about being a DJ is feeling [____9____]

5 💬 Over to you
Look at the list of jobs. Who should earn most/least? Why? Put them in order. Then compare your ranking with the class.

☐ a DJ
☐ a pop star
☐ the conductor of an orchestra
☐ a doctor
☐ a college lecturer

Writing: *formal transactional letter*
▶ *Part 1*

1 Sample writing task

1 Read the task.

1 What do you have to do?
2 Who will you write the letter to?
3 What style should you use?

Writing task

You have seen this advertisement for a music festival in an English-language magazine. You would like to go to the festival when you visit Britain in the summer. However, the advertisement does not give you all the information you would like. Look at the advertisement and your notes. Then write a letter, asking for further information.

which bands playing?

Rockwave Summer Festival

accommodation nearby?

Upton Park, Somerset
July 15th–17th

Experience real entertainment with 3 days of continuous music!

Entrance £45

discounts for students?

need to book long time in advance?

Tickets and further information from
Rockwave Entertainment
P.O. Box 3008, London N12 6QT

Write a letter in 120–180 words in an appropriate style.

2 Answer these questions.

1 When and where will the festival take place?
2 How much do the tickets cost?
3 How long will the concert last?
4 Where can you write to get tickets and information?

3 Look at the handwritten notes. Expand them into questions.

Example:

Is there any accommodation near the venue?

4 Can you think of two other questions you might like to ask?

2 Read a sample letter

1 Read the letter that one student wrote to Rockwave Entertainment.

1 Why does the writer begin *Dear Sir or Madam* and end *Yours faithfully*?
2 What is the main topic of each paragraph?

Para. 1 Reason for writing
Para. 2 ....
Para. 3 ....
Para. 4 ....

2 Underline all the questions in the letter.

1 Did the writer ask all the questions in the task?
2 Which extra question(s) did he ask that were not in his notes?
3 Which questions are indirect questions?
4 Why does the writer use indirect questions in his letter?

Dear Sir or Madam

I am writing to ask for more information about the Upton Park Rockwave Festival in July, which was advertised in our local English paper. I am coming to Britain in July, and I would really like to go to the festival.

First, I would like some more information about the festival. Could you please let me know which bands are playing? I would also like to know what time the performances start and end each day.

Next, I wonder if you could send me some information about accommodation? Is there a Youth Hostel near Upton Park, for example? As I am a student, I am interested in something which is not too expensive.

Finally, could you let me know if we need to book tickets a long time in advance or if we can buy them on the day of the concert? I would also like to know whether there are discounts for students.

I look forward to hearing from you.

Yours faithfully,

MARIO GONZÀLEZ
Mario Gonz lez

Over to you

3 Writing strategy

Complete the notes.

▶▶ *transactional letters*

When you write a transactional letter:
- make sure you read the whole .... carefully before you begin.
- include all the points you have been given.
- use .... questions when you want to be polite.
- use .... style when writing to a stranger.

4 Writing task

1 Read the task.

1 What is the advert about?
2 Who will read your letter? What style should you use?
3 What information do you want?

2 Can you think of two more questions you'd like to ask? Add them to the notes on the advert.

Writing task

You have seen this advertisement in the local paper. Read the advertisement and the notes you have made beside it. Then write to the Station Manager saying you are interested and asking for more information.

☆ **Rock FM**, ☆
your local English language radio station, is organising an open day.

when and where exactly?

Come and find out about:
- *how we produce radio programmes*
- *the equipment we use*
- *the sort of people who work for us*
- *how to get a job in radio*
- *our special training programmes*

Plus! A chance to meet a ☆ famous DJ! ☆

which DJ? will he/she give a talk on his/her work?

how much exactly? *Special rates* for students

For more information, please contact: The Station Manager, Rock FM, PO Box 222

Write a letter in 120–180 words in an appropriate style.

5 Language practice

1 Expand the handwritten notes in Exercise 4 into indirect questions, beginning with the following phrases:

Could you tell me ...
I would also like to know ...
Could you please let me know ...

Example:

Could you tell me what time the open day will begin?

2 Now add two more indirect questions you could ask about the radio open day.

6 Plan your letter

Make a paragraph plan using the ideas below. Write notes. You can add two of your own questions.

Para. 1
Introduction: Why I am writing/Where I saw the advertisement
Useful phrases:
I am writing to ask for (some more) information about / to enquire about ...

Para. 2
Topic: Questions about the open day: when and where?
Useful phrases:
First, / To start with, I would like to know ...

Para. 3
Topic: Questions about the DJ: which DJ? will he or she give a talk?
Useful phrases:
Also, I wonder if you could tell me ...

Para. 4
Topic: How much for students?
Useful phrases:
Finally, could you ...

Closing remark: I look forward to hearing from you.

7 Write

Now write your letter. Follow the ▶▶ *Writing strategy*. How will you begin and end the letter?

8 Check your work

Are the grammar, spelling and punctuation correct?

▶▶ **WB** p.50

10 Success

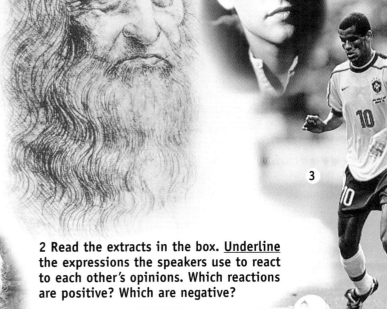

Speaking ▶ *Parts 3 and 4*

1 Discussion

1 Look at the pictures of people who have been very successful in their field. Match the names to the pictures.

a) Agatha Christie
b) Leonardo da Vinci
c) Picasso
d) Rivaldo
e) Leonardo DiCaprio
f) Nicola Horlick

2 Why are they famous?
Example:
Leonardo DiCaprio is a film actor.

3 What would you like to be famous for?
Example:
I'd like to be a famous sports personality.

2 🎞 Listen

1 Look at the list of factors which could be important for success. Then listen to two students talking about them. Tick the ones they both think are important.

- good looks
- hard work
- talent
- support from parents
- good luck
- knowing people who can help you

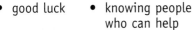

2 Read the extracts in the box. <u>Underline</u> the expressions the speakers use to react to each other's opinions. Which reactions are positive? Which are negative?

reacting to opinions

A: What do you think about good looks?
B: I don't think it's very important ...
A: I think it is because ...
B: That's true, but ...
A: So, hard work – you need to work hard, don't you think?
B: Yes, but ... I think it's more important to ...
A: I suppose it's quite useful. What about ... ?
B: Yes, it's important, but it's not that important.
A: Don't you think so? I think ...
B: That's a good point.

3 Listen again. What reasons do the speakers give for their ideas?

3 💬 Speaking task: *prioritising*

1 Talk together and decide which factors in Exercise 2.1 <u>you</u> think are important. Be sure to react to your partner's opinions.

2 Now choose three and put them in order of priority.
Example:
The most important factor for success is ...
Next, I'd put ...
I'd put ... before ...

3 Compare your ideas with the class.

4 💬 Discussion

1 How important is education to help you achieve success?
2 Are there any successful people that you especially like or admire?

 WB p.51

83

Reading ▸ Part 2

1 Predict

1 Read the title and sub-heading of the text, and the picture caption. What do you think the main idea of the text will be?

a) Geniuses are born with a special talent that other people don't have.

b) Geniuses achieve success through hard work rather than a special talent.

2 What's your opinion?

2 Read for general understanding

1 Read the text once quite quickly.

1 What do Dineshi, the Yusof children and Mozart have in common?

2 Who is Professor Howe?

3 What does the example of Billy Sidis show about genius?

4 Is this statement true or false according to the text?

'Anyone can be a genius if he or she works hard enough.'

2 Have you changed your opinion in Exercise 1?

3 Read for detail

Read the text again carefully paragraph by paragraph and answer these questions. <u>Underline</u> the parts of the text that help you.

Paragraph:

1 When did Dineshi start to write?

2 What does *environment* mean in lines 19, 26 and 39?

3 According to Professor Howe, why are Dineshi and the Yusof children geniuses?

4 How does the case of Mozart support Professor Howe's ideas?

5 What skills did Billy Sidis lack?

6 What is the golf champion's opinion about luck?

The Secret of GENIUS

For years people have said that geniuses are born with a special talent. New research challenges that view.

Richard Woods reports.

She looks like any other little girl in her first year at school: a smart uniform, a happy smile and a bag of books. But Dineshi, a five-year-old from west London is so clever that she seems almost unreal. With an IQ* of 160, Dineshi knew the alphabet, the days of the week and the months of the year when she was one and a half. She started reading just before her second birthday and writing just after it. 'When she was a baby, I realised she was exceptionally bright,' says Dineshi's mother, 'so I tried to provide an **environment** to help her develop intellectually. I started giving her lessons and she enjoyed them.'

Mr and Mrs Yusof from Coventry know all about creating an **environment** that encourages intellectual development. Mr Yusof gave up his job to educate their children at home. They were encouraged to read books from an early age and they watch television only occasionally, usually for 'educational' programmes. Sufiah, the eldest daughter, went to university when she was 13. Her brother started his university studies at 12. Their mother said: 'You must have the correct **environment** – the schooling, the family, the support, they must all come together.'

By comparison with others, such children seem incredibly intelligent. But according to Professor Michael Howe, a psychologist at Exeter University, they do not have an inborn superhuman talent. Their remarkable achievements are the result of practice, persistence, and an encouraging environment. Would these children have achieved so much if their parents hadn't given them so much attention? Professor Howe doesn't think so.

The case of Wolfgang Amadeus Mozart seems to support Professor Howe's theory. Mozart was composing music by the age of five, and at six or seven he was giving professional concerts around Europe. Most people believe this was the result of inborn genius. But Professor Howe claims that Mozart's childhood compositions are largely arrangements of other composers' work. Most importantly, according to Professor Howe, his father was an extremely ambitious music teacher who made his son practise more than three hours a day. By the time he was six, he had probably spent 3,500 hours studying music.

*IQ = Intelligence Quotient: a measure of intelligence

Thomas Edison, inventor of electric light, said genius was 99% perspiration, 1% inspiration.

Are geniuses happy? As a child
85 in the early 1900s, Billy Sidis was
described as 'the most remarkable
boy in the United States'. Brilliant
at languages, he taught himself
Latin at four and could read and
90 speak eight languages when he
was six. At eleven, he gave a
lecture to the University of
Harvard Mathematical Club. He
was a genius until everything
95 began to go wrong. His parents
had pushed him to develop his
exceptional intelligence, but had
totally neglected other important
skills. For example, Sidis did not
100 know how to dress himself
properly even by the time he was
an adolescent. Finally, he suffered
a breakdown.

There are plenty of people who
105 have high IQs but never achieve
anything great. They are bright,
but they lack the drive to get on:
motivation. Thomas Edison, the
inventor of electric light, said
110 genius was 99% perspiration, 1%
inspiration. According to Professor
Howe, we should all be able to
excel if we try hard enough. The
following anecdote illustrates his
115 point. A famous golf champion had
produced some amazingly good
shots. 'I wish I had been as lucky
as you were,' said one of his
opponents at the end of the day.
120 'It's funny,' said the golf
champion, 'the harder I practise,
the luckier I get.'

4 Reading strategy

▶▶ *multiple-choice questions*

For multiple-choice questions, you have to choose the best answer from given options.
- Find and underline the parts of the text that answer the questions before you look at the options.
- Then choose the option that is closest to your answer.

Choose the option A, B or C which best answers the questions in Exercise 3. Use the clues to help you.

1 A when she was five years old
   B when she was two years old
   C when she was one and a half

Clue: *Did she start writing before or after her birthday?*

2 A personal qualities and talents
   B your physical surroundings
   C the conditions in which you live/that affect your life

Clue: *What examples of 'environment' does Mrs Yusof mention?*

3 A They have intelligent parents.
   B They have had a lot of support.
   C They were born intelligent.

Clue: *Look at the last part of paragraph 3 (line 55). Which phrase means the same as a word in one of the options?*

4 A He was a natural genius.
   B He was very ambitious.
   C He put a lot of time into his studies.

Clue: *Look at the last two sentences of paragraph 4.*

5 A physical skills
   B intellectual skills
   C social skills

Clue: *What was he unable to do?*

6 A Luck has nothing to do with winning.
   B Luck is more important than practice.
   C He won because he is a lucky person.

Clue: *What word could you use instead of 'luckier' in line 122?*

5 Vocabulary: *near synonyms*
1 Find:
a) three adjectives that mean the same as *clever*. (paras. 1/6, 3, 5).
b) two adjectives that mean the same as *unusual*. (paras. 3, 5).
What nouns do they describe?

2 Find:
four adverbs that mean *very* or *unusually* (paras. 1, 3, 4, 6).
What adjectives do they make stronger?

6 ◯ Over to you

1 Should parents push their children to achieve a lot or let them go at their own pace?
2 Would you like to be taught by your parents at home?

▶▶ **WB** p.51

Grammar: *third conditional, wish*
▶ *p.184*

grammar file 11

A Third conditional: unreal situations in the past

1 *If Rivaldo* **hadn't trained** *hard, he* **wouldn't have become** *a great footballer.* (but he did train hard)

2 *If Ellen MacArthur* **had been** *less brave, she* **wouldn't have sailed** *around the world alone.* (but she was brave)

B *may/might/could* + *have* + past participle: possibility

3 *Ian Fleming* **could/might have written** *more James Bond novels if he had lived longer.* (it's possible)

C *wish* + past perfect: wishes about the past

4 *I* **wish** *I* **had learned** *to play the piano.* (but I didn't)

5 *Georgia* **wishes** *she* **hadn't lost** *her Discman.* (but she did)

Note: For emphasis, we can use *if only* instead of *wish*.

! *What's wrong?*

1 *Elvis wouldn't have become famous if he wouldn't have been a great singer.* X

2 *If Steven Spielberg didn't become a Hollywood producer, he wouldn't have made E.T.* X

3 *I wish I wouldn't have given all my CDs away.* X

---

1 Third conditional

Fill in the gaps using the verbs in brackets.

1 Neil Armstrong was an experienced astronaut. If he *hadn't been* so experienced, the Space Agency *wouldn't have chosen* him to walk on the moon. (not be/not choose)

2 Mother Teresa cared about poor people. She .... to India if she .... to help them. (not go/not want)

3 The Beatles were great song-writers. If they .... so talented, they .... superstars. (not be/not become)

4 Princess Diana was famous all over the world. If she .... Prince Charles, she probably .... so famous. (not marry/not be)

5 Mozart died very young. If he .... so young, he .... many more symphonies. (not die/write)

2 Wishes about the past

1 Put the verbs in brackets into the correct form.

1 I wish we *had heard* (hear) about the concert earlier. We *would have bought* (buy) tickets.

2 I wish I .... (know) there was a James Bond film on last night. I .... (stay in) to watch it.

3 I wish I .... (bring) my camera. I .... (could/take) some photos of the band.

4 My mum wishes she .... (go) to drama school when she was younger. She .... (might/become) a big star!

5 My friend wishes he .... (wait) outside the stage door. He .... (could/get) Robbie Williams' autograph.

6 I wish you .... (come) to the party. You .... (meet) some really nice people!

2 ⟲ What wishes and regrets do you have about the past?

3 Transformations

Complete the second sentence so it has a similar meaning to the first sentence, using the word given. Do not change the word given. Use between two and five words.

1 I'm sorry I shouted at you. **wish**
I .... at you.

2 He wouldn't have succeeded without your help. **if**
He wouldn't have succeeded .... him.

3 Paul regrets missing the party. **wishes**
Paul .... the party.

4 I went to the concert because my friend gave me a ticket. **not**
I wouldn't have gone to the concert if .... me a ticket.

5 We got Björk's autograph because we went to the stage door. **would**
We .... Björk's autograph if we hadn't gone to the stage door.

6 Bob got a part in the film because his father was the producer. **have**
If his father hadn't been the producer, Bob .... a part in the film.

7 My friend regrets selling his guitar. **wishes**
My friend .... his guitar.

▶▶ WB p.52

Vocabulary building

1 Word formation: *adjectives and nouns*

1 Make adjectives from these nouns and verbs and put them in the correct column below according to the ending. Be careful of spelling changes.

1 optimism   3 hope   5 ambition   7 please
2 profession   4 energy   6 influence   8 fame

-al	-ant	-ful	- (t)ic	-ous

2 Make nouns from these adjectives and verbs, and put them in the correct column.

1 motivate   3 brilliant   5 creative   7 tolerate
2 disappoint   4 inspire   6 violent   8 lonely

-(at)ion	-(an)ce / -(en)ce	-ment	-ness	-(it)y

3 🗩 Use the word in CAPITALS at the end of each sentence to form a noun or adjective that fits in the gap. Then say if you think the sentences are true or false.

1 To be a success, it's important to have .... from your parents. ENCOURAGE

2 Everybody is born with the same level of .... INTELLIGENT

3 Reading widely can aid your .... development. INTELLECT

4 Parents should be .... not to push their children too hard. CARE

5 You need .... as well as brains to become a genius. DETERMINE

4 Add the words you formed to the correct columns above.

2 🗩 Discussion

1 Looking back at the past 20 years, who do you think is / was:

• the most brilliant scientist or inventor?
• the most important world leader?
• the most dangerous leader?
• the most courageous person?
• the most famous actor?
• the most influential writer or poet?
• the most successful singer or musician?
• the most glamorous model or actress?

2 Discuss your choices with a partner and say why you chose those people.

3 Word–formation task

1 What do you know about Nelson Mandela? Read the text below to check.

2 Use the word in CAPITALS underneath to form a word that fits in the space. Decide if you need a noun, adjective or adverb. There is an example at the beginning (0).

NELSON MANDELA

Nelson Mandela has been one of the most **(0)** *inspirational* figures of the last 100 years. He grew up in South Africa, when black people were considered less **(1)** .... than white people. He refused to accept this unpleasant situation and fought for **(2)** .... . The government put him in prison, but this only increased his **(3)** .... to change the system. He received extremely harsh **(4)** .... but never allowed himself to hate anyone. He was **(5)** .... freed after 27 years, thanks to the persistence and loyalty of his supporters. When he became the President of South Africa, Mandela didn't want revenge, but offered his enemies **(6)** .... instead. He showed the world that **(7)** .... is not the right way to solve problems. His tremendous courage, tolerance and **(8)** .... make him a hero of our times.

0 INSPIRATION	3 DETERMINED	6 FORGIVE
1 IMPORTANCE	4 TREAT	7 VIOLENT
2 EQUAL	5 FINAL	8 GENEROUS

3 Add the nouns and adjectives you formed to the correct columns in Exercise 1.

4 Verbs + prepositions

Underline the preposition that follows the gap in each sentence. Then fill in the gaps with a verb from the list in its correct form.

accuse / succeed / discourage / forgive / insist / contribute

1 Instead of taking revenge, the Indian leader Gandhi *forgave* his enemies <u>for</u> treating him harshly.

2 Actress Julia Roberts .... on filming a scene again and again until she thinks it's right.

3 Politicians often .... the press of telling lies about them.

4 A good football manager will try to .... his players from smoking.

5 The famous psychologist Freud has .... greatly to our understanding of the human mind.

6 Steve Redgrave .... in winning his fifth Olympic gold medal for rowing, despite having diabetes.

▶▶ WB p.53

Listening ▶ *Part 4*

1 Before you listen

1 Read the instructions for the Listening task. What are you going to hear?

2 Read the statements 1–7. Which of the following topics a)–f) do you expect to hear them talking about? Match them to the statements.

a) what it is like being well known   .....

b) the support they have had from their family .....

c) living away from home   .....

d) the advantages of being twin sisters   .....

e) how their career as singers started   .....

f) their plans for the future   .....

3 Listening for parallel ideas ▶▶ Unit 9 p.80
Think of other ways of expressing the underlined ideas in statements 1–7.

Example:
<u>enjoy</u>: *like, love, think it's great*

2 Listening strategy

▶▶ *recognising positive and negative statements*
Listen carefully for positive and negative forms of verbs and other expressions.

1 Read these extracts from the recording. <u>Underline</u> the negative words and expressions.

1 we <u>hardly</u> ever meet fans except when we're back home with the family

2 they keep ringing us up and writing to us, which isn't much fun

3 You keep a bit of home with you when you go away, so you don't feel alone.

4 But none of our relatives went into music as a career.

5 they didn't try to put us off, they supported us.

6 what he said didn't make us change our minds.

2 🔊 Listen to the extracts. Are the negative forms easy or hard to hear?

Listening task

You will hear an interview with Katie and Sally Lloyd, twin sisters who sing in a successful girl band. Decide which of the statements 1–7 are TRUE and which are FALSE. Write T for TRUE and F for FALSE in the boxes.

1 The twins <u>enjoy</u> meeting their fans. | 1 |

2 The twins <u>like hearing</u> from distant <u>relations</u>. | 2 |

3 The twins sometimes <u>feel lonely</u> in London. | 3 |

4 The twins come from a family of <u>professional musicians.</u> | 4 |

5 The twins' parents <u>encouraged them</u> in their choice of career. | 5 |

6 The twins were <u>grateful for</u> their brother's <u>advice</u>. | 6 |

7 The twins' brother <u>introduced them to people</u> in the <u>music business</u>. | 7 |

3 🔊 Listening task

1 Listen to the recording and do the task.

2 Listen again and check your answers.

4 💬 Over to you

What are the advantages and disadvantages of becoming well known? Think about lack of privacy, loneliness, etc.

Writing: *story* ▶ *Part 2*

1 Sample writing task

Read the task.

1 Who is going to read the story?

2 Who will be the main character in the story?

Writing task

Your teacher has asked you to write a story beginning with the words:

As soon as Peter read about the competition, he knew he had to take part.

The best stories will be published in the school magazine.

Write your story in 120–180 words.

2 Brainstorm ideas

Think of answers to these questions. Then compare your ideas with other pairs.

1 Who is Peter?

2 What sort of competition did he enter?

3 Why was he so keen to enter?

4 What happened on the day of the competition?

5 Did he win?

6 How did he feel?

7 How does the story end?

3 Read a sample story

1 Read the story. The paragraphs are mixed up. Number them in the correct order 1-4.

2 Now answer the questions in Exercise 2 above.

3 When you write a story:

a) set the scene. (**Where** did it happen? **When**?)

b) introduce the main character(s). (**Who**?)

c) give more background information/explain what led up to the main event(s). (**Why**?)

d) describe the main event(s). (**What** happened?)

e) end the story. (**Outcome**/**Result**)

Does the writer do all of these things in the story?

☐ As soon as Peter read about the competition, he knew he had to take part. 'Enter our talent competition', the advertisement said, 'and become a star.'

☐ Then, out of the crowd, he <u>heard</u> a girl shout: 'Go on! You're great!' Others joined in. Suddenly, Peter's confidence <u>returned</u>. When he finished his act, everyone <u>stood up</u> and <u>cheered</u>. It was incredible. He had won! But where was the mystery girl? And who was she? He had to find her!

☐ On his big day, Peter felt extremely nervous. He <u>had to</u> perform in front of three judges and 50 other competitors. Halfway through his song, he <u>froze</u>. 'I can't do it,' he thought, 'Let me out of here!'

☐ For as long as he could remember, Peter <u>had dreamt</u> of stardom. He wanted to see his name in lights, to appear on TV, and to be adored by fans. He<u>'d been taking</u> guitar lessons for years. He still wasn't very good but he had a strong singing voice – and he was a great dancer! 'This time next week,' he told himself, 'I'll be a star.'

4 Tenses and time expressions

1 Look at the <u>underlined</u> verbs in the sample story. What tenses does the writer use:

a) to describe background events?

b) for the main events?

2 Circle the time expressions that signal the sequence of events.

Example: *As soon as*

5 Starting and finishing your story

1 Read the first paragraph of the story again. How does the writer make the reader want to read on? Tick one or more of the following:

a) He starts the story in an original way.

b) He gives a summary of the whole story.

c) He uses direct speech to make events more vivid.

2 Read the final paragraph again. How does the writer make it interesting? Tick one or more of the following:

a) He repeats what he said in the introduction.

b) He leaves us wondering what happens next.

c) He writes an exciting or unexpected ending.

6 Writing skills: *punctuation*

1 There are five different sorts of punctuation in this extract from the story. Can you name them all?

'I can't do it,' he thought. 'Let me out of here!'

2 Punctuate the following sentences. Put capital letters where necessary.

1 oh no she exclaimed my photo is in the paper

2 i dont want to be a famous singer the pop star said

3 my ambition she said is to become a great actress

4 dont be silly john said you cant act at all

5 look he added thats madonna shes a good actress

6 the tv company want you to appear on their talent show mum shouted

7 Writing skills: *time linkers*

<u>Underline</u> the correct word or phrase in each pair.

1 *In the start/At the start* of the story, we have no idea what is going to happen.

2 *At first,/In the first place,* Peter felt nervous but he relaxed in the end.

3 Peter didn't want to perform in front of all those people, but *at the end/in the end* he agreed.

4 Peter didn't know the girl in the audience, but he met her *after/afterwards.*

5 He couldn't believe what had happened. He was famous *at last/at least*!

Over to you

8 Writing strategy

Complete the notes.

▶▶ *writing a story*

When you write a story:

• use the past continuous and the .... to describe background events.

• use the past .... to describe the main events.

• you can make the beginning of the story interesting by ....

• you can make the end of the story interesting by ....

• you can use direct speech.

9 Writing task

Read the task.

1 Who will read the story?

2 Who is the main character in the story?

3 What style of writing is suitable for your story?

Writing task

You have decided to enter a short story competition. The rules say that the story must begin with the words:

When a TV company came to film in her village, Monika didn't realise she would soon be famous.

Write your story in 120–180 words.

10 ⬭ Brainstorm ideas

Answer these questions. Note down your ideas and compare them with a partner.

1 Who is Monika?

2 Which village does she live in? Where?

3 Why did a TV company come to film in her village?

4 How did Monika get involved? What did she do? How did she feel?

5 What happened next?

6 How did the story end?

11 Plan your story

Use the headings below to help you organise your ideas into a plan.

<u>Introduction</u>

<u>Background information</u>

<u>Main events</u>

<u>Ending</u>

12 Write

Now write your story. Use the plan you made in Exercise 11. Follow the ▶▶ *Writing strategy*. Remember to use a range of time linkers.

13 Check your work

Have you used past tenses correctly? Are the spelling and punctuation correct?

▶▶ WB p.55

11 Lifestyles

Speaking ▸ *Part 2*

1 💬 Discussion

How have the lives of teenagers changed over the last 100 years? Look at the photos, which show young people 100 years ago and today.

Which of the young people are more likely to:

- get married young?
- leave school at 14?
- travel abroad?
- have no more than two children?
- work in an office?
- have a summer holiday every year?

2 📼 Listen

1 Listen to a student comparing and contrasting photos 1 and 2. Tick the points he mentions.

- family
- holidays
- clothing
- free time

2 Listen again. Complete the sentences in the box.

> *describing and speculating*
> In this picture there are some young people.
> They don't seem ...
> They look as if they ...
> I think they are probably ...
> In the second picture, there are teenagers as well.
> I get the impression from the picture that ...
> They seem to be ... , so I guess ...
> They don't look ...

3 Which young people does the speaker think are happier?

3 💬 Speaking task: *photos*

Look at photos 3 and 4.

Student A: Compare and contrast the photos, and say who you think is enjoying their school life more.

Student B: Compare and contrast the photos, and say which picture represents a better learning situation in your opinion.

4 💬 Discussion

1 How interested are you in learning about the past?
2 How much do you know about the early life of your grandparents?
3 What is the best thing about being a teenager today?

▶▶ WB p.56

Reading ▶ Part 3

1 Predict

Look at the title of the article opposite and the photos. What do the photos tell you about the Inuit way of life a) in the past? b) today?

2 Read the text

1 Read the text once.

1 How did the Inuit get food in the past?

2 What were their clothes made of?

3 How did they travel around?

4 Did they go to school?

5 Who were the most important people in the community?

6 How have these things changed?

2 Now discuss these questions.

1 Which culture does Jimmy think he belongs to, the Inuit culture or modern US culture?

2 Why are the Inuit losing their traditional culture, according to him?

3 How does he feel about the changes? What does he think should be done?

3 Reading strategy

▶▶ *linking expressions*

Pay attention to linking expressions at the beginning of sentences. They will help you understand the logical connection between sentences and paragraphs.

Examples:

Instead must be preceded by a contrasting idea.

Another must add an idea to one in the sentence or paragraph before.

1 The sentences in the box below have been removed from the text. Read them and <u>underline</u> the introductory linking expressions. What relationship do they signal with the sentence before?

1 contrasting idea   3 reason/result   5 adds another idea
2 time   4 emphasises the previous idea

2 Now look at the gaps in the text and decide where the sentences fit. There is one extra sentence which you do not need to use.

A Another thing we could learn is how to speak our language properly.

B Back then, just getting to the next village would take hours or even days.

C As well as that, most students these days watch many hours of TV.

D In fact, they would eat almost anything they could catch.

E So I would have to ask one of them to show me.

F As a result, we end up not knowing enough about our culture and language.

G <u>But in spite of</u> all these things, I am still an Eskimo.

16-year-old Jimmy Ulujuk is a Native American and lives in Alaska. In our series on other cultures, he describes how his Inuit people are losing their traditional way of life.

Who am I today? Am I a traditional Inuit or a modern American? Look at me: my face looks like an Eskimo, but I'm

5 wearing a T-shirt, jeans and a baseball cap. Look at the things I'm doing these days. I attend the local High School, where I study American subjects with American teachers. Spaghetti is my

10 favourite food. I play basketball, volleyball and go cross-country running, just like all American kids. Basketball is one of the things I'm good at. Nothing ever gets in the way

15 of my basketball practice! **0 G**

I still do some of the traditional things my ancestors used to do. For example, the town where I live is part of the traditional hunting

20 grounds of my ancestors. In the past, my ancestors would travel all over these mountains. They had to travel constantly to get food and clothing. In those days

25 they used to hunt caribou, moose, bears, even rabbits for food. **1 ☐** It was especially difficult in cold weather. Sometimes

30 if there was a bad winter, they would starve.

Land of the Inuit

Their tools and musical instruments were handmade – drums, knives, spears, shovels, combs and much more. They used animal skins to make clothes. Our elders still know how to make the best clothes and tools. They
35 are the most important people in our community and act as the leaders of our tribe. I would love to make a traditional drum for myself but the trouble is, I don't know how. **2**▭ They know all the traditional ways, and give advice to any member of the tribe who needs it.

Most of us high school students today in AKP are losing our traditional
40 culture. Why? The main problem is, there have been too many changes. One big change is transport. In the winter, people use their snow machines to get around, while in the past they used to use dog teams. People fly to the nearest big town to go shopping. **3**▭ It must have been hard, but maybe travelling slowly was better. People had time to look around, so
45 they had closer contact with their environment.

The first school in the 1950s was another big change. We started being educated by Americans then. Today, we are even supposed to learn our own language and traditions in school. But our attention is usually focused on the American side of things. **4**▭ I get on really well with
50 my grandmother, but when she is talking to me in our Inuit language, I can't understand her sometimes. This makes me feel left out of our Inuit culture. When I see the elders today, I wish I could learn what they learned. Maybe all the students feel that way. We'll probably lose our language in the next generation. We could do something about it, but
55 what, and how?

The only way things will change is if we spend more time with our parents and elders. They could teach us the things they used to do. **5**▭ We would probably learn a lot of sentences, instead of the simple words they teach us in school. Although it would be nice for this to happen, it
60 probably won't. It's up to everyone to make an effort, but no-one's doing anything about it. I think we should try before it's too late.

4 Vocabulary: *expressions with get*

1 Read the text and the sentences in the box again. Find all the expressions with the verb *get*.

get — *food / clothing*
— *in the way of*

2 ▶▶ *guessing meaning from context* Unit 1 p.9, Unit 2 p.17

Use the context to work out what the expressions mean. Then match them to their meanings below.

a) to reach, arrive at
b) to have a friendly relationship with
c) to stop sb. from doing sth.
d) to travel
e) to obtain

5 ⬭ Over to you

1 Do you think the Alaskan Inuit culture and language can be preserved?

2 How important do you think it is to preserve customs and traditions?

▶▶ WB p.56

Grammar: *present and past habits* ▶ pp.181/182

grammar files 4, 7

A Present habit

- **present simple + frequency adverbs**

1 *I **play** basketball **every weekend**.*

- **present continuous + *always*: annoying habits**

2 *My sister is **always teasing** me about my hair.*

B Past habit

- ***used to*: past actions and states**

3 *I **used to** fight with my brother as a kid.* (action)

4 *I **didn't use** (NOT ~~didn't used~~) to like my older sister.* (state)

- ***would*: past actions only**

5 *My grandmother **would** tell us bedtime stories.*

Compare: *I used to be (NOT ~~would be~~) shy.*

C Past continuous or *used to*?

Compare:

6 *I **used to play** kids' games when I was little.* (past habit)

7 *I **was playing** a computer game when you **rang**.* (single action interrupted by another action)

! What's wrong?

1 *I was often staying with my grandparents when I was little.* ✗

2 *I would be scared of dogs before I got my own.* ✗

3 *I used to fall off my bike yesterday.* ✗

1 **Questions and answers**

1 Complete the answers using present simple/continuous, *used to* or *would*.

1 **A:** Do you go abroad often?
   B: No, but my father .... regularly. (travel)

2 **A:** Do you get on well with your brothers and sisters?
   B: Yes, although we .... a lot in the past. (fight)

3 **A:** How many cinemas are there in this town?
   B: There .... five or six, but now there are three. (be)

4 **A:** Did your parents read to you as a child?
   B: Yes, they .... me a story every night. (read)

5 **A:** Do you like your cousin?
   B: No, he .... what I do. (always/criticise)

2 ⬭ **Ask and answer the questions. Change the answers so they are true for you.**

2 ***used to* or past continuous?**

Underline the correct option in each pair.

1 I *used to go/was going* downstairs when I tripped and fell.

2 We *used to live/were living* in the country.

3 I *used to spend/was spending* all my money on sweets when I was younger.

4 *Did you use to fight/Were you fighting* with your brother when I rang?

5 *Did you use to collect/Were you collecting* autographs as a kid?

3 **Error correction**

1 Read the text below. What was life like for the writer's great-grandmother?

2 Read the text again and look carefully at each line 1–10. Three lines are correct. Tick them. The other lines each have a word which should not be there. Underline it. There are two examples at the beginning (0 and 00).

MY GREAT-GRANDMOTHER

0 My great-grandmother, Anna, was really pretty as a girl and she ✓

00 had lots of admirers. Her parents were wealthy and they <u>were</u> used

1 to take her to England for a holiday every year. They would always

2 used stay in the same hotel. The owner of the hotel had a son, Peter,

3 and they fell in love! When they got married, she had to leave her

4 native Poland. She was being very homesick at first. She didn't

5 like living in this strange country. She would to cry for hours every

6 single morning! But things they gradually became easier for her. Life

7 was hard in those days. There wasn't any electricity so she was used

8 to do all the washing and cleaning by hand. She had twelve children!

9 Families didn't used to be big then so twelve wasn't unusual. When

10 I think how life used to be in those days, I'm feeling very glad I did
    not live then!

▶▶ **WB** p.57

Vocabulary building

1 True or false?

1 How many of these statements do you agree with?

1 Life is a lot easier for teenagers than it used to be.

2 Being a teenager wasn't as much fun in the past as it is today.

3 Life is more dangerous today than it was 100 years ago.

4 Life was much better before motor cars were invented.

5 The more money teenagers have, the worse they behave.

6 Life was a great deal less stressful in the past than it is now.

2 Complete the rules.

- We add *-er/-est* to regular adjectives that have .... syllable.

- We drop the *-y* and add *-ier/-iest* to adjectives that have .... syllables, e.g. *easy – easier*.

- We use *more/the most, less/the least* with adjectives that have .... or more syllables.

- Some adjectives are irregular, for example: ....

- We use (not) ..... + ... when comparing two things which are similar or equal in some way.

- We use words like *a lot*, ... and .... to make comparatives stronger.

Note: We use *the ..., the ...* with two comparatives (e.g. *the easier ..., the better ...*) when the second fact depends on the first.

3 Reword any sentences in Exercise 1.1 that you disagree with.

Example:

Life is much harder for teenagers than it used to be.

2 Comparatives and superlatives

1 Read the text opposite.

1 Who is the text about?

2 What are the advantages and disadvantages of their way of life?

2 Now fill in the gaps with the correct form of the adjective in brackets. Add any other words necessary.

3 💬 Over to you

Compare your life with that of Miguel, a young person from the tribe. Think about the points below.

- education
- entertainment
- danger
- fitness
- family life
- excitement
- luxuries
- health
- daily life
- technology

Example:

I think his life is a lot more exciting than mine/than my life (is).

Last night I watched one of (1) .... (good) programmes I've seen on TV for ages. It was about an Indian tribe in the Brazilian jungle. They are one of (2) .... (primitive) communities on Earth and their lives have hardly changed in a thousand years. They hunt wild animals and eat wild berries. Some berries in the jungle are (3) .... (poisonous) in the world, but the Indians can identify the safe ones!

Their lives are a lot (4) .... (hard) .... ours. They have no modern technology so, for them, communicating with other people is much (5) .... (difficult) .... for us. There are no cars in the forest so things are (6) .... (quiet) there.

Their pace of life is much (7) .... (slow) – and they're not nearly (8) .... (competitive) .... we are. They are also a great deal (9) .... (sociable) .... we are. Young people have to hunt and cook, so they work much (10) .... (hard) .... we do but their lives are probably not (11) .... (stressful) .... ours in other ways. In the end, they are just (12) .... (happy) .... teenagers in any city!

4 Transformations

Complete the second sentence so it has a similar meaning to the first sentence, using the word given. Do not change the word given. Use between two and five words.

1 Life was shorter in the past. **long**

In the past, people didn't live .... they do now.

2 Living in the jungle isn't as easy as living in the city. **is**

Living in the jungle .... living in the city.

3 The pace of life is much faster in the city than in the country. **far**

The pace of life in the country is .... in the city.

4 I've never seen such a good documentary before. **have**

That was .... ever seen.

5 I can't tell stories nearly as well as my grandfather does. **much**

My grandfather can tell stories .... me.

6 Miguel can run much more quickly than me. **fast**

I can't run .... Miguel.

7 I've never eaten such disgusting food. **was**

It .... food I have ever eaten.

8 Life is noisier than it used to be. **as**

Life isn't .... it used to be.

▶▶ **WB** p.58

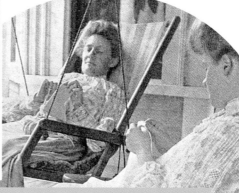

Listening ▶ Part 1

1 Before you listen

▶▶ *listening for a purpose*
Unit 1 p.12

1 Look at the Listening task. Read questions 1–6 and <u>underline</u> the words that tell you:

a) what the situation is.
b) what you need to listen for.

2 Read the options A–C and think about words or phrases you can listen for.

2 📼 Listening strategy

▶▶ *working out the main idea from details*

People don't always state their main message explicitly. You have to work it out from the details. Listen carefully to the expressions they use. What message do they give?

1 Listen to Question 1 and tick the option A, B or C which you think is correct.

2 Now read these extracts from the recording. Which is the correct answer? <u>Underline</u> the phrases that tell you.

'*I was really looking forward to this part of the course. ... I thought we were going to learn more about their way of life today, not just ... . I wish the teacher had shown us some slides ...*'

3 Listen again to check.

3 📼 Listening task

1 Listen to the rest of the task and choose the best answer. You will hear each extract twice.

2 Compare your answers. What parts helped you decide?

4 💬 Over to you

Speaker 6 talks about differences of opinion between himself and his parents. What do you and your parents disagree about?

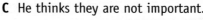

Listening task

You will hear people talking in six different situations. For questions 1–6, choose the best answer A, B or C.

1 You hear a boy talking about a lesson at school.
   What does he say about the lesson?
   A It was disappointing.
   B It was boring.
   C It was long.

   [1]

2 You hear a girl talking about her great-grandmother.
   What does she say about her?
   A She was wealthy.
   B She was good-looking.
   C She was ambitious.

   [2]

3 You hear a woman talking about a tradition.
   What is the woman doing when she speaks?
   A giving advice
   B telling a story
   C apologising

   [3]

4 You hear a man talking about the Welsh language.
   What is he doing when he speaks?
   A suggesting ways of learning Welsh
   B explaining how the Welsh language survived
   C criticising people who aren't interested in languages

   [4]

5 You turn on the radio and hear the beginning of a talk.
   What is the talk about?
   A the surnames of famous people
   B the history of surnames
   C common surnames in Britain

   [5]

6 You hear a boy talking about differences of opinion between him and his parents.
   What does he say about these different opinions?
   A He thinks they are a good thing.
   B He thinks they are funny.
   C He thinks they are not important.

   [6]

Writing: *composition* ▶ *Part 2*

1 Sample writing task

1 Read the task.

Writing task

Your class has been discussing national customs and traditions and whether it's important to keep them alive. Your teacher has asked you to write a composition, giving your opinion.

Write your composition in 120–180 words.

2 Do you think national customs and traditions are still important? Should we keep them alive? Why/ Why not? Tell a partner.

2 Read a sample composition

1 Read the composition opposite.

1 What is the writer's opinion?

2 What are the main points of his argument? Underline them.

3 Which examples/illustrations does he give to justify his argument?

2 Discuss the style.

Does the writer use a) formal b) informal style? Why?

<u>Some people think</u> that our national customs and traditions are no longer important. I disagree with this idea. I believe it is very important to keep our traditions alive.

<u>To start with</u>, I think that these customs unite a country culturally. They remind us about our history and the character of our people. They are a way of celebrating the things that make our country different.

<u>Secondly</u>, many customs bring people together socially. When people sing and dance together, they really get to know each other. In our village, for instance, we have a big party on our National Day. It's a time to forget arguments and make new friends. <u>What's more</u>, everyone can join in – the young and the very old.

<u>Finally</u>, I think that our festivals bring colour into our lives and make life more interesting. They attract tourists, so they are important financially, too!

<u>In conclusion</u>, I think customs and traditions are extremely important in the life of a country. It would be a pity if we let them die.

3 Linking expressions

Replace the <u>underlined</u> phrases with a phrase from the box.

To sum up,
People sometimes suggest
Last but not least,

In the first place,
Furthermore,
In the second place,

4 💬 Over to you

Do you agree or disagree with the writer? Have you changed your opinion in Exercise 1?

5 Writing skills: *linking expressions*

1 Read the text below. Choose phrases from the box to fill in the gaps. There may be more than one possible answer.

furthermore	for instance	to start with
in conclusion	what's more	in the first place
to sum up	for example	first of all also

In my opinion, traditions are no longer important. Why? Well, (1) ...., some of our customs are really out of date. In the past, (2) ...., British men used to raise their hats when they met a woman. That just seems silly now.

It's the same for other traditions. These days, nobody can remember old folk songs and dances. They're out of date. (3) ...., when people try to do them, I think they just look ridiculous.

(4) ...., I would say that in the twenty-first century we need to look forward, not back. It's time we left the past – and our old-fashioned traditions – behind us.

2 Can you think of any other alternatives to fit any of the gaps?

Over to you

6 Writing strategy

Complete the notes.

▶▶ *writing a composition*

When you write a composition in which you are giving your opinion:

- note down three or four main .... that you can develop.
- state your opinion clearly in the .... and again in the ....
- deal with each main point in a separate ....
- include some .... to explain/illustrate your ideas.

7 Writing task

Read the task and <u>underline</u> the main topic of the composition.

> **Writing task**
>
> **Your class has been discussing the following topic:**
> *Young people today are totally selfish. They are only interested in their possessions.*
>
> **Your teacher would like you to write a composition, saying if you agree or disagree with the statement.**
>
> **Write your composition in 120–180 words.**

8 ⬭ Brainstorm ideas

Tick the statements that you agree with and think of examples to support your opinion. Then discuss your ideas with a partner.

1 Young people only think of themselves.
2 Young people care a lot about the environment.
3 Most young people just want to make money when they leave school.
4 Young people do a lot to help others, especially old people.
5 Young people really envy families who have big houses and cars, and they're desperate to have the same.
6 Most young people think friends and family are more important than material things.
7 Young people want the latest fashions and equipment and are not interested in anything else.

9 Plan your composition

Make a plan like the one below. Choose two or three of the ideas you agree with from Exercise 8. Add reasons/examples to justify your opinion.

Para. 1 (Introduction)
My opinion: ....
Para. 2
Topic: ....
Topic sentence: ....
Details: ....
Para. 3/4
Topic: ....
Topic sentence: ....
Details: ....
Final para. (Conclusion)

10 Write

Write your composition. Follow the ▶▶ *Writing strategy*. **Remember to use linking expressions to introduce your main points and examples.**

11 Check your work

Have you stated your opinion clearly? Are the grammar, spelling and punctuation correct?

▶▶ **WB** p.60

12 Inventions

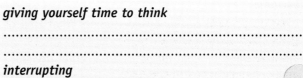

Speaking ▸ *Part 3*

1 Quiz

1 Look at the pictures of some inventions and discoveries that have changed our world. Match the pictures to the items 1–10 in the quiz.

2 Now try the quiz. Can you match the questions to the answers?

TEST YOUR KNOWLEDGE!

1 When was **the aeroplane** invented?

2 Who made **the cinema** possible?

3 In what country were **paper and ink** invented?

4 What nationality was the inventor of **the mechanical clock**?

5 When was **the World Wide Web** introduced?

6 Who invented **the combustion engine** for cars?

7 Where was **the hamburger** created?

8 Who was **the telephone** invented by?

9 What nationality was the man who discovered **the technique of vaccination**?

10 Who invented **the lever**?

A In the early 20th century
B China
C British
D Alexander Bell
E Dutch
F August and Louis Lumière
G Archimedes
H In 1989
I The USA
J Gottlieb Daimler and Karl Benz

2 🔊 Listen

Listen to two students talking about the importance of some of these inventions in their everyday lives.

1 Which inventions do they talk about? Tick the pictures.

2 Listen again. What do they say about each invention? Complete the sentences.

1 Without .... , we'd have to ....

2 .... means you can ....

3 If they hadn't invented ...., we wouldn't be able to ....

4 It makes our life ....

5 .... lets us ....

3 Listen to the rest of the discussion.

1 What expressions does each student use to give him/herself time to think? Write them in the box below.

2 The second student interrupts her friend at one point. What expression does she use? Write it down.

giving yourself time to think

....

....

interrupting

....

3 💬 Speaking task: *selecting*

1 Talk together and choose two inventions which are most important in your lives. Use expressions from Exercise 2.

2 Tell the class what you have decided.

▸▸ **WB** p.61

99

Reading ▶ Part 4

1 Predict

1 You are going to find out some information about four inventions. Look at the title of the article, the sub-headings, and the photos.

1 Who could each invention be useful for?

2 What problem do you think each invention was designed to solve?

2 The words in the box are from the article. Can you guess which words relate to which invention?

> clockwork   (bicycle) handlebars   a licence   a screen
> a spring   dialogue   indestructible   professional
> be impressed by sth.   manufacture   haul (water)
> challenge sb. to do sth.   roll sth. along the ground

2 Reading strategy

▶▶ *predicting where to find information*

To help you locate information in a long text quickly, try to predict which part of the text you are most likely to find it in.

1 For each question 1–12 opposite, <u>underline</u> key words so you know what to look for.

2 Decide which section of the text (A–D) you will probably find the information in. (One question has more than one answer, so you will need to choose two sections.)

3 ▶▶ *scanning for parallel expressions* Unit 8, p.66. Scan that section, using the key words you've <u>underlined</u> to help you find parallel expressions, as in the example (0). If you can't find the information, look at the next most likely section.

Here are some clues to help you.

Questions:

1 What do you call someone who studies? What kind of places do people study at?

2 Think of another word for *basic*. What other *devices* might be mentioned in the text?

4 Someone who has a physical disability is dis............ .

Which invention

must be operated by <u>someone with special training</u>?	**0**	**C**
was invented by a young person while he was still studying?	**1**	
copies very basic technology from another device?	**2**	
is made from material that is extremely strong?	**3**	
helps people who have a physical disability?	**4**	
has improved the lives of people in very poor communities?	**5**	**6**
requires the owner to have a special document before it can be used?	**7**	
is now sold all over the world?	**8**	
was built in less than a month?	**9**	
was considered by others to be impossible at first?	**10**	
provides employment for physically handicapped people?	**11**	
was thought up by somebody who works for a newspaper?	**12**	

3 Vocabulary: *word formation*

1 Find words in the texts to complete the sentences.

1 The car which Vaios designed collapses. It's *collapsible* .

2 You can carry the car in a suitcase. It's ....

3 Vaios' tutors didn't think he could achieve his aim. They didn't think it was ....

4 Poor people can afford Trevor Bayliss' wind-up radio. It's ....

5 People in Africa need a source of water they can rely on. They need a .... source of water.

6 The Q-drum has no parts that you can remove. It has no .... parts.

7 It's hard to destroy the material which the Q-drum is made of. It's almost ....

2 Can you guess what these words mean?

1 drinkable 2 comprehensible 3 convertible 4 reversible

4 💬 Over to you

If you could invent something to make life easier for other people, what would you invent?

▶▶ **WB** p.61

TECHNOLOGY

What's new?

Claire Shapiro writes about some recent inventions that really benefit ordinary people.

A THE WIND-UP RADIO

When British inventor Trevor Bayliss invented the wind-up radio, his goal was to provide an affordable means of communication to people in Africa. There, radio is the main method of distributing information, but electricity is scarce and batteries are expensive. Trevor's brainwave was to take the idea behind the simple, old-fashioned wind-up clock and apply it to the radio. The result: a clockwork radio. You just wind up the spring and it will play for up to an hour. Unfortunately, no British manufacturer was interested in Trevor's invention, so he started his own company, BayGen, with two partners. They set up a factory in South Africa, which employs disabled people. In 1996 BayGen began selling the radios worldwide. They are also distributed by aid organisations such as the United Nations and the Red Cross. BayGen is now planning to apply the wind-up principle to other products. It could transform the lives of many people who don't have access to even simple technology.

B THE PORTABLE CAR

Just imagine owning a car that you can carry around! Vaios Panagiotou, a mechanical engineering student at Brighton University, has built the world's first car that's collapsible and fits into a suitcase. It weighs 20 kilograms, measures just 80 x 60 x 11 centimetres and is powered by a two-stroke engine. Featuring bicycle handlebars as the steering wheel, seven gears, headlights and traffic direction indicators, this remarkable car can reach speeds of up to 56 kilometres per hour on the streets of the university campus. It took Vaios only 15 days to build. 'My tutors challenged me to do it,' Vaios says. One tutor added: 'We have been extremely impressed by what Vaios has achieved. When he first showed us his designs, we thought it wasn't achievable. He has managed to make the design a reality.' However, the police have told Vaios that he won't be allowed onto public roads without a vehicle licence.

C SUB-TITLES FOR THEATRES

Millions of deaf people in the USA are unable to fully enjoy films and live theatre performances. In 1997, Don DePew, a New York reporter, came up with a way to help. His idea was to provide 'real-time' sub-titles which

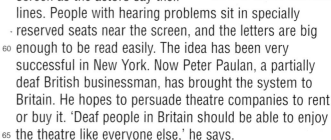

can be read by deaf people while they watch a performance. How is this done? The dialogue of the play is typed into a computer before the show. During the performance, a <u>professional computer operator</u> sits near the stage. He listens to the actors and displays the dialogue on a screen as the actors say their lines. People with hearing problems sit in specially reserved seats near the screen, and the letters are big enough to be read easily. The idea has been very successful in New York. Now Peter Paulan, a partially deaf British businessman, has brought the system to Britain. He hopes to persuade theatre companies to rent or buy it. 'Deaf people in Britain should be able to enjoy the theatre like everyone else,' he says.

D THE Q-DRUM

Water is Africa's life-blood. But millions of Africans live many kilometres from a reliable source of clean water, and village women spend much of their time hauling water to their homes in open containers. So South African architect Hans Hendrikse and his brother Piet, an engineer, invented the Q-Drum. The Q-Drum is a plastic drum shaped like a car-wheel. It can be filled with water and rolled easily along the ground using a rope passed through the middle. Apart from the screw-top lid, it has no removable parts, and is made of almost indestructible material. So it has a life-span of over 10 years. 'Now life is easier,' says Grace Tombane, who has been using the Q-Drum for the past three years. 'Even the small children can use the drum. They make a game of it.' The Q-Drum now has an international patent and a factory has been set up in the neighbouring country of Zimbabwe to manufacture it on a large scale.

Grammar: *the passive* ▶ *p.186*

grammar file 16

A The passive
- *be* + past participle (+ *by*)

1 *The wind-up radio **was invented by** Trevor Bayliss.*
2 *It **is** now **being manufactured** in South Africa.*
3 *Thousands of radios **have been sold** worldwide.*

- modal + *be* + past participle

4 *The wind-up principle **can be applied** to other products.*
5 *More products that help ordinary people **should/must be developed**.*

B *make/let/be allowed to*

Compare:

6 *They **made** the designer **redesign** the boat.*
▶ *The designer **was made to redesign** the boat.*
7 *They **don't let** Vaios **drive** his car on public roads.*
▶ *Vaios **isn't allowed to drive** his car on public roads.*

! What's wrong?

1 *The Model-T car it was built by Ford.* ✗
2 *The CD player was invented by them about forty years ago.* ✗
3 *The scientist wasn't let to build the robot.* ✗

---

1 Sentence transformation

Put these sentences into the passive, starting with the words given. Add *by* only when it is important and informative.

1 Thomas Edison invented the light bulb.
The light bulb ..*was invented by Thomas Edison*.. .

2 Scientists are building a new space satellite.
A new space satellite ....

3 They design new cars every year.
New cars ....

4 Bill Gates developed the 'Windows' programs for computers.
The 'Windows' programs for computers ....

5 They must test all new drugs.
All new drugs ....

6 The machine exploded while they were testing it.
The machine exploded while it ....

7 They should give that inventor the Nobel prize.
That inventor ....

8 They will find a cure eventually.
A cure ....

2 Rewriting

<u>Underline</u> the object of the sentences. Then rewrite the sentences in the passive. Add *by* only when it is important and informative.

1 Alexander Fleming discovered <u>penicillin</u>.
Penicillin was discovered by Alexander Fleming.

2 Someone has just invented a 'miracle' washing machine.
3 They didn't let the inventor speak to the press.
4 Someone will soon design a thinking robot.
5 The Government must support inventors financially.
6 They are going to build a new road round the town.
7 They are making car manufacturers introduce more safety features.
8 Why didn't they let us go to the exhibition?
9 When did they invent the first computer?
10 Someone should congratulate the scientists on their work.

3 Open cloze

1 Read the text below. What is important about the dates 1874 and 1876?

2 Read the text again and think of the word that best fits each space. Use only one word in each space. Most of the words you need are auxiliary verbs. There is an example at the beginning (0).

HOW THE PHONE WAS INVENTED

Nowadays, mobile phones **(0)** ...*are*.. used **(1)** .... people all over the world. They're popular because they can **(2)** .... taken anywhere. Billions of phones **(3)** .... been sold in the past few years. But do you know how and when the phone **(4)** .... invented?

The first telephone was developed in Boston USA **(5)** .... Alexander Graham Bell. Bell's mother was deaf, so he was very interested in speech and sound. The idea for the phone came to him quite suddenly while he **(6)** .... staying with his parents in 1874. He told his father about **(7)** .... , and they discussed the possibilities together. Bell's idea **(8)** .... tested by using a wire set up between two rooms. The invention worked! But Bell still wasn't sure whether messages **(9)** .... be sent over long distances. He needn't have worried. In 1876, the very first long-distance phone call was made.

Are mobile phones safe? Scientists are worried that people's health may **(10)** .... damaged if they use the phones too often. Tests are still **(11)** .... carried out. When the results have **(12)** .... published, people can decide for themselves.

▶▶ **WB** p.62

Vocabulary building

1 Word formation:
compound nouns

1 Match a word in box A with a word in box B to form the names for some common household appliances. One is written as one word.

A

fridge	tin	microwave
mobile	screw	tumble
vacuum	video	

B

opener	dryer	cleaner
driver	oven	phone
recorder	freezer	

2 Read these descriptions. Which appliances above do they describe?

1 It's large and square and made of metal. You find it in the kitchen. You cook food in it.

2 It's light and made of plastic. It has rows of buttons. You call your friends on it.

3 ⏣ Now describe the other appliances in Exercise 1.1. The words in the box below may help you. Can your partner guess which object you are describing?

Size/shape: square round triangular rectangular flat cylindrical

Material: plastic rubber metal

Special features: a lid a slot a compartment a handle a hose a control panel

2 Lexical cloze

1 Read the text below. How clear are the instructions?

2 Read the text again and decide which answer A, B or C best fits each space. There is an example at the beginning (0).

0 **A** orders **B** instructions **C** commands

⚡ O P E R A T I N G   I N S T R U C T I O N S ⚡

Congratulations on choosing a 'Sound Blaster' radio/CD player

Just follow the simple (0) $\underset{\sim}{B}$... in this (1) ..... , then sit back and enjoy the sound sensation.

First, (2)..... two AA batteries into your machine or (3)..... the machine into a wall socket. Press the ON/OFF (4)..... to turn on the machine. A red light will appear.

To (5) ..... the radio, just move the lever up to the correct position. You can adjust the sound by turning the green (6) ..... marked 'Volume' to the appropriate number. To operate the CD player, simply select 'CD' by pressing the red (7)..... and the CD tray will open. The tray will close automatically (8) ..... you put your CD in, and the music will start. When you have finished

listening, you can (9) ..... the CD from the machine by pressing the switch marked with two arrows. Do not leave CDs in the machine for long (10) ..... .

To (11) ..... your machine, simply press 'OFF' and the red light will (12) ..... .

1	**A** propaganda	**B** brochure	**C** leaflet
2	**A** enter	**B** push	**C** insert
3	**A** plug	**B** hammer	**C** screw
4	**A** label	**B** switch	**C** indicator
5	**A** operate	**B** make	**C** search
6	**A** handle	**B** lid	**C** knob
7	**A** dial	**B** plug	**C** button
8	**A** as far as	**B** as long as	**C** as soon as
9	**A** eject	**B** move	**C** unplug
10	**A** ages	**B** times	**C** periods
11	**A** turn down	**B** turn off	**C** turn in
12	**A** go out	**B** go away	**C** go down

3 ⏣ Over to you

Try and explain to a partner how to operate:

a computer *or* a mobile phone *or* a simple machine you often use.

4 Prepositional phrases

Complete the phrases in *italics* with words from the list.

use / trial / stock / display / order / control / sale / guarantee

1 'Please use the stairs. The lift is *out of* ...., I'm afraid.'

2 'All our computers are *in* .... at the moment. Can you wait a few mintues?'

3 The new drug is still *on* .... – we must be sure it's safe before it can be sold.

4 My CD player is *under* .... so if it goes wrong, the makers will repair it free of charge.

5 Some of the first cars ever built are *on* .... at the Science Museum.

6 The car in the window is a show model – it's not *for* ....

7 The shop hasn't got the video I want *in* .... but they're going to order it.

8 On icy roads, a car can easily skid and go *out of* ....

▶▶ **WB** p.63

Listening ▶ Part 2

1 Before you listen

You are going to hear a radio programme about inventions in the USA in the 1920s. Look at the photos, which show a typical home at that time.

What would be different in a picture taken today?

2 Predict

▶▶ *predicting the information you need* Unit 8 p.70

Look at the Listening task and read the sentences. Decide what kind of information you need to fill in the gaps.

3 🖭 Listening task

▶▶ *listening for parallel ideas* Unit 9 p.80

1 Listen to the recording and complete the sentences using no more than three words or a number in each space.

2 Compare your answers with a partner.

3 Listen again and check and complete your answers.

Listening task

You will hear a talk on the subject of inventions. For questions 1–10, complete the sentences.

All through the twentieth century, life was changing as a result of inventions and [＿＿＿＿＿ **1**]

In the 1920s, important changes affected [＿＿＿＿＿ **2**], entertainment and the home.

Ford cars were famous for being small, cheap and always [＿＿＿＿＿ **3**]

Henry Ford sold more than [＿＿＿＿＿ **4**] cars in the 1920s.

In the 1920s, cinemas were built in many [＿＿＿＿＿ **5**], far from anywhere.

The first film made with sound was called [＿＿＿＿＿ **6**]

In the 1920s, many film stars lost their jobs because their [＿＿＿＿＿ **7**] were not good.

Before the 1920s, the main form of evening entertainment for families was [＿＿＿＿＿ **8**] at home.

When it was first invented, people used to listen to the radio in [＿＿＿＿＿ **9**]

Like today, most new inventions in the 1920s were [＿＿＿＿＿ **10**] at first.

4 Listening strategy

▶▶ *dealing with unknown words*

When you are listening for specific information, you don't have to understand every single word.

• Don't panic if you can't understand everything.
• Focus on the information you need.

Look at the extracts from the tapescript on p.178. Underline any unfamiliar words. Did you need these words to do the listening task?

5 💬 Over to you

What did you learn from the radio programme that you didn't know before?

Writing: *report*
▶ *Part 2*

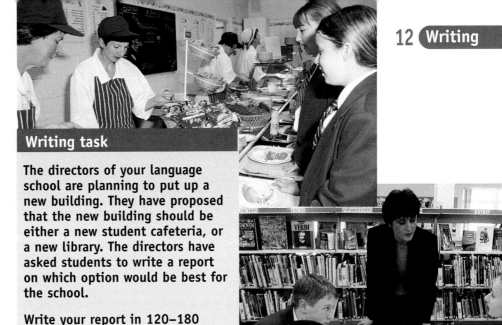

1 Sample writing task
Read the task.

1 Who will read your report?

2 What style should you use?

3 What is the purpose of the report? Underline the two options you have to write about.

Writing task

The directors of your language school are planning to put up a new building. They have proposed that the new building should be either a new student cafeteria, or a new library. The directors have asked students to write a report on which option would be best for the school.

Write your report in 120–180 words.

2 💬 Brainstorm ideas

1 Think about the advantages and disadvantages of each option in the writing task and add more notes to the table below.

	Cafeteria	*Library*
Advantages	*good meeting place*	*good for quiet study*
Disadvantages	*need more staff*	*expensive to buy books*

2 Which option would you recommend?

3 Read a sample report

1 Read the report opposite and fill in the gaps using a suitable linking expression from the box.

What's more   Although   However   On the other hand
Therefore   In addition   Also

2 Answer these questions.

1 Which option does the writer recommend?

2 What reasons does the writer give for this recommendation?

3 Do you agree with the writer?

3 Discuss the style.

1 There are three sentences that are too personal and informal for a report. Find them and cross them out.

2 Why does the writer use the second conditional (*would*) so often?

To: The Director of Studies
Subject: New school building
Date: 14 May

The purpose of this report is to recommend which building would be best for the school.

A The student cafeteria

The main advantage of a new cafeteria is that students would have a place to meet socially as well as buy food and drink. I know that I often want to just relax somewhere between lessons. (1) ...., students can share their knowledge with each other, which will help their progress in class.

(2) .... , we would need staff to do the cooking and cleaning.

B The library

This is an excellent idea, because students would be able to study in a quiet place. At home, I have to share my room with my sister, so I need somewhere quiet to do my homework. (3) .... , if we had a library, we would have lots more books and resources than we have now. This would help us do research for projects.

(4) ...., it would be expensive to buy a large amount of books, magazines, cassettes and videos.

Conclusion

(5) .... a library would be useful, it is not essential because many students can find the information they need on the Internet at home. Actually, I haven't got the Internet, but many of my friends have. (6) ...., I would recommend the cafeteria because it is more important for students to have somewhere to meet.

4 Writing skills: *contrast linkers*

Rewrite sentences 1–4 below using *although*, *however* or *in spite of*.

Example:

The library would be expensive, but I would still recommend it.

a) *Although the library would be expensive, I would still recommend it.*

b) *The library would be expensive. However, I would still recommend it.*

c) *In spite of the fact that the library would be expensive, I would still recommend it.*

1 All students would benefit from having a library, but I would recommend the cafeteria.

2 The cafeteria would be convenient, but is not the most important thing for students.

3 The library has lots of resources, but many students prefer to study at home.

4 The cafeteria would be convenient, but it would not be used enough, in my opinion.

Over to you

5 Writing strategy

Complete the notes.

▶▶ *writing a report*

When you write a report where you have to choose the best option, you should:

• discuss the .... and .... of each option.

• use linking expressions like .... and .... to link and contrast your ideas.

• state your .... in the conclusion.

6 Writing task

1 Read the task below.

1 Who will read your report?

2 <u>Underline</u> the two options you have to write about.

3 What must you include in your report?

7 Plan your report

1 Note down some good reasons for choosing a) a gymnasium and b) a video room. Then note down at least one disadvantage with each.

• Which of the two options would you choose? Why?

• Which are you going to recommend in your report? Why?

2 Look at the ideas one student thought of. Did you think of different ideas? If so, add them to the list.

	Gymnasium	*Video room*
Advantages	*healthy* *good fun* *relieve stress*	*educational* *relaxing* *a change from books*
Disadvantages	*too expensive* *needs a teacher or trainer there all the time*	*students may take videos away*

3 Tick two or three of the best ideas which you can use in your report and make a plan. Add notes on the proposal you recommend.

<u>Introduction</u>

<u>A Gymnasium</u>

Advantages: ....

Disadvantages: ....

<u>B Video Room</u>

Advantages: ....

Disadvantages: ....

<u>Conclusion</u>

I would recommend ....
because ....

Writing task

Your teacher has just given this notice to the members of your class.

From: The Director of Studies

To: All students

Subject: New facilities

We propose to improve the service we offer to students this year. A sum of money is now available to spend on either a new gymnasium or a new video room. Which of these two projects do you think would be more useful for the students in the school? Please write a short report giving your recommendation, with reasons for your choice.

Many thanks,

G. Smith

Write your report in 120–180 words.

8 Write

Now write your report. Follow the ▶▶ *Writing strategy*. Remember to start your report in the correct way and to use headings.

9 Check your work

Have you given a reason for your recommendation? Are the grammar, spelling and punctuation correct?

▶▶ **WB** p. 65

Progress test 3

1 Lexical cloze

For questions **1–12**, read the text below and decide which answer **A**, **B** or **C** best fits each space. There is an example at the beginning **(0)**.

Example:

0 **A** at   **B** in   **C** by

MULTI-CULTURAL BRITAIN

Britain **(0)** *B.* the twenty-first century is a multi-cultural society. Britain's most **(1)** ... meal is curry, not roast beef, and people in London speak 307 **(2)** ... languages! That's more languages than in any **(3)** ... city in the world! The children and grandchildren of immigrants to Britain have **(4)** ... become part of multi-cultural Britain. Ethnic groups today make **(5)** ... about 5.6% of Britain's population.

You can see **(6)** ... of multi-cultural Britain everywhere. There are many Black and Asian people in sport, politics and the media. School children in ethnic minority schools can learn languages **(7)** ... Bengali, and some schools **(8)** ... Muslim, Hindu and Jewish special days, as well as the more traditional holidays, such as Christmas and Easter. British sports teams are full **(9)** ... players from overseas. Clothes **(10)** ... lifestyles from other parts of the world have become fashionable in recent years.

Multi-culturalism is a good thing and young people feel very **(11)** ... about it. Many young people **(12)** ... today's more relaxed atmosphere to the way of life in the past.

2 Open cloze

For questions **13–24**, read the text below and think of the word which best fits each space. Use only one word in each space. There is an example at the beginning **(0)**.

THE SOUNDS OF MUSIC

Popular music today makes great use **(0)** ...*of*.... an invention called the electronic synthesiser. The synthesiser is **(13)** .... electrical instrument that can produce the sounds of many different musical instruments, **(14)** .... as the electric guitar, piano or drums. It was invented **(15)** .... Harry Olson and Herbert Belar as long ago **(16)** .... 1955. However, the first commercial synthesiser did not become available **(17)** .... another nine years.

A synthesiser is played with a keyboard, **(18)** .... a piano. Inside, there are electronic components **(19)** .... produce an electronic signal. The keyboard controls the frequency of the signal and the sound level, which comes out of a loudspeaker connected **(20)** .... the synthesiser.

If the synthesiser had not **(21)** .... invented, we would not **(22)** .... had the revolution in music which has taken place in the last 50 years. When musicians realised what they could do with **(23)** .... new invention, the sounds of music changed completely. Now, they could produce an enormous range of sounds from just one instrument. Popular music would never **(24)** .... the same again.

1 **A** popular	**B** favourite	**C** loved
2 **A** varied	**B** different	**C** unlike
3 **A** other	**B** one	**C** another
4 **A** yet	**B** still	**C** now
5 **A** out	**B** up	**C** on
6 **A** customs	**B** traditions	**C** signs
7 **A** such	**B** as	**C** like
8 **A** celebrate	**B** socialise	**C** rejoice
9 **A** with	**B** of	**C** up
10 **A** also	**B** and	**C** or
11 **A** positive	**B** certain	**C** helpful
12 **A** like	**B** prefer	**C** want

3 Key word transformations

For questions **25–32**, complete the second sentence so that it has a similar meaning to the first sentence, using the word given. **Do not change the word given.** You must use between two and five words, including the word given. There is an example at the beginning **(0)**.

Example:

0 You mustn't spend so much money.
stop

You must ..*stop spending*..... so much money.

25 What kind of music do you like best?
favourite

What's .... music?

26 When does the match start?
tell

Can you .... match starts?

27 Are we going to the cinema?
if

Could you tell me .... to the cinema?

28 I wanted to learn Italian but I didn't.
wish

I .... Italian.

29 If Franco hadn't scored the goal, they wouldn't have won the match.
so

Franco .... they won the match.

30 We lived in China when I was younger, but now we live in Australia.
used

When I was younger we ....,
but now we live in Australia.

31 The Egyptians divided the day into hours.
was

The day .... the Egyptians.

32 Christina's mother doesn't let her stay out after midnight.
allowed

Christina .... stay out after midnight.

4 Error correction

For questions **33–44**, read the text below and look carefully at each line. Some of the lines are correct, and some have a word which should not be there. If a line is correct, put a tick (✓) next to it. If a line has a word which should not be there, underline the word. There are two examples at the beginning **(0 and 00)**.

A STAR IS BORN

0 You may not have heard of handsome Jose Marlotti, but that is all ✓
00 about to change. Marlotti is going to be the hit of the year when <u>some</u>
33 two films are starring the young Spanish-American actor hit cinemas
34 across Europe during the next a few months. Success for the young
35 actor is assured, with his good looks, talent, intelligence and
36 professional approach to his work. When I asked to him if he had
37 always wanted to be act, he replied that it had been his ambition
38 ever since he could remember. His parents had been encouraged him
39 to complete his school studies before he went to drama school in the
40 Madrid, and his Spanish father now he works as Jose's manager.
41 Jose's American mother says that in the past she wished if he
42 had gone to university because she wasn't sure how to successful
43 he would be. But now of course that has all changed and she is
44 happy for that her son is enjoying life as an international film star.

5 Word formation

For questions **45–52**, read the text below. Use the word given in capitals underneath the text to form a word that fits in the space in the text. There is an example at the beginning **(0)**.

LIBRARY OF KNOWLEDGE

For over 15 years, *Active Mind* has been the world **(0)** *leader*. in reference publishing. The new *Active Mind* CD provides **(45)** .... with an enormous library of knowledge as well as **(46)** .... from experts. This multi-media CD includes a **(47)** .... search engine, and a complete A–Z list of articles, providing a **(48)** .... source of useful **(49)** .... than ever before. Ask any question, and the search engine **(50)** .... processes your query and scans millions of words to find the articles most **(51)** .... to answer your question. Now, with our very **(52)** .... development you can go online to access even more knowledge from **(53)** .... websites around the world, as well as from *Active Mind Online*. Register now for free special offers.

0	**LEAD**	**49**	**INFORM**
45	**USE**	**50**	**CAREFUL**
46	**GUIDE**	**51**	**LIKE**
47	**POWER**	**52**	**LATE**
48	**GREAT**	**53**	**SELECT**

13 Survival

In 2000, a small group of volunteers spent a year on a remote, uninhabited Scottish island with no modern technology and no contact with the outside world. Their experiences were filmed and shown on TV.

Speaking ▶ *Parts 3 and 4*

1 Discussion

1 Look at the photo and read the information.

Would you volunteer to do something like this? Why/Why not?

2 What do you think the volunteers had to learn to do in order to survive? Think of ideas to add to this list:

How to light a fire
How to build a shelter

2 💬 Speaking task: *prioritising*

If you had to spend a year on the island, what would you take with you? Look at the pictures and decide which three things would be most useful. Use expressions from the box.

expressing purpose

... is/are important because ...

We can/could use ... to (light a fire).

... would be very useful for (cutting firewood).

We'll need ... in case (we get lost)/so that we can (find our way around).

Maybe ... is more important because ...

The most important thing is ...

3 Listen

1 Listen to two students discussing the following questions. What do they say?

1 What personal qualities would you need to survive in difficult conditions?
2 How well would you cope?
3 What would you miss most from your everyday life?

2 Listen again. Tick the expressions in the box they used:

a) when they didn't know a word.
b) when they didn't understand a word.
c) to give an explanation.

asking for/giving explanations

I'm sorry? I didn't understand the question.
I'm sorry, I don't understand what ... means.
How do you say that ... ?
I don't know the word/term in English.
You know, ...
I mean .../What I mean is ...

4 💬 Discussion

How would <u>you</u> answer the questions in Exercise 3.1?

▶▶ **WB** p.68

109

Reading ▸ Part 1

1 Predict

Read the title and sub-heading, and look at the photos.

1 Who is the text about? What are they going to do?
2 Why do you think they are going to do this?
3 What dangers and hardships could they face?

2 Skim

▶▶ *skimming* Unit 2, p.16

Skim the text quickly.

Paragraph:

1 What was the boys' crime? In what way is their punishment unusual?
2 What kind of place are they going to?
3 What help will they get?
4 How will people know if the boys are all right?
5 What will they have to give up?
6 What is the advantage of this punishment?

3 Reading strategy

▶▶ *focusing on main points*

Headings summarise the main idea of each section or paragraph in a text. When you have to match headings to paragraphs:

- identify the main point of the paragraph.
- don't focus on details.
- decide which heading summarises the main point.
- look for phrases that express the main idea in different words.

1 Read the text again, paragraph by paragraph. Match the pairs of headings to the paragraphs 1–5. Underline the parts of the text that are paraphrased or summarised in the headings.

A a) Unsuitable clothing   b) A good chance of survival

B a) A tough environment   b) Dangerous animals

C a) A first crime   b) A traditional punishment

D a) Learning how to amuse yourself   b) Living without TV

E a) Surviving the first few days   b) Tools for survival

2 Decide which of the heading options a) or b):

- summarises the main idea of the paragraph.
- just focuses on a detail in the paragraph.

3 Now write your own heading for paragraph 6. Compare your headings with other students.

Alone in the wilderness

Equipped only with sleeping bags and tools, two teenagers face 18 months alone in the wilds of Alaska. Find out why in our special report.

1

They'll have sleeping bags, and tools for cutting firewood and gathering food. But they'll have no way to contact the outside world during more than a year of **exile**[1] in the wilderness. 17-year-
5 old Adrian Thomson and Peter Guthrie belong to the Tlingit Indian tribe of Alaska. Earlier this year, they pleaded guilty to robbing a pizza delivery man. As this was their first offence, the State judge decided not to send the youths to prison.
10 Instead, in the first case of its kind, he invited the tribal elders to punish them in accordance with Indian tribal custom. The elders decided to banish the boys for 18 months to separate islands off the Alaskan coast.

2

15 A year on one of these **uninhabited**[2] islands will be no holiday for the youths. Most of the islands are very mountainous, and are covered with thick forests. They are part of the Tongass National Forest, and are inhabited only by wildlife,
20 including black bears and wolves. The seas around the islands are rich in fish, and whales and seals are a common sight. The climate is slightly warmer than the rest of Alaska, but the boys will be facing a winter of snowstorms and
25 heavy rainfall, with average temperatures as low as minus six degrees Centigrade.

3

The boys will be given some basic equipment, but tribal officials would not say if they would be given guns for hunting and protection against
30 wild animals. They said each boy would have forks for **digging up**[3] shellfish, axes and saws for cutting firewood, and some food to get them through the first few days. They will have sleeping bags and each will build a small shelter,
35 which will be equipped with a wood **stove**[4] for cooking and heat. Apart from these things, the boys will have to survive on their own, using whatever they can find.

4

Can these youngsters live through their **ordeal**⁵?
40 Guthrie and Thomson seem much like teenagers anywhere else in the United States, wearing reversed baseball caps, and clothes inspired by MTV. Although they don't look ideally suited to life in the wild, the tribal elders said that the two would survive. The boys
45 have been taught how to live off the land since they began to walk. They will be checked on **periodically**⁶, but there will be no way for them to contact the outside world even in case of emergency.

5

The day they were told the news about their sentence,
50 the teenagers were **lounging**⁷ in the sun. One was listening to music on his Walkman, and the other was playing a video game. The two boys will have to forget about things like these when they start their life on the islands. When asked what they would do for
55 entertainment, Peter said: 'It's going to be hard without TV and computer games. I haven't really thought about what I'll do.' Adrian seemed less concerned. 'Sure, I'll miss my music when I'm alone, but there'll be a lot to do and a lot to think about.'

6

60 Although exile may seem like a **tough**⁸ punishment, the elders believe that it will be good for the boys. It will teach them that criminal behaviour is wrong, and it will also build character. 'Prison is a bad environment. The boys would learn bad attitudes from other
65 criminals,' said one elder. 'With this punishment, they will learn to be independent and to face difficulties alone. It will make them more responsible members of our society. They will also have time to really think about what they have
70 done. We are confident that it will convince them never to commit another crime when they
75 are set free.'

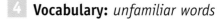

4 **Vocabulary:** *unfamiliar words*

1 Find words 1–8 in the article. Use the following context clues to help you work out what they mean.

1 Look for an explanation at the end of the paragraph.
2 Is the word formed from any other word you know?
3 What do we use a *fork* for?
4 The purpose is explained in the text.
5 Think about the situation. Is living alone on an island something easy and pleasant or not?
6 Think about the situation. Will the boys be checked on often or from time to time?
7 Think about the activities which the boys were doing.
8 What does the linking word *Although* suggest?

2 Now complete these definitions.

a) A place that is .... has no-one living there.
b) A .... is a piece of equipment that you cook on or heat a room with.
c) If you do something .... , you do it fairly regularly but not frequently.
d) .... is when someone is forced to leave their town or country and live somewhere else.
e) If something is .... , it is difficult.
f) If you .... something .... , you remove it from under the earth with a tool.
g) If you .... , you stand or sit in a relaxed way.
h) An .... is a very unpleasant experience.

5 **Vocabulary:** *crime*

1 Match the verbs in column A to phrases in column B. There may be more than one answer.

	A	B
☐	1 plead	a) somebody to prison
☐	2 send	b) somebody free
☐	3 commit	c) guilty/innocent
☐	4 set	d) somebody (to prison/exile)
☐	5 sentence	e) a crime

2 Number the actions in the order they happen.

6 💬 **Over to you**

What do <u>you</u> think? Is the tribal punishment fair? Why/Why not? Do you agree that it will *build character*?

▶▶ **WB** p.69

Grammar: *reported speech* ▶ *p.185*

grammar files 13, 14

A Reporting statements

Direct speech	Indirect speech
1 'I**'m** lucky to be alive!' the survivor **said**. ▶	The survivor **said** (that) **he was** lucky to be alive.
2 'My boat **sank** yesterday,' he **told us**. ▶	He **told us** (that) his boat **had sunk the day before**.
3 'I **must** phone **my** parents,' he **said**. ▶	He **said** (that) he **had to** phone **his** parents.

B Reporting questions

Direct questions	Indirect questions
• **Wh- questions**	
4 '**How** did **you** keep **warm**?' we asked him. ▶	We asked him **how he'd kept** warm.
• **Yes / No questions**	
5 '**Did you** feel **scared**?' we **wanted to know**. ▶	We wanted to know **if/ whether** he had felt scared.

! What's wrong?

1 The explorer said he has broken his leg yesterday. X

2 They asked him how long had he been waiting. X

3 He said me that he was lost. X

1 Reported statements

1 Two teenagers have been found in the jungle after getting lost. Read what they said to a reporter.

1 'We were exploring with a group of tourists, but we decided to go off on our own.'

2 'We've been alone in the jungle for six days.'

3 'We've been eating nothing but berries.'

4 'We both cut our feet but otherwise we're not hurt.'

5 'We're really lucky to be alive!'

6 'We're looking forward to seeing our parents.'

2 Now report what they said using a reporting verb from the list.

said / explained / told the reporters / admitted

1 *The teenagers explained that they had been exploring with a group of tourists, but they ...*

2 Direct and reported questions

1 Write the direct questions which the reporter asked the teenagers in Exercise 1.

1 How/you/get lost?

   How did you get lost?

2 How long/you/be/here?

3 What/you/eat?

4 you/hurt yourselves/while/you/ in/jungle?

5 How/you/feel/now/about your adventure?

6 What/you/look forward to doing next?

2 Now report the questions above using a reporting verb from the list.

asked them / wanted to know / wondered

1 *The reporter asked them how they had got lost.*

3 Error correction

1 Read the text below.

1 Who is it about? What has he done?

2 Why did he do it? Do you think his explanation is the real reason?

3 What was the most difficult part of his experience?

2 Read the text again and look carefully at each line 1–12. Two lines are correct. Tick them. The other lines each have a word which should not be there. Underline it. There are two examples at the beginning (0 and 00).

SMALL BOAT, BIG SEA

0 54-year-old Jim Shekhdar today became the first man to row across ✓

00 the Pacific alone. As he came ashore, he told <u>to</u> reporters that he

1 did not believe there was anything particularly courageous about his

2 achievement. Mr Shekhdar has joked that he had gone on the trip as

3 it was enough hard to get away from his wife on dry land. During his

4 nine-month journey, Jim was forced to eat packet food. He explained

5 that he can could not open any of the tins he had taken because he

6 had been forgotten to pack a tin opener. He said one of his worst

7 experiences it was when sharks attacked his boat. He had to fight

8 them off with a stick. He said reporters that he had enjoyed the

9 first couple of months at sea but he has had started to feel lonely

10 eventually. When a reporter asked Mrs Shekhdar if will she would

11 allow her husband to go to sea again, she said that she could not to

12 make that decision. 'If he wants that to go, he will,' she said.

3 💬 Why do you think people do things like this?

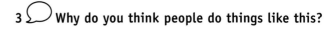

WB p.69

Vocabulary building

1 Words that go together

1 Match a word in column A with a word in column B.

	A		B
1	send	a)	animals
2	chop	b)	a hole
3	dig	c)	a shelter
4	hunt	d)	a fire
5	build	e)	a distress signal
6	light	f)	wood

2 Complete the sentences using the expressions above.

1 We had no matches so we rubbed sticks together to *light a fire*.

2 We used an axe to ...., and we put that on the fire.

3 We tried to .... to a passing ship but it did not see us.

4 We had nothing to eat so we had to .... – mostly rabbits!

5 To keep our food cool, we had to .... in the sand and bury it.

6 It was cold at night but we were able to .... to sleep in.

3 💬 **Where do you think the people were? What happened to them?**

2 Phrasal verbs

1 Read the text carefully. Then fill in the gaps with a phrasal verb from the box in the correct form.

come up with	run out of	come across
make do with	get over	carry on

Man survives nine days in dinghy

Shipwreck survivor Luke Kelly spent nine days adrift in a dinghy in heavy seas. He set sail in a yacht from Spain but a fire in the engine forced him to abandon ship. The boat sank in minutes.

There was no food on the dinghy so he had to (1) .... the chocolate he found in his pocket. After seven days he (2) .... water, and had nothing to drink. He waved to passing ships but none came to help him. He felt desperate but he knew he had to (3) .... trying to get help. Then he (4) .... a can of engine oil floating in the water. When he saw it, he (5) .... an idea which saved his life. He removed his jacket, soaked it in the oil and set fire to it. A passing ship saw the fire and came to his rescue. Luke was taken to hospital suffering from exposure. It will take him a long time to (6) .... his ordeal.

2 Match the phrasal verbs to their meanings below.

a) continue   c) find by chance   e) recover from

b) manage with   d) have no more left   f) think of

3 Lexical cloze

1 Read the text below. What advice does it offer?

2 Read the text and decide which answer A, B, C or D best fits each space. There is an example at the beginning (0).

0   **A** unless   **B** provided   **C** depending **D** despite

ADVICE FOR TOURISTS

Tourists may explore the trail unaccompanied, **(0)** *B*.. they keep to the following guidelines.

- Before you set **(1)** .... on the jungle trail, make sure you **(2)** .... someone where you are going and what time you **(3)** .... to be back.
- Take a **(4)** .... of the trail with you – and make sure that you can **(5)** .... it!
- Keep to the main **(6)** .... through the jungle.
- Stay together! Then, if you **(7)** .... your way, rescuers will be able to **(8)** .... you more easily.
- Make sure you **(9)** .... suitable clothing – a sun hat and thick boots are a necessity!
- If you **(10)** .... a fire to cook food, take **(11)** .... to extinguish it completely before you carry **(12)** .... with your walk.

1	**A** out	**B** away	**C** over	**D** down
2	**A** talk	**B** report	**C** tell	**D** say
3	**A** think	**B** know	**C** expect	**D** suppose
4	**A** plan	**B** diagram	**C** guide	**D** map
5	**A** interpret	**B** read	**C** translate	**D** utilise
6	**A** roads	**B** avenues	**C** streets	**D** paths
7	**A** mistake	**B** lose	**C** miss	**D** forget
8	**A** search	**B** discover	**C** find	**D** hunt
9	**A** carry	**B** wear	**C** fetch	**D** put
10	**A** light	**B** set	**C** do	**D** burn
11	**A** warning	**B** attention	**C** notice	**D** care
12	**A** on	**B** away	**C** off	**D** out

▶▶ WB p.71

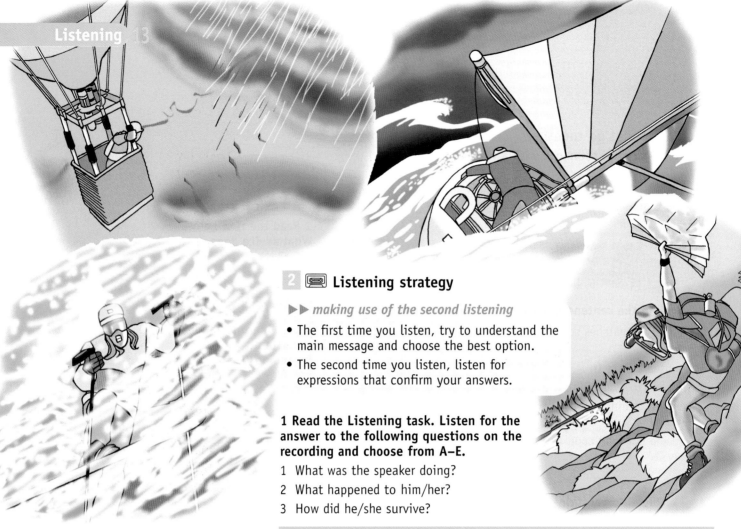

Listening ▶ Part 3

1 Before you listen

1 Read the instructions for the Listening task.

1 How many people are you going to hear?

2 What topic are they going to talk about?

2 Look at the pictures of people in dangerous situations. Use the words in the box to talk about:

1 what is happening/has happened in each picture.

2 what the people could do to survive in those situations.

> get lost/lose your way
> hurt/injure yourself
> run out of food
> land   sink
> be blown off course
> send a distress call
> keep moving

2 🔊 Listening strategy

▶▶ *making use of the second listening*

- The first time you listen, try to understand the main message and choose the best option.
- The second time you listen, listen for expressions that confirm your answers.

1 Read the Listening task. Listen for the answer to the following questions on the recording and choose from A–E.

1 What was the speaker doing?

2 What happened to him/her?

3 How did he/she survive?

Listening task

You will hear four different people describing a dangerous situation. Choose from the list A–E how each person survived. Use the letters only once. There is one extra letter which you do not need to use.

A My previous experience helped me.

B My calls for help were answered.

C I remained very calm throughout.

D I followed some useful advice I had heard.

E I knew what to do because I had read about it.

Speaker 1 [ ] **1**

Speaker 2 [ ] **2**

Speaker 3 [ ] **3**

Speaker 4 [ ] **4**

2 Listen again. For each extract, answer these questions.

1 Why did Speaker 1 decide to follow the river?

2 What did Speaker 2 do to attract attention?

3 Why did Speaker 3 know what to do in this situation?

4 How did Speaker 4 know about digging a hole?

3 Do you need to change any answers in Exercise 2.1?

3 💬 Over to you

Think of a situation in your life when you were very lucky. What happened? Tell the class.

Writing: *story* ▶ *Part 2*

1 Sample writing task
Read the task.

1 Who is going to read the story?
2 Where will you put the sentence given?
3 What kind of story will you write?
 a) a story with a happy ending
 b) a story that ends in disaster

Writing task

The editor of a student magazine has invited students to send in a story. The story must end with these words:

The nightmare was over. We were safe at last.

Write your story in 120–180 words.

2 Brainstorm ideas

1 Decide what kind of story it will be.

a) adventure c) disaster
b) mystery d) crime

2 Think of answers to these questions. Then compare your ideas with other pairs.

1 What happened?
2 Who was involved?
3 When did it happen?
4 Where?
5 Why did it happen?
6 How did the main character(s) feel?
7 How did the story end?

3 Does your story fit the ending given in the writing task?

3 Read a sample story
Read the story.

1 What are the answers to the questions in Exercise 2.2? Are any of the ideas the same as yours?
2 Did you find the story interesting? Why?
3 How would <u>you</u> have felt in this situation? Have you ever been in a similar situation?

Have you ever been in real danger? I have. It happened last year while I was on holiday in Scotland.

I was touring with my family and my friend, Conrad. We were driving along the wild coast that borders the West of Scotland. One day, my dad stopped the car near a deserted beach. He and my mum settled down to sunbathe, but Conrad and I wanted to explore. We promised to be back in two hours.

We walked farther than we intended. When we turned back, we had a horrible shock! Where the land had been earlier, there was now just sea. I heard Conrad gasp: 'Oh no. What are we going to do now?' We were trapped!

There was no way up the cliffs but we climbed onto the highest rocks we could find. We shouted at the tops of our voices, but nobody came. The sea got closer and closer as the tide came in. Eventually, the waves reached our feet, and then our waists. We were frantic. Then, miraculously, a lifeboat appeared round the bay. The nightmare was over. We were safe at last.

4 Adding interest

1 Here are some features of a good story.

A good story uses:
• interesting details.
• vivid vocabulary to make the story come alive.
• direct speech.

2 Find the interesting words and expressions in the story that mean the same as:

1 natural, unaltered by people
2 empty, with no people present
3 got comfortable
4 planned
5 say in a shocked voice
6 unable to escape
7 very loudly
8 surprisingly and wonderfully

3 Which of the words you found are:

a) adjectives?
b) adverbs that tell us how something happened?
c) a reporting verb that tells us how someone said something?

5 Tenses

<u>Underline</u> the verbs in the story.

1 How many different tenses are used in the story?
2 Which tense is used to describe the background to events?
3 Which tenses are used to describe actual events?

6 Writing skills: *vocabulary*

Read this short story. Replace the underlined words with more vivid ones from the box.

> miraculously   screamed   huge
> yelled   exhausted   great
> frantic   glorious

It was a <u>nice</u> summer day that morning so we decided to go to the beach.

It got windier in the afternoon and the waves were really <u>big</u>. We could hardly hear each other in the wind. 'Let's go surfing,' I <u>said</u>. At first it was <u>nice</u> in the sea. But then we realised we were too far from land. We became really <u>worried</u>. 'I'm drowning!' Sam <u>said</u> in terror.

Then, <u>luckily</u>, a helicopter appeared. The pilot pulled us from the sea. We were <u>tired</u>, but we were safe.

Over to you

7 Writing strategy

Complete the notes.

▶▶ *writing a story*

When you write a story:

- use .... vocabulary and lots of detail to bring the story to life.
- use a variety of tenses like the .... and the .... but do not use the .... perfect tense to describe finished events.

8 Writing task

Read the task.

1 Who is going to read your story?
2 Who is the central character?
3 Should the story have a happy or a sad ending?

Writing task

You have decided to enter a short story competition for the school students' magazine. The rules say you must end the story with these words:

When I thought about the day's adventures, I smiled. Everything had come out right in the end!

Write your story in 120–180 words.

9 💬 Brainstorm ideas

1 What could the story be about? Choose from these ideas, or think of your own.

a) A time you got lost
b) A day when you helped someone out of a dangerous situation
c) A trip that went wrong at first

2 Answer these questions. Make notes.

1 What exactly were your 'day's adventures'? What happened?
2 Who was involved besides you (if anyone)?
3 When did it happen? Where? Why did it happen? What was the background?
4 What did you do? How did you feel?
5 How did it 'come out all right in the end'?

10 Write

Now write your story. Follow the ▶▶ *Writing strategy*.

11 Check your work

Will your story interest readers? Are the grammar, spelling and punctuation correct?

▶▶ WB p.72

14 Animal kingdom

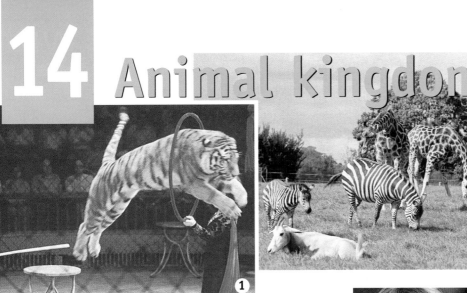

Speaking ▶ *Part 2*

1 About you

1 Do you enjoy going to the zoo? Why/Why not?

2 Have you ever been to a circus? What did you think of it?

3 Do you or your family have a pet? Who chose it? Who looks after it?

2 Vocabulary: *words that go together*

1 Match a verb in column A with a phrase in column B. There may be more than one possibility.

A	B
1 jump through	a) a wild animal
2 be	b) tricks
3 train	c) in captivity
4 stroke	d) on a lead
5 keep (an animal)	e) a pet
6 tame	f) in a cage
7 teach (an animal)	g) a hoop

2 Look at the photos 1–4. Which phrases from Exercise 2.1 can you use to talk about each photo?

Example:

In the first photo, I can see a tiger jumping through a hoop.

3 💬 Speaking task: *photos*

Student A: Look at photos 1 and 2, which show wild animals in different settings. Compare and contrast them and say which of the animals seem to have a better life.

Student B: Look at photos 3 and 4, which show domestic animals in different settings. Compare and contrast them and say which animals you think are more important for people.

4 📼 Listen

1 Read these questions. Write *Yes* or *No* next to each one, according to your opinion.

1 Is it cruel to keep wild animals in captivity?

2 Is it acceptable to use animals for entertainment?

3 Do you think pets are an important part of family life?

2 Now listen to two students discussing question 1.

1 What is their opinion?

2 How do they support their ideas?

3 Listen again. Tick the phrases they use to introduce examples/reasons.

> *introducing examples/reasons*
> For example/For instance, …
> Besides, …   Also, …
> You can see in the picture that …
> Everybody knows that …
> I've read about/that …

4 Who do you agree with?

5 💬 Discussion

Now discuss Questions 2 and 3 in Exercise 4.1. Make sure you support your ideas with reasons and examples. Use phrases from the box.

▶▶ WB p.73

Reading ▶ Part 2

1 Predict

1 Look at the title and sub-heading of the article and the photos.

1 Why do you think the men in the cage are there?

2 How do you think they are feeling?

3 Is this something you would do? Why/Why not?

2 Which of these adjectives best describe sharks in your opinion?

dangerous   beautiful   frightening
cuddly   unpredictable   graceful

2 Read for general understanding

Read the text once quite quickly.

1 How did the writer feel about sharks before he went shark diving?

2 Why did he decide to go shark diving?

3 What effect did the experience have on him?

3 Reading strategy

▶▶ *understanding the writer's purpose*

You will find it easier to understand a text if you know why it was written. While you are reading, ask yourself these questions:

• Does the writer want to give me factual information?

• Does the writer want to express his/her personal feelings and opinions?

• Does the writer want to persuade me to share his/her views?

Answer the questions in the strategy box about this text. Find examples to support your answers.

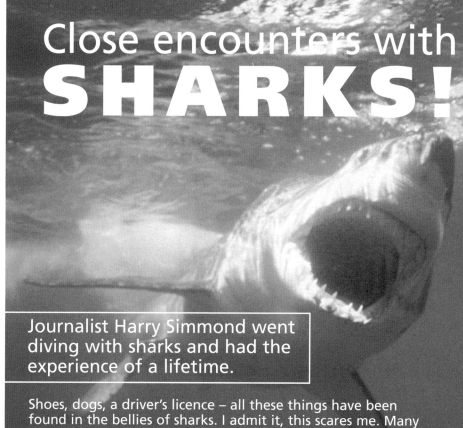

Close encounters with SHARKS!

Journalist Harry Simmond went diving with sharks and had the experience of a lifetime.

Shoes, dogs, a driver's licence – all these things have been found in the bellies of sharks. I admit it, this scares me. Many people share my fear. The horror movie 'Jaws', made in 1975, firmly established the shark's reputation as an **unpredictable**,
5 **aggressive** man-eater. However, the facts don't support this image. Only five to ten people a year die in shark attacks. The truth is, sharks are misunderstood; most sharks are harmless to people unless you provoke them.

   To find out more, I'm on my way to Geyser Rock, where I'll
10 soon be getting close to one of the biggest sharks of all. Geyser Rock is a small island off the southern tip of South Africa and it's home to an enormous colony of fur seals. Seals are the favourite food of the Great White shark, so it's one of the best places in the world to see this uncommon species.
15 Finding sharks is surprisingly difficult, so you need to go to places which they visit regularly. I'm sitting in an 8-metre catamaran, and behind me is a cage made of 3mm steel mesh. In half an hour I'll be inside the cage under the water, surrounded, I hope, by a crowd of Great Whites.

20   Many people are critical of cage-diving. They claim that some of the cages used for the dives are unsafe, and some guides are unqualified. Using bait to attract sharks also encourages them to associate humans with food, they say. Soon, someone will get seriously hurt. Just one fatal attack
25 on a diver could reinforce the belief that sharks are cold-blooded killers and this would undermine worldwide efforts to protect them from overfishing. But it seems to me there are strong arguments in favour of shark-diving. It can help to destroy some of the myths about sharks and change public
30 attitudes towards them. If every shark-diving trip is informative and educational, people who see sharks are more likely to support conservation efforts.

And now at last I'm at my destination and it's time for my dive. Feeling pretty nervous, I put on
35 a wetsuit, snorkel and mask and lower myself into the cage. My guide, Ken, warns me to hang on tight, then releases the rope. The cage sinks down into the sea, swinging violently from side to side from the force of the waves. At first I can
40 see nothing because of all the bubbles, and I begin to panic. But after a few moments the bubbles clear. I stare out into the murky water, trying to catch sight of a shark. To attract them, Ken has tied a piece of meat to the cage. But all I
45 can see are a few fish swimming lazily below me. I begin to relax.

Then suddenly the cage is jolted violently from behind. I struggle to turn around and find myself face to face with an enormous mouthful of
50 razor-sharp teeth. Less than a metre away from me is a huge Great White shark. Briefly, we make eye contact. I am paralysed with fear and my heart is beating fast. As I watch, the creature swallows the meat. Then it turns and swims off
55 with a graceful movement. It is probably after larger prey. The fact is, sharks are much too fussy about what they eat to take much interest in divers.

That experience has changed the way I see the
60 world. Since then, every time I sit on a train or walk into a room, I want to shout: 'I've had a close encounter with a Great White shark!' For me, it has destroyed the image of the shark as ferocious killer. Now I hope I can persuade others
65 to revise their attitudes to these amazing creatures.

4 Multiple-choice questions

▶▶ *multiple-choice questions* Unit 10, p.85

For questions 1–6, choose the answer A, B or C which you think fits best according to the text.

1 Many people are afraid of sharks because
 A sharks are known to be very aggressive.
 B the facts about sharks are not widely known.
 C shark attacks on people are common.
2 Why did the writer go to Geyser Rock?
 A to observe a particular type of shark
 B to study fur seals
 C to find out what sharks like to eat
3 What is the writer's view of cage-diving?
 A It could increase the risk of shark attacks on people.
 B It could make people even more afraid of sharks.
 C It could lead to greater understanding of sharks.
4 How did the writer feel when he went into the water?
 A worried
 B relaxed
 C terrified
5 Why did the shark swim away?
 A It was frightened.
 B It was looking for more food.
 C It didn't like the meat.
6 What was the writer's purpose in writing this article?
 A to change the reader's opinion about sharks
 B to share a holiday adventure with the reader
 C to warn the reader about the dangers of shark-diving

5 Vocabulary: *adjectives*

1 Find all the adjectives the writer uses to talk about sharks in the text.

unpredictable — **shark** — *aggressive*

2 Which words are:

a) positive in meaning? b) negative in meaning?

6 ⬤ Over to you

1 Have you changed your ideas about sharks after reading this article?
2 What conservation programmes do you know about in your country?

▶▶ **WB** p.73

Grammar: *structures after reporting verbs*
▶ *p.186*

grammar file 15

A Reporting verbs followed by *that* clause

1 'The rabbit has escaped!'
▶ We **realised that** the rabbit had escaped!

2 'You left the door open.'
▶ They **complained that** he had left the door open.

B Commands, requests, offers, advice
• verb (+ object) + *to*–infinitive

3 'I'll buy you a dog.'
▶ My father **offered to buy me** a dog.

4 'Don't touch the spider!'
▶ He **advised/asked/told/warned us not to touch** the spider.

C Verbs followed by more than one structure
• verb + *-ing* OR *that* (+ *should*)

5 'Let's go to the park.'
▶ They suggested **going/that we (should) go** to the park.

• verb + *to*–infinitive OR *that* clause

6 'I'll help.'
▶ I agreed/promised **to help/that I would help.**

• verb + *-ing* OR *that* clause

7 'I did it!'
▶ He admitted **doing/that he had done** it.

! What's wrong?

1 He advised Tom to not pick the spider up. ✗

2 My friend asked that I feed her cat. ✗

3 My sister suggested us to get a puppy. ✗

---

1 Reporting verbs

1 Read the statements below. Which speaker is:

a) threatening to do something?
b) refusing to do something?
c) giving a warning?
d) agreeing to do something?
e) making a suggestion?
f) denying something?
g) giving advice?

1 'Don't let the bird out of the cage, or it'll escape,' Mum said.
2 'I didn't let the rabbit out!' my brother said.
3 'No, I won't clean the hamster's cage,' Erica said.
4 'Take more care of your dog or I'll give it away,' said Mum.
5 'Your cat is too fat. Put it on a diet or it will get ill,' said the vet.
6 'Why don't we take the dog for a walk?' said my sister.
7 'OK, I'll look after your puppy while you're away,' said my friend.

2 Rewrite the statements in reported speech using an appropriate reporting verb. Sometimes there is more than one correct answer.
Example:

1 *Mum warned me not to let the bird out of the cage or it would escape.*

2 Sentence completion

Complete these sentences so they are true for you.

1 My friend has offered ....
2 After dinner, Mum always asks ....
3 My parents have promised ....
4 I would advise my friends not to ....
5 I have persuaded my parents ....

3 Transformations

Complete the second sentence so that it has a similar meaning to the first sentence, using the word given. Do not change the word given. Use between two and five words.

1 'Please feed the cat, John,' Mrs Smith said. **asked**
Mrs Smith .... the cat.

2 'No, I won't buy you a pet, Thomas,' Mum said. **refused**
Mum .... a pet.

3 'Why don't we take the boat out?' Mr Brown said. **taking**
Mr Brown .... out.

4 'I'll look after your pets during the holidays, shall I?' **to**
Our neighbour .... our pets during the holidays.

5 'Yes, I lost the keys!' **admitted**
Daniel .... the keys.

6 'I wouldn't touch the snake if I were you, Kate,' I said. **warned**
I .... the snake.

7 'Oh no, I forgot to put the cat out!' said my brother. **realised**
My brother .... to put the cat out.

8 'Please Harry, don't tell my parents what happened,' Sarah said. **begged**
Sarah .... her parents what had happened.

▶▶ **WB** p.74

Vocabulary building

1 Verbs + prepositions

1 Underline the preposition that follows the gap. Then fill in the gaps with a verb from the list.

suspect / object / blame / prevent / insist

1 Pet owners should be *prevented* from keeping dangerous animals in their homes.

2 If you .... anyone of dealing in endangered animals, you should report them to the police.

3 We should .... on people cleaning up the mess their pets make in the street.

4 I don't .... people for wanting to keep dogs but they're a nuisance if you live in a town.

5 I would strongly .... to my neighbours keeping poisonous snakes in their home.

2 ⟳ Do you agree or disagree with the statements above?

2 Open cloze

1 Read the text below.

1 How many different types of pet does it mention?

2 Would you keep any of these animals as pets?

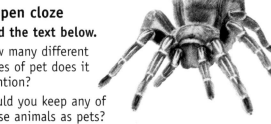

2 Read the text again and think of the word that best fits each space. Use only one word in each space. Most of the words you need are prepositions. There is an example at the beginning (0).

IS IT A PET?

Most people who are looking **(0)** ...*for*... a pet choose a domesticated animal, such **(1)** .... a dog, a cat or a rabbit. But these types **(2)** .... animal do not appeal to everybody. Some people prefer animals that are much **(3)** .... exotic! Animal-lover Roy Smith keeps a tarantula **(4)** .... the corner of his living room. Tarantulas are poisonous spiders, but that doesn't stop Roy **(5)** .... picking his spider up and stroking it. In fact, he lets **(6)** .... crawl all over him!

Another of our readers, Mary Boxer, has an amazing collection of snakes, including a six-foot boa constrictor. Last year **(7)** .... snake got out **(8)** .... its cage and hid in her neighbours' flat. They were terrified when they spotted it and still haven't forgiven her **(9)** .... allowing it to escape!

Jacky Merton is crazy **(10)** .... bats. Bats are wild animals, of course, and should not be kept **(11)** .... captivity. But Jacky's bats are all injured. She takes care **(12)** .... them for a few weeks, then releases them into the wild as soon as they recover.

3 Word formation: *nouns from adjectives and verbs*

1 Make nouns from these adjectives and verbs, using the endings below. Be careful of spelling changes.

1 cruel	4 patient	7 aggressive
2 conserve	5 possible	8 fit
3 please	6 entertain	9 behave

-(at)ion -ce -iour -(i)ty -ment -ness -ure

2 Which nouns form the negative by adding *dis-/im-/mis-*?

3 Sometimes you need to make a change inside the word. Can you make nouns from these words? Use your dictionary to help.

Adjectives

1 proud 2 strong 3 young 4 true

Verbs

5 choose 6 believe 7 prove 8 live

4 Word-formation task

Read the text below. Use the word in CAPITALS underneath to form a word that fits in the space. Decide if you need a noun or an adjective. Be careful! One space needs a negative form. There is an example at the beginning (0).

GUIDE DOGS FOR THE BLIND

There has been a great **(0)** ·*improvement*· in the lives of blind people since the first guide dogs were trained. Guide dogs give blind people **(1)** .... because they act as their owner's 'eyes'. Not every dog has the right temperament for this work, so trainers have to be careful in their **(2)** .... The dogs need to be extremely **(3)** .... They must enjoy their work, too, because a dog only works well if he is enjoying **(4)** .... When they start training, the dogs are young so their trainers need to show **(5)** .... towards them. If the dog misbehaves, trainers need to show their **(6)** .... with a sharp word or signal. However, with a little **(7)** .... , the dogs soon learn. Guide dogs show tremendous **(8)** .... and owners rarely need to reprimand them.

0 IMPROVE	**3** INTELLIGENCE	**6** PLEASE
1 CONFIDENT	**4** LIVE	**7** ENCOURAGE
2 CHOOSE	**5** FIRM	**8** LOYAL

▶▶ WB p.75

Listening ▸ *Part 4*

1 ⬭ Before you listen

You are going to hear an interview with a famous wildlife photographer. Look at the photos.

1 What animal can you see?
2 How aggressive do you think it is?
3 What equipment is the photographer using?
4 What dangers does he face?
5 Why do you think he does this kind of work?

2 Listening strategy

▸▸ *focusing on the information you need*

When answering multiple-choice questions:

- concentrate on the question (your purpose for listening) the first time you listen, and ignore information you don't need.
- the second time you listen, choose the answer that expresses the same meaning as the recording.

1 Read the interviewer's questions below. Underline the key words in each question.

1 What kind of information do you need to listen for in each case?
  a) a fact   c) a reason
  b) an opinion   d) a feeling
2 Can you predict any of the answers?

1 How do you feel when you get really close to wild animals?
2 What do you do if elephants become aggressive?
3 You got very close to lions on one occasion. Why didn't they attack you?
4 What do you think of sprays that hide the human scent?
5 What are the disadvantages of watching animals from a high platform?
6 Why did you once go into a lake full of crocodiles?

2 ▭ Listen to the recording once. Note down brief answers to the questions above.

3 ▭ Multiple-choice task

1 Now look at the multiple-choice answers below. Which option A, B or C is the closest to your answers in Exercise 2?

Listening task

1 When he's close to wild animals, he feels
  A nervous.
  B confident.
  C proud.   ☐ 1

2 If elephants become aggressive,
  A he leaves the area.
  B he throws things at them.
  C he stands still and waits.   ☐ 2

3 The lions didn't attack him on one occasion because
  A they couldn't see him properly.
  B they had smelt other animals.
  C they were in search of water.   ☐ 3

4 He thinks *Up Close* is
  A useless.
  B expensive.
  C dangerous.   ☐ 4

5 Watching animals from a high platform is
  A uncomfortable.
  B time-consuming.
  C risky.   ☐ 5

6 He went into a lake full of crocodiles because
  A he wanted to take a shot of a crocodile.
  B he was unaware that there were crocodiles.   ☐ 6
  C he was interested in the habits of crocodiles.

2 Listen again and check your answers.

4 Over to you

The following jobs all involve working with animals:
zoo-keeper / vet / lion-tamer / jockey / shepherd / farmer
Which do you think is
a) the most interesting? c) the most rewarding?
b) the most dangerous?   d) the most tiring?

Writing: *article* ▶ *Part 2*

1 Sample writing task

Read the task and <u>underline</u> the key points.

Writing task

You have seen this notice in a student magazine.

> *CALLING ALL ANIMAL LOVERS*
>
> **Do you like animals?**
>
> We invite readers to write and tell us which animal you think makes the best pet.
>
> *We will publish the three most interesting articles.*

Write your article in 120–180 words.

2 💬 Brainstorm ideas

1 What animals do people keep as pets in your country? Tick the list below.

1 dog   4 parrot   7 lizard
2 cat   5 hamster   8 others?
3 rabbit   6 snake

2 Think of reasons why each animal might make a good pet.
Example:

Animal	*Why it makes a good pet*
cat	– *easy to look after*
	– *no need to take it for walks*
	– *affectionate*
	– *independent*

3 Which animal do you think makes the best pet? Have you got one in your home? Why/Why not?

3 Read a sample article

Read the article. The topic sentences are missing from the article. Ignore them for now.

1 Does the writer mention any of your ideas?

2 What reasons does the writer give for his/her choice?

Who could resist a dog?

Are you thinking of getting a pet? Maybe you're wondering what kind of animal would be best for you? Well, there's only one pet worth keeping, in my opinion – and that's a dog. Why? I'll tell you.

(1) .... It can easily be trained to guard the house. This means that you can go out at night and feel secure. Burglars won't go near a house if they hear a dog barking.

(2) .... Many people love having a dog for company. Dogs are so intelligent that they seem to understand their owners. Because of this, lots of people treat their dogs like members of the family.

(3) .... Let me add one more reason just to prove my point. You'll need to go to the park to exercise your dog. While you're there, you'll meet other dog owners and make lots of new friends. Get a dog and your life could change in ways you've never dreamt of!

4 Topic sentences

In an article, topic sentences need to be vivid and personal to make the reader interested. Look at the topic sentences below. Choose the best one for paragraphs 2–4 of the sample article in Exercise 3.

Paragraph 2

a) Just imagine how much safer you would feel with a dog.

b) A dog makes people feel safer.

Paragraph 3

a) Dogs are friendly.

b) What about the friendship a dog can offer you?

Paragraph 4

a) Have I convinced you that a dog makes an ideal pet?

b) A dog makes an ideal pet.

5 Style

Look at the sample article again. Which of the following are true and which are false?

When you write an article:

1 your style should be formal and impersonal.

2 you can use questions to involve the reader.

3 you can address the reader directly.

6 Writing skills: *linkers of reason/result/ contrast*

Link the sentences below by using an appropriate introductory expression from the box.

This means (that)   In spite of this,
This is why   This is because

1 Dogs are full of energy. They need lots of exercise.
   Dogs are full of energy. This means they need lots of exercise.
2 It's not difficult to train most dogs. They always respond to firmness and encouragement.
3 Owning a dog is a big responsibility. I have never regretted getting one.
4 Most dogs make good pets. They are loyal and obedient and love company.
5 Dogs are not as independent as cats. Dogs make better pets.
6 Dogs can hear things that humans can't hear. They can guard your home.

Over to you

7 Writing strategy
Complete the notes.

▶▶ *writing an article*

When you write an article giving your views on a topic, you should:

• check who you are writing the article for and use the correct ....
• support your views by giving .... of what you mean.
• divide your article into .... and make sure each of these has a topic ....
• make some of your topic sentences more .... by using questions (real or rhetorical).

8 Writing task
Read the task and <u>underline</u> a) where your article will be published b) the main topic of the article.

> **Writing task**
>
> **You have seen this advertisement in your school magazine.**
>
> **Write your article in 120–180 words.**

> **CALLING ALL WRITERS**
> Could you write an article for our school magazine?
> Write an article, giving us your views on the topic below and we will publish it next week.
> *Which two wild animals do you think need most protection in the world? Why?*

9 Brainstorm ideas
1 Name some of the wild animals that you know are endangered around the world.
2 Which two species should we try to protect most?
3 What do you know about these animals?
4 Why are they in danger?
5 How do you think we should protect them?

10 Plan your article
Choose the most important issues you have just discussed and make a paragraph plan using the ideas below.

Para. 1 (Introduction)
Many animals are in danger. Which should we help first?
Para. 2
Topic: The first animal I would choose
Topic sentence: ....
Reason(s) why it needs protecting: ....
Para. 3
Topic: The second animal I would choose
Topic sentence: ....
Reason(s) why it needs protecting: ....
Para. 4 (Conclusion)
Brief summary and request to readers to get involved.

11 Write
Now write your article. Follow the ▶▶ *Writing strategy*.

12 Check your work
Are the grammar, punctuation and spelling correct?

 WB p.77

15 Fashion

Speaking ▶ Part 2

1 About you

1 How important are clothes to you?

2 What influences your choice? Think about price, fashion, comfort, friends, family, etc.

2 Vocabulary

Look at the photos. Who is wearing the following?

casual clothes
a smart suit
a long-sleeved sweatshirt
a knee-length skirt
baggy trousers
sports clothing   evening dress
a headscarf   trainers

3 💬 Discussion

1 What are the people saying about themselves through their choice of clothes? Match these statements to the photos.

a) 'I'm informal but smart.'

b) 'I don't care what other people think.'

c) 'I like to spend a lot of money on clothes.'

d) 'I like to be comfortable.'

e) 'I want to shock people.'

f) 'I pride myself on my appearance.'

g) 'I like to keep up with the latest fashions'.

2 Which statement would best describe you?

⑥

4 📼 Listen

1 Listen to a student talking about two of the photos.

1 Which photos did he compare and contrast?

2 Which clothes would he <u>least</u> like to wear?

2 Listen again and tick the phrases he uses to express his opinions about clothes. Which are negative? positive? neutral?

expressing opinions
I hate .../can't stand ...   I don't mind ...
I would never wear anything like that.
I couldn't possibly ...
I wouldn't be seen dead in ...
I'd definitely wear ...
I'm very choosy about what I wear/buy.

3 What's <u>your</u> opinion about the people in the photos he describes?

5 💬 Speaking task: *photos*

Choose two photographs.

Student A: Compare and contrast the clothes and say which you would least like to wear.

Student B: Compare and contrast the clothes and say which ones you think are most comfortable.

6 💬 Discussion

1 Do you think it matters what people wear a) in their free time? b) for important occasions like weddings, job interviews? Why?

2 Is there too much pressure on young people to wear name brands?

▶▶ **WB** p.78

Reading ▸ Part 3

1 Predict

1 Look at the title and sub-heading of the article opposite. What do these colours mean to you?

2 Now scan the text to find these colours. What does the article tell you about them?

2 Read the text

Read the text once all the way through and discuss these questions.

Section:

0 When did colour become important?

1 How did cosmetics first develop?

2 What do you think a *transfer* is (line 28)?

3 Why should we be careful about the colours we wear?

4 Why do you think white is the *colour of sorrow* in traditional Asian cultures?

5 What advice does the writer give about choosing colours?

6 Do you agree with the ideas in the last paragraph of the article?

3 Reading strategy

▸▸ *predicting what comes next*

As you read, use grammatical and lexical links to help you predict what is coming next. This will help you read faster and with greater understanding.

1 Seven sentences have been removed from the text. Read the sentence before and after each gap carefully and decide what kind of information is missing. Choose the correct option a) or b) below. Key words in the text have been underlined to help you.

Question:

0 a) example	b) explanation ✓
1 a) example	b) contrasting idea
2 a) contrasting idea	b) result
3 a) explanation	b) example
4 a) contrasting idea	b) example
5 a) example	b) result
6 a) contrasting idea	b) explanation

The Power of COLOUR

Today, fashion dictates not only the clothes we wear, but the colours, too. Did you know that colours have had important meanings since ancient times?

If you take a stroll around the fashion department of any high street store today, you'll be dazzled by the variety of <u>colours</u>, patterns and textures available. <u>However, there is nothing all that new in</u>
5 <u>this.</u> **0** **H** For the Ancient Egyptians, the Celts in Britain, the Aztecs in South America, <u>colour</u> was an important part of life.

In many ancient civilisations, people painted coloured circles and lines around their eyes and
10 mouths. Originally they did this to please the gods and scare away evil spirits. But they soon realised that colour could be used to make their faces and bodies beautiful – and cosmetics were born. They were first used <u>to distinguish between</u> different
15 tribes, and also <u>between males and females.</u> <u>Women</u> used colour and pattern to emphasise their body shape. **1** By contrast, men tended to use designs that emphasised their strength and skill.

Body painting is one of the most ancient arts of
20 humankind and today it is coming back into fashion. <u>Until recently, only men</u> used tattoos on their bodies. **2**
Girls who prefer not to have tattoos paint
25 patterns on their hands and faces with henna, or use removable transfers to decorate their
30 arms and legs. Like their ancient ancestors, they are pursuing an ideal of beauty.

35 Eventually, the colours of our clothes became just as important as those used for painting the body. Clothes are a symbol of power. The power in the clothes affects both the person who wears them and the people around him or her. So it's important to <u>choose the colours you wear carefully.</u> [3] [ ] <u>But if</u> you wear <u>it</u> too long, you
40 can start to feel impatient or aggressive. The colour green, on the other hand, is known to calm the nerves and soothe emotions.

The mysterious Aztec and Maya civilisations were not familiar with wool, linen or silk, some of our most
45 popular modern fabrics. But they dyed their textiles with great artistry. For them, every colour had a meaning, either positive or negative. For example, <u>yellow</u> was the symbol of the sun and
50 of ripe corn growing in the fields, and <u>blue</u> meant the wearer had royal ancestors. <u>Red</u> stood for blood. [4] [ ]
In ancient Egypt, <u>gold</u> was the colour of the Sun god and the symbol of power.
55 In traditional Asian cultures, <u>white</u> is the colour of sorrow. The blue of the sky, the red of the sun and the paleness of the moon were associated with religious rituals, legends and poetry.

60 With the passing of time, fashion has become increasingly international.
Today, the same fabrics, colours and designs are available all over the world. Fashion dictates not only the clothes we wear, but the colours, too. <u>Every colour under the sun</u> is available in today's style
65 parade. [5] [ ] The best thing is to go for the colours that suit you best. Choose a colour that doesn't make your complexion look too pale, one that doesn't clash with your hair colour, one that reflects your personality. And remember that colours can influence the way you feel. Wear colours that make you feel confident and relaxed.

70 Just as in ancient times, the right clothes give you power, make you look good, and help to identify you as part of your group.
Today, however, <u>you don't have to be wealthy</u> to look stylish. [6] [ ]

2 Now read the sentences A– H in the box below and choose the sentence which fits each gap. Underline the words in each sentence that help you decide. There is one extra sentence which you do not need to use. There is an example at the beginning (0).

A This is because the high street has put style within reach of all of us.

B Pink, lilac, strawberry-red, pea-green, bright orange – which one should you choose?

C Now, however, they can be seen on many women and girls, too.

D For example, ancient Celtic women painted their bodies blue.

E Did you know, for example, that wearing a red sweater or jacket can increase your energy levels?

F Black symbolised war and death.

G We feel we have to buy them because the shops are full of them.

H <u>The truth</u> is that ancient peoples already recognised the magical power of <u>colour</u>.

4 **Vocabulary:** *word sets*
1 Find three different types of fabric or textile in the article. Can you think of any more types of fabric?

2 What fabrics are you wearing now? Do you have a favourite fabric?

5 ⬭ **Over to you**
Note down your three favourite colours.

Then turn to p.178 to see how your colour choices match your personality. Do you agree with the colour experts?

Grammar: *impersonal statements, the causative*
▶ *pp.186–187*

grammar file 16

These reporting verbs are often followed by an impersonal structure: *say, believe, claim, consider, know, think.*

People know that the Incas made amazing gold jewellery.

▶ **It is known that** the Incas **made** amazing gold jewellery.

▶ The Incas **are known to have made** amazing gold jewellery. (in the past)

┌─ **! What's wrong?** ─────
1 *The colour green is thought that it is a restful colour.* X
2 *It is said that Cleopatra she bathed in milk.* X

1 Impersonal statements

Rewrite these sentences in the impersonal form.

1 Many people believe that colours influence the way we feel.
It is believed that *colours influence the way we feel* .

2 Experts say the Egyptian Pharaohs wore clothes made of gold.
The Egyptian Pharaohs are said to
....

3 People used to think that painting your face scared away bad spirits.
It ....

4 They say that rock star Elton John spent a million pounds on clothes in one year.
Elton John ....

5 We know that the American Indians painted their bodies before battle.
The American Indians ....

6 Today, people consider that denim jeans are a bit old-fashioned.
Today, denim jeans ....

grammar file 17

• *have/get* + object + past participle
1 *'Do you cut your hair yourself?'*
  *'No, I **have it cut** (by the hairdresser).'*
2 *'Did you shorten those trousers yourself?'*
  *'No, I **had/got them shortened** (by a professional tailor).'*

┌─ **! What's wrong?** ─────
1 *He's going to the optician's to test his eyes.* X
2 *I'm planning to get cut my hair.* X

2 have/get something done

Complete the questions using *have* or *get* and a verb from the list. Ask and answer the questions with a partner.

pierce / tattoo / cut / paint / dye / take out

1 How often do you .... your hair ....?
2 Would you like to .... any part of your body ....?
3 Would you ever .... your tongue ....?
4 Have you ever .... a tooth ....?
5 What colour would you like to .... your bedroom ....?
6 What would your parents say if you .... your hair .... purple?

3 Error correction

1 Read the title of the text below. What does *colour therapy* mean? Read the text to find out.

2 Look carefully at each line 1–12. Four lines are correct. Tick them. The other lines each have a word which should not be there. <u>Underline</u> it. There are two examples at the beginning (0 and 00).

COLOUR THERAPY

0 Colour therapy has a very long history. It is believed that the ✓
00 Ancient Egyptians <u>they</u> were the first people to think that colour
1 was important. They have looked at nature and copied its
2 colours in many areas of their lives. Their leaders had done the
3 floors of their temples painted green, to resemble the grass that
4 grew along the River Nile. The colour blue is thought to be have
5 been important to them as well. The Ancient Romans used colour to
6 show how important they were. Their rulers had their clothes be
7 made from purple cloth. Purple dye was expensive, so this showed
8 they were being rich and powerful. Nowadays, colour is extremely
9 important to us, too. In the shops, experts tell us which colours we
10 should wear if we want to feel good. It is being believed that the
11 colours around us they can influence our lives. Because of this,
12 many companies are having their offices be painted in colours that
will make their employees work better.

▶▶ **WB** p.80

Vocabulary building

1 Adjective order

1 Look at the table, which shows the normal word order for descriptive adjectives.

1	2	3	4	5	6
opinion	size/shape/participles	colour	pattern	origin	material
crazy pretty	tiny tight/loose long-sleeved	dark- blue	striped checked	Italian French	velvet denim

2 Now rewrite these sentences putting the adjectives into the correct order.

1 At the weekends I usually put on my trousers. (blue/favourite/cotton)

2 The model is wearing a jacket. (leather/red/gorgeous)

3 All the members of the band wore trousers. (velvet/tight/black)

4 The bride wore a wedding dress. (silk/long/white)

5 The woman was wearing a shawl. (woollen/lovely/green)

6 My friend was wearing a skirt. (ankle-length/fashionable/linen)

2 Over to you

Describe:

a) the clothes you are wearing today.

I'm wearing a plain cotton top and black denim trousers.

b) the most embarrassing outfit you have ever worn.

c) the worst outfit you have ever seen a pop star wear.

3 Choosing the right word

Complete each sentence with one of the words in its correct form.

1 wear/carry/put on/get dressed

a) I'm nearly ready – I've just got to .... my coat.

b) My grandparents always .... walking sticks when they go out.

c) Are you going to .... jeans to the party?

d) I always wash before I .... in the morning.

2 fit/suit/match/go

e) Your shirt doesn't .... your jacket. It's the wrong colour.

f) I've lost weight so my trousers don't .... me any more.

g) I'm looking for a sweater to .... with these blue trousers.

h) What do you think – does this dress .... me or does it look awful?

4 Lexical cloze

1 Read the text below. What did pop star Elton John sell? Why?

2 Read the text again and decide which answer A, B, C or D best fits each space. There is an example at the beginning (0).

0 **A** did **B** made **C** won **D** had

SALE OF THE CENTURY

Pop star Elton John (0) ..*B*. thousands of dollars recently by selling a collection of his clothes and stage **(1)** .... . The outfits on **(2)** .... included some amazing wigs and some of the brightly-coloured jackets and shirts he **(3)** .... for his live concerts. Elton is not as slim as he was when he first started singing, **(4)** .... some of the clothes he bought then don't **(5)** .... him any more. He had bought so many clothes **(6)** .... the years that there can't have been any room left in his **(7)** .... ! But that was not why he **(8)** .... the sale. His real motive was to **(9)** .... money for his favourite charities.

As a singer, Elton has **(10)** .... wanted to entertain people. His clothes are meant to surprise and even shock his audience. He doesn't care if the colours don't **(11)** .... or whether he's dressed in the **(12)** .... style. As one of the 'old men' of rock, his clothes are now part of rock history. And that is why fans of all ages were so **(13)** .... to buy the items in the recent sale.

1	**A** costumes	**B** robes	**C** customs	**D** dresses
2	**A** sold	**B** sale	**C** rent	**D** hire
3	**A** dressed	**B** carried	**C** put	**D** wore
4	**A** as	**B** however	**C** so	**D** but
5	**A** match	**B** suit	**C** fit	**D** go
6	**A** along	**B** over	**C** since	**D** through
7	**A** wardrobe	**B** cabinet	**C** shelf	**D** suitcase
8	**A** offered	**B** put	**C** sold	**D** held
9	**A** rise	**B** raise	**C** take	**D** lift
10	**A** ever	**B** always	**C** even	**D** every time
11	**A** agree	**B** suit	**C** clash	**D** match
12	**A** latest	**B** last	**C** recent	**D** late
13	**A** optimistic	**B** interested	**C** keen	**D** hopeful

▶▶ WB p.81

Listening ▶ *Part 2*

1 Before you listen

1 Read the instructions for the Listening task. What are you going to hear?

2 Look at the list of factors below. Which three do you think are the most important for a successful model? Why?

- being beautiful
- being tall
- being thin
- being sociable
- being young
- being able to work long hours
- being able to travel away from home

2 Predict

▶▶ *predicting the information you need* Unit 8 p.70

Look at the listening task and read the sentences. Decide what kind of information you need to fill in the gaps. Ask yourself questions like these.

Question:

1 Why was Clara not successful? What qualities do models need?

2 What kind of contract does Clara offer? For a certain time?

3 What quality is most important in a model?

4 What does Clara need models for? What different types of modelling are there?

Now you continue.

3 🖭 Listening task

1 Listen to the recording once and complete the sentences using no more than three words. Remember to listen for meaning.

Listening task

You are going to hear an interview with a former model, who now finds new models for the fashion industry. For questions 1–10, complete the sentences.

Clara <u>was not successful</u> as a model because she was [1   ] for the job.

<u>If a possible new model does well in an interview</u>, Clara offers them a [2   ] contract.

<u>The most important quality</u> Clara looks for in new models is the right [3   ]

People often <u>lose interest</u> when they hear that Clara only needs models for [4   ]

Clara often has to tell new models to <u>change</u> their [5   ]

The <u>worst problem</u> for a model is lack of [6   ]

Clara <u>compares</u> new model Susan Bell to a nineteenth-century [7   ]

Susan Bell <u>is not doing a lot of modelling</u> now because she is [8   ]

Vernon, a well-known male model, <u>used to have a job as a</u> [9   ]

Clara's <u>ideal method of keeping up to date</u> with fashion is to look at [10   ]

2 ▶▶ *listening for parallel ideas* Unit 9 p.80

How did Clara express the <u>underlined</u> words in Questions 1–10 on the recording? Match them to these extracts. The first one has been done for you.

a) I wasn't very good at it. *1*

b) the most difficult thing is that

c) last year he was working as a

d) to do something different with

e) my favourite way to keep up to date

f) become less enthusiastic

g) if the interview goes well

h) she looks a bit like

i) something that's essential

j) isn't working much

3 Now listen again and check your answers.

4 Over to you

Here are some ideas many people have about models. Do you agree or disagree with them? Why?

'*Models are too thin and make young people feel bad about their figures.*'

'*Models aren't very intelligent.*'

'*If you're a model, your career will be over by the time you're 25.*'

Writing: *composition* ▶ *Part 2*

1 Sample writing task

1 Read the task.

1 What is the topic?

2 Who is going to read your composition? What style should you use?

3 Do you have to a) write in favour of the statement b) write against the statement c) consider arguments for <u>and</u> against?

Writing task

You have had a class discussion on fashion and clothes. Now your English teacher would like you to write a composition, discussing both sides of this statement:

Young people should be allowed to wear what they like.

Write your composition in 120–180 words.

2 ◯ What's your opinion?

1 Should young people be allowed to wear what they like?

2 Can you think of any situations when this would not be a good thing?

2 Read a sample composition

1 Read the composition. The paragraphs are mixed up. Number them in the correct order 1–4.

2 <u>Underline</u> the phrases that helped you to decide. Can you think of any alternatives to these phrases?

3 Paragraph organisation

1 Read the sample composition again. Which paragraph:

a) gives the arguments against the statement in the task? .....

b) states the writer's opinion; suggests a solution/ a way forward? .....

c) gives the arguments in favour of the statement? .....

d) introduces the topic and shows there are two sides to the question? .....

2 Answer these questions.

1 Does the writer use a topic sentence for each paragraph?

2 How many arguments does the writer make in favour of allowing people to wear what they like? How many arguments against?

3 What reasons or examples does he give to justify each of his arguments?

3 Match sentences from the sample composition with the plan on the right.

☐ However, there is another side to the question. To start with, clothes such as designer jeans are very expensive. Parents can't buy clothes like this all the time. Also, fashions can be silly or even dangerous. Having a stud put in your tongue, for example, could cause an infection and make you really ill.

☐ Many young people argue that they should wear what they like but adults disagree. So who is right? Let us think about both sides of the question.

☐ In conclusion, I would say that young people should be able to choose what they wear most of the time, but not always. I think adults and young people have to discuss the situation in a reasonable way, and compromise when there are problems.

☐ On the one hand, I think that teenagers should have a say in what they wear. Fashion is important to young people and peer pressure is strong. If young people are made to wear old-fashioned, boring clothes they will feel 'different' and get depressed.

Para. 1 (Introduction)
State that there are two sides to the argument.
Para. 2
Topic sentence: ....
Argument(s) for: ....
Reasons/examples: ....
Para. 3
Topic sentence: ....
Argument(s) against: ....
Reasons/examples: ....
Final para. (Conclusion)
Restatement of my opinion plus comment/ reason/further comment.

4 ◯ Discussion

Do you agree with the writer's opinions? Why/Why not?

Over to you

5 Writing strategy
Complete the notes.

▶▶ *writing a balanced composition*

When you write a composition showing both sides of a question:

- set out the problem in the .... and show that there are .... on both sides.
- separate the arguments for and .... the question into different ....
- make sure you give .... to justify your arguments.
- summarise your arguments and suggest a compromise or a solution in the ....

6 Writing task
Read the task.

1 What topic do you have to write about?

2 Do you have to a) argue for <u>or</u> against the topic
b) consider both sides of the question?

> **Writing task**
>
> **After a class discussion about clothes and fashions, your English teacher has asked you to write a composition, giving arguments for and against this statement:**
>
> *We can't judge people from the clothes they wear.*
>
> **Write your composition in 120–180 words.**

7 💬 Brainstorm ideas
1 Discuss these questions with a partner.

1 Think of your friends/members of your family. What kind of clothes do they wear? Do they wear different clothes for different occasions?

2 Do you think their clothes show their personalities or are they different underneath? Give examples.

3 Have you ever judged someone because of their clothes, then changed your mind later? Explain how it happened.

4 How long does it take to really get to know someone?

2 Note down some reasons:

a) why we sometimes judge people from their clothes.

b) why it is not always a good idea to do this.

> <u>*Why we sometimes judge people from their clothes*</u>
> *– clothes = first thing we notice about a person*
> ....
> ....
> <u>*Dangers of judging people from their clothes.*</u>
> *– people can't always afford clothes they want*
> ....

8 Plan your composition
Make a plan like the one on p.131. Choose the best ideas from your notes for Exercise 7.2.

9 Writing skills: *introductions and conclusions*
1 Look at the introductions below. Which one is not suitable? Why not?

A
> I don't agree with this statement.

B
> Some people always judge others from the way they dress. Should they do this? I think there are two sides to the question.

2 Look at these conclusions. Which one:

1 does not round off the composition well? .....

2 is not the right length? .....

3 summarises the writer's opinion clearly? .....

C
> In conclusion, I believe that we have to be careful about judging people from their clothes. Clothes can tell us quite a lot, but we should not rely on clothes alone when we judge a person's character.

D
> To sum up, I think there are arguments for and against this statement.

3 Now, think of your own introduction and conclusion. Note them down.

10 Write
Write your composition using your plan in Exercise 8. Follow the ▶▶ *Writing strategy*.

11 Check your work
Are the grammar, spelling and punctuation correct?

▶▶ **WB** p.82

16 Our environment

Speaking ▶ Parts 3 and 4

1 How much do you know?
Look at the photo and read the caption. What's the link between the polar bear, climate change and saving energy?

2 Quiz
Do the quiz in pairs.

> Are you doing your bit to help the planet? Try our fun quiz and find out if you're a Super Saver or an Energy Waster. Tick any of the following statements that you agree with.

- I walk, cycle or use public transport whenever possible.
- If I remember, I turn off the TV, lights and heaters when I'm not using them.
- I take old newspapers, bottles and cans to the recycling centre regularly.
- I love fast food so I get my parents to buy pizzas and hamburgers instead of locally-grown food.
- I encourage my parents to buy energy-efficient products.
- I sometimes put on an extra sweater if I'm feeling cold, but it's easier to turn the heating up.
- I get my parents to drive me to school and the shops whenever possible.
- I prefer reading a book to playing computer games or watching TV.
- I like to leave all the lights on in the house – it looks much cosier.
- I sometimes buy energy-efficient batteries for my Discman and computer games.
- I throw empty drink cans in the bin.
- I always have a shower, not a bath, to save water.

▶▶ Check your scores on p.178.

CUT POLLUTION! SAVE ENERGY!

3 🔊 Listen
1 Your local Environment Action group plans to publish a leaflet to inform young people about ways to save energy. Listen to two members of the group discussing what to include in the leaflet. What do they decide is most important?

2 Here are some of the expressions they use as they go through their list of ideas. Listen again and number the expressions in order as you hear them.

discussing options/making decisions
- ☐ I think maybe ... is a better idea.
- ☐ Let's see, what choices have we got?
- ☐ We must put ... in the leaflet.
- ☐ So we need one more thing.
- ☐ OK, so we've decided ...
- ☐ We should definitely include ...

4 💬 Speaking task: *decision making*
Talk to each other and decide what <u>you</u> would include in the leaflet. Use ideas in the Quiz. Then compare your ideas with the class.

5 💬 Discussion
Are there any special facilities or activities in your town to make it more environmentally friendly?

▶▶ WB p.83

Reading ▸ *Part 4*

1 Think about the topic

Read the title and sub-heading of the article, and look at the photo.

1 What traffic problems are there where you live, or in the nearest city?

2 How do they affect your daily life?

3 Has anything been done to solve the problems? If so, what?

4 What ways can you think of to reduce the number of cars in cities?

2 Skim and scan

1 Read the headings A–E.

1 Which five cities did the writer visit?

2 What do you know about any of these cities?

2 Skim and scan the texts quickly.

1 Are any of your ideas for solving traffic problems mentioned?

2 What others are mentioned?

Answer the questions by choosing from the cities A–E. The cities may be chosen more than once. When more than one answer is required, these may be given in any order. There is an example at the beginning (0).

Which city do the following statements refer to?

It is the only city in the country to have such a system.   **0** **B**

The majority of people travel by bike.   **1** ☐

There is a special bus service to the centre that costs nothing.   **2** ☐

People can only use their cars on certain days.   **3** ☐

You pay the same for your ticket wherever you travel in the city.   **4** ☐

Only people who live in the city centre can drive there.   **5** ☐

Drivers leave their cars outside the city centre.   **6** ☐ **7** ☐

A new transport system is under construction.   **8** ☐

Shoppers don't need to carry their purchases around with them.   **9** ☐

You can buy stamps or make a phone call at a bus stop.   **10** ☐

Cyclists have special roads just for them.   **11** ☐ **12** ☐

---

3 Multiple-matching task

Read the task. For each statement 1–12:

• underline the key words that tell you what information to look for. *What are the key words in the example (0)?*

• predict which section will most probably have the information you need. (Two questions have two answers, so you will need to look in more than one text.)

• scan the section you have chosen to find the information you need. Look for parallel expressions.

   Find the expression in text B that matches the key words in the example.

• when you think you have found the answer, read carefully to check it's correct.

4 Vocabulary: *compound adjectives*

1 Make adjectives using the underlined words below, as in the example. Then check your answers in the text.

1 A system that is easy for people to understand

   an easy-to-understand system

2 A street that is only for pedestrians.

3 A street that is only for bicycles.

4 A street that goes two ways.

5 A town centre that is free of traffic.

2 Can you write adjectives for the following?

1 A street where cars go one way only.

2 A stereo system that is easy to use.

3 A drink that is free of sugar.

5 💬 Over to you

Read this statement. Think of arguments for and against. What's your opinion?

'All cars should be banned from our cities.'

▶▶ **WB** p.83

A tale of five cities

There are millions of cars on the road today. How do cities cope with this?
We visited five cities that have found solutions to their traffic problems.

A ▸ CURITIBA, BRAZIL

Curitiba has very few traffic jams, even though it has more cars per person than any other Brazilian city except Brasilia. This
5 is because the authorities have developed an efficient bus network to transport people rapidly around the city. Main roads have special lanes for
10 buses only, so that they do not get caught in traffic jams. Services are regular and frequent, and it is quick and easy to switch from one bus
15 route to another. Every two kilometres there are bus terminals, equipped with newspaper stands, public telephones, post offices and
20 shops. There is a fixed fare for all the journeys within the city. It is a simple, easy-to-understand system, and it works. Nearly 75 per cent of commuters in
25 Curitiba travel by bus.

B ▸ MILAN, ITALY

In Milan, cars need a permit to enter the city centre. Only residents and some employers can obtain a permit, so very
30 little traffic now drives in or out. Nearly everyone parks on the edge of the restricted area and heads for the centre on foot. As a result, Milan now has
35 many pedestrian-only shopping streets, and this has led to an increase in shopping in the city centre. Grass and trees have been planted, and many other
40 improvements have also been made. The permit scheme is now recognised as a great success. The <u>scheme is unique to Milan</u>, but it is thought that
45 similar car bans and pedestrian schemes will have spread to other Italian cities by the end of the decade.

C ▸ DELFT, HOLLAND

The town of Delft in Holland has solved its traffic problems
75 by encouraging people to cycle. In 1980, separate bike lanes were created on all major routes, as well as 12 kilometres of bike-only two-way streets,
80 two special tunnels, and three new bridges for cyclists. Government rules require all shops to provide parking spaces for bicycles. Offices have to
85 provide one secure bicycle space for every three employees, and each house must have a bicycle garage. In the first three years of operation, the average
90 number of kilometres driven by car owners in Delft dropped by 6 per cent. In the rest of the country that number rose on average by 15 per cent. More
95 than 50 per cent of all trips in Delft are now made by bicycle.

D ▸ ATHENS, GREECE

In Athens, car owners are only
50 allowed to drive into the city centre every other day. They must match the final number of their car number plate to the day's date – if the date is an
55 even number, and so is the final number of the number plate, then they can enter the inner-city area. The same goes for odd number plates and odd dates.
60 This means that 50 per cent of all cars must stay at home each day. Pollution is measured every day, and when the levels of pollution get too high, all cars
65 are banned from entering the city centre. However, as the new underground railway is completed and extended, it is hoped that soon more
70 commuters will be travelling by Metro. If so, it may be possible to lift the present traffic restrictions.

E ▸ LÜNEBURG, GERMANY

Traffic jams and growing pollution in this historic German city forced the local council to
100 take action in 1990. To encourage people to leave their cars at home, regular fast public transport was introduced, and bicycle paths and wider
105 pavements were built. The town centre became traffic-free, apart from cars for the disabled. A 'park-and-ride' system offers a free car park on the outskirts
110 of the town, and a free bus service into the centre. There is also a place to leave shopping in the town centre, so people can walk around without their
115 bags, and pick them up when they leave. This efficient system has led to a 15 per cent increase in the use of public transport, a 60 per cent increase in cycling,
120 and a 10 per cent increase in walking.

Grammar: *the future (2)*
▶ *p.182*

grammar file 8

A Future continuous:
will/may/might + be + -ing

Actions in progress at a point in the future:

1 *People **may/might be cycling** to work in a few years' time.*
2 *This time next year, **I'll be studying** for my final exams.*

B Future perfect: will/may/might + have + past participle

Events completed before a point in the future:

1 *By the end of the decade, many cities **will have banned** cars.*
2 *By 3000, we **may/might have used up** the Earth's natural resources.*

! What's wrong?

1 *This time next year I will study in Britain.* ✗
2 *By the time I am 25, I will find a job!* ✗

---

1 Future simple or future continuous?

1 Put the verbs in brackets into the correct form.

This time next month I (1) .... (work) in southern Spain, as a wildlife volunteer. In a few weeks from now, I (2) .... (learn) about different species of birds and animals and (3) .... (help) to conserve the marshes. I (4) .... (be) there for three weeks. While I am there, I hope I (5) .... (get) the chance to visit Coto Doñana, which is a fantastic wildlife reserve. If I enjoy the experience, maybe I (6) .... (do) it again next year. As soon as I get back, I (7) .... (tell) you all about it.

2 💬 **Would you like to work on a similar wildlife project?**

2 Future perfect

Fill in the gaps with *will*, *may* or *might* + the verb in brackets, depending how sure you feel about the statement. Then compare your answers with a partner.

1 By the year 2050, scientists .... (invent) computers that can think and feel.
2 By the time I am 30, I .... (become) world famous!
3 By the middle of this century, astronomers .... (find out) more about how the universe was formed.
4 By the end of this century, many animals .... (become) extinct.
5 By the year 2050, biologists .... (identify) most plants on this planet.
6 By the year 2080, I hope we .... (stop) polluting our planet.

3 💬 Future continuous or future perfect?

Use the prompts to make questions. Use the future continuous or the future perfect. Then ask a partner for his/her opinion.

1 people/build/houses under the sea 100 years from now?
2 we/use up/all the world's oil 30 years' time?
3 people/live/on other planets in a few years' time?
4 computers/replace/teachers/in a few years from now?
5 you/still/live/in this town 10 years from now?

4 Open cloze

1 Read the text below. What does the writer predict for the future?

2 Read the text again and think of the word that best fits each space. Use only one word in each space. Most of the words you need are auxiliary verbs or prepositions. There is an example at the beginning (0).

HOW I SEE THE FUTURE

By the start of the next century, I imagine that life on Earth will (0) *have* changed a great deal. The world's population (1) .... have grown enormously, and people will probably (2) .... living in much larger cities. They (3) .... even have built cities under the sea! We may have run out of oil and coal (4) .... the end of this century. If this happens, we will have (5) .... develop new energy sources. (6) .... a hundred years' time, we may be using more natural resources, like solar power and wind power.

Sadly, by the end (7) .... this century, the world's rain forests may (8) .... been cut down. Many species of animals and plants may disappear with them. I also think that pollution will probably have (9) .... worse. In the future, our cities may (10) .... covered with glass domes to keep the air clean.

On the other hand, people are likely to be living longer. A hundred years (11) .... now, doctors may have learnt how to cure disease and how to grow spare body parts. They could even have created a bionic man (12) .... the year 3000!

---

3 💬 **What's your opinion?**

▶▶ **WB** p.84

Vocabulary building

1 Word formation

1 Complete the table. Use your dictionary to help you.

Verb	Noun	Positive adjective	Negative adjective
1 conserve	....	xxx	xxx
2	practice	....	....
3	....	destructive	xxx
4 endanger	....	....	xxx
5	threat	....	....
6 pollute	....	....	....
7	safety	....	....
8	....	....	unrecycled

2 ⏺ Now fill in the gaps with a word from the table. Don't use the same word twice. Then, ask and answer questions with a partner.

1 Do you .... all your rubbish or do you just throw it away? Why?

2 Is the air in your town/village clean or is there a lot of .... ?

3 What animals are in .... of extinction?

4 Do you think we still have plenty of time to .... our planet? Why/Why not?

2 Word-formation task

1 Read the text below. What is 'Greenpeace'?

2 Use the word in CAPITALS underneath to form a word that fits in the space. Decide what kind of word you need. Be careful! One space needs a negative form. There is an example at the beginning (0).

JOIN GREENPEACE NOW

'Greenpeace' is an internationally famous (0) *environmental* organisation. We work to save our planet in very (1) .... ways. We want to warn people about the dangers that (2) .... our world. We want to stop the (3) .... destruction of the tropical rain forests. We want to stop power stations from releasing (4) .... gases into the atmosphere. It is important to protect wildlife and we have many (5) .... projects. We must save (6) .... animals such as turtles and pandas from extinction. Their habitats are disappearing (7) .... quickly. We have to persuade governments to make the right (8) .... so that we can protect these wildlife areas. The sea is very (9) .... so we have to act quickly here, too. At Greenpeace, we can make an important (10) .... to the future of our planet. Why not join us today?

0 ENVIRONMENT	**4** HARM	**8** DECIDE
1 PRACTICE	**5** CONSERVE	**9** POLLUTE
2 THREAT	**6** DANGER	**10** CONTRIBUTE
3 SENSE	**7** EXTREME	

3 Phrasal verbs

Replace the words in *italics* with a phrasal verb from the box in the correct form.

> keep on doing sth.
> cut sth. down
> use sth. up
> look after sth.
> give sth. off
> cut down on sth.

1 If we don't *take care* of our planet, the human species may not survive.

2 If people *destroy* all the rain forests, the land will become dry and useless.

3 We must *reduce* the amount of fossil fuel we burn as it causes pollution.

4 Cars *produce* poisonous fumes, so we should use them less.

5 We are polluting the sea and if we *continue* doing this, many sea creatures will die.

6 Before long, we will have *finished* all the Earth's natural resources.

4 Choosing the right word

1 Underline the correct word in each pair.

1 We must encourage more people to save energy by *circulating/recycling* rubbish.

2 We need to make sure our rivers are *save/safe* from pollution.

3 There should be stronger *laws/rules* to stop ships polluting the sea.

4 We must conserve wildlife areas, or many animals may *become/get* extinct.

5 Many *specialities/species* of animals will disappear unless we stop people from hunting them.

6 Unless we stop building new roads, we will destroy the *countryside/ nature*.

2 Which of the issues above do you think is the most important?

▶▶ **WB** p.86

Listening ▶ *Part 4*

1 Before you listen

1 Read the instructions for the Listening task.

1 What are you going to hear?

2 What are *solar panels*, and what are they for?

3 How common are they in your area?

2 Read the statements 1–7. What do you need to listen for? Turn the statements into questions.

1 Why did Simon start .... ?

2 Why did he get help from .... ?

3 What did he want to .... ?

4 Why did the school .... ?

5 How important was .... ?

6 Does Simon think he is the right .... ?

7 Does Simon feel .... ?

3 Can you predict any of the answers to the questions?

2 🖭 Listening strategy

▶▶ *don't choose your answer too soon*

Listen to more than one sentence before you decide on your answer in case the next part gives you different information.

1 Read the clues for Questions 1–3. The first sentence may mislead you if you decide on your answer too soon. The second sentence introduces the information you need.

2 Now listen to the first part of the recording and decide if the statements are TRUE or FALSE. Compare your ideas with the class.

Listening task

You will hear an interview with a high school student who has been working on a project to install solar panels at his school. Decide which of the statements 1–7 are TRUE and which are FALSE. Write T for TRUE and F for FALSE in the boxes.

1 Simon started the project because he'd enjoyed learning about solar energy at school. | 1 |

Clue: *That's what many people think, ... The truth is ...*

2 Simon thinks the experts helped him because they could see he was taking the idea seriously. | 2 |

Clue: *My dad's help was important ... . But I think ...*

3 Simon's main purpose was to make students more aware of environmental issues. | 3 |

Clue: *Well, yes, that. But what I really wanted ...*

4 Simon believes the school agreed to the project in order to save money on fuel. | 4 |

5 Simon says the help of the school secretary was useful in getting the project started. | 5 |

6 Simon thinks he is the right person to teach children about saving energy. | 6 |

7 Simon feels he should make up his mind about his future studies now. | 7 |

3 🖭 Listening task

1 Listen to the rest of the recording and complete the task.

2 Now listen to the whole recording from the beginning. Check your answers.

4 💬 Over to you

What could your school do to save money on electricity? Think about turning off lights, closing windows in winter, etc.

Writing: *transactional letter* ▶ *Part 1*

1 Sample writing task

Read the task.

1 Who are 'you'?
2 Who is Vicky Davies? What is she offering to do?
3 Do you know Vicky well? What style should you use when you write to her?
4 Underline the information Vicky Davies wants (five questions).

Writing task

You are the Secretary of the Eco-Club at your school. You saw this advertisement in a local paper recently and wrote for more details.

Eco-Action Group

Are you worried about the state of the environment? Would you like to know more? We are willing to give talks and free video shows to interested groups!

For more details, please contact:
**Ms Vicky Davies
P.O. Box 4990
Birmingham B12 9QY**

You received this reply:

Thank you for your interest in our talks. We would be happy to come to your school. Could you let us know which date you prefer, what time you would like the talk, and how many students will be coming? We will need a TV and video. I wonder if you have this equipment at the school? Let me know if not, and we can bring our own. Finally, could you send a map showing where your school is?

Yours sincerely

Vicky Davies

Vicky Davies

Reply to Vicky Davies, answering her questions, and making arrangements for the talk. Write a letter of 120–180 words in an appropriate style.

2 Read a sample letter

Read the letter that was written in reply to Vicky Davies. (The introduction and conclusion are missing.) Did the writer include all the information asked for? Look back at your notes in Exercise 1 and check.

Dear Ms Davies,

(1) ....

We would like to have the talk on Wednesday, November 15th, if this is convenient for you. Lessons finish at 3 p.m. and the school closes at 4.30 p.m., so if possible we would like the talk to last for about an hour, from 3.15 to 4.15 p.m. About 50 students will be coming. We have both a TV and a video recorder in school, so there is no need for you to bring any equipment.

I enclose a map, as you asked. Our school is very close to the city centre, and it is easy to find. If you come by car, you will find plenty of parking spaces in the grounds behind the school.

(2) ....

Yours sincerely,

Marcus Hunt

Marcus Hunt

3 Introductions and conclusions

1 Which of these introductions would be most suitable for the letter? Why?

A

It was great to hear from you! So glad you can come.

B

Thank you very much for your letter, and for agreeing to come and talk to our school. We are grateful for the chance to learn more about the environment.

2 Which of the following makes the most suitable conclusion? Why?

C

I hope that I have given you all the information you asked for. If you need to ask about anything else, please do not hesitate to contact me.

D

Once again, thanks a lot for agreeing to come. I think it's going to be great! See you soon!

Over to you

4 Writing strategy

Complete the notes.

▶▶ *writing a transactional letter*

When you write a transactional letter to make arrangements:

- carefully read all the material you are given and keep checking back to make sure you haven't forgotten any ....
- check who is going to read your letter and make sure the letter is written in the correct ....

5 Writing task

Read the task.

1 Who are 'you'?

2 What is your group planning?

3 Who has written to you? Why? What does he/she want to know? What information do you need to give?

4 How well do you know the person you are going to write to? How informal can you be?

6 Plan your letter

Make a paragraph plan using the ideas below. Write notes.

Para. 1

Introduction: Thank Paula for her letter/for volunteering to help.

Useful phrases: Thank you for your letter asking about ...

Para. 2

Topic: Details about the working weekend: when; where/what time we will meet; how we'll be travelling

Useful phrases: Here are the details about ...

Para. 3

Topic: What to wear/bring

Useful phrases: There are one or two more things that perhaps I should mention. First of all, ...

Para. 4

Topic: Let me know if you need any other information/you definitely plan to come with us.

Useful phrases: Please let me know if ... . I would be grateful if you would ...

7 Write

Now write your letter. Follow the ▶▶ *Writing strategy*.

8 Check your work

Are the grammar, spelling and punctuation correct?

Writing task

You are the secretary of a voluntary environmental group. Your group is planning a working weekend to clean up some of your local beaches. You have received a letter from someone who would like to take part in the project. Read the letter and the notes you have made. Then write a reply of 120–180 words in an appropriate style.

Dear .... ,

I read that your group is planning a working weekend to clean up some of our local beaches. I would like to volunteer to help you in the project. Could you send me some more details, including when the weekend will be and whether you can provide transport? I would be grateful for any other information you can give me, too.

I look forward to hearing from you.

Yours sincerely,

Paula Santorini

Notes

Working weekend:

– Sat. Jan. 30th – Sun. Jan 31st. (all volunteers welcome!)

– Meet outside Town Hall Sat & Sun 7.00 a.m. sharp.

– Transport: by our own minibus.

Remember – wear old clothes and bring strong boots, gloves

– bring packed lunch and plenty to drink!

▶▶ WB p.87

Progress test 4

1 Lexical cloze

For questions **1–12**, read the text below and decide which answer **A, B, C** or **D** best fits each space. There is an example at the beginning **(0)**.

Example:

0 A a   **B** an   **C** the   **D** some

NO ORDINARY TEENAGER

Christiana Tugwell is not **(0)** *B.* ordinary person. She is the leader of an environmental campaign which wants to **(1)** ... builders from destroying an area of woodland in southeast England and **(2)** ... wildlife. The campaigners have **(3)** ... tents on the land and Christiana speaks to people on her mobile phone from **(4)** ... the camp. But the most surprising **(5)** ... is that Christiana is only 15 years old.

Christiana's first protest was against the fast food industry **(6)** ... she was only nine years old. Then in 1999 she went to court to stop 60 houses being **(7)** ... on nearby woodland. Now she is living in a tent and helping to construct tunnels under the earth, **(8)** ... it is impossible for the developers to start work.

Christiana's mother **(9)** ... her daughter to continue campaigning. Today, **(10)** ... of them think that more people should help to conserve the environment. 'I'm only 15 and I've managed to come **(11)** ... with this campaign,' Christiana says. Unless people like her **(12)** ... campaigning, in ten years' time much more will have been destroyed.

1	**A** stop	**B** end	**C** finish	**D** halt
2	**A** polluting	**B** saving	**C** conserving	**D** endangering
3	**A** put up	**B** put out	**C** put off	**D** put down
4	**A** on	**B** in	**C** into	**D** inside
5	**A** reason	**B** thing	**C** thought	**D** explanation
6	**A** as	**B** when	**C** if	**D** since
7	**A** made	**B** done	**C** built	**D** had
8	**A** in order to	**B** even though	**C** so that	**D** in case
9	**A** decides	**B** conserves	**C** contributes	**D** encourages
10	**A** both	**B** any	**C** all	**D** some
11	**A** on	**B** in	**C** up	**D** away
12	**A** make up	**B** carry on	**C** get by	**D** move to

2 Open cloze

For questions **13–24**, read the text below and think of the word which best fits each space. Use only one word in each space. There is an example at the beginning **(0)**.

MAN'S BEST FRIEND

Man's best friend won't just keep you company, he'll also improve your chances **(0)** ....*of*.... finding a partner. Psychologists from Warwick University **(13)** .... the UK **(14)** .... discovered that a dog helps people to **(15)** .... new friends. It doesn't matter what you look like, people are more likely to speak to you if you are with **(16)** .... cuddly canine friend.

June McNicholas, one of the university team, took a dog **(17)** .... her for five days as she went around town, and recorded the number of times she spoke **(18)** .... strangers – an amazing 156 times. About 60 per cent of **(19)** .... meetings were with the opposite sex. But in another week when June walked around alone, **(20)** .... only spoke to new people 50 times. A male colleague then did the **(21)** .... experiment. Sometimes the man dressed smartly, and **(22)** .... other times he was scruffy. But it didn't matter how he was dressed, he met ten times the number of people he **(23)** .... normally meet **(24)** .... he didn't have a dog at his side. 'It shows that dogs are good ice-breakers,' June McNicholas says.

3 Key word transformations

For questions **25–32**, complete the second sentence so that it has a similar meaning to the first sentence, using the word given. **Do not change the word given.** You must use between two and five words, including the word given. There is an example at the beginning **(0)**.

Example:

0 You mustn't spend so much money.
stop

You must ..*stop spending*..... so much money.

25 'I've been protesting for three months,' the campaigner explained.
had

The campaigner explained that she .... for three months.

26 I asked the designer what had made her so successful.
you

'What .... so successful?' I asked the designer.

27 'Does Francesca like snakes?' we wanted to know.
if

We wanted to .... snakes.

28 That tiger was really frightening.
by

I was really .... that tiger.

29 We know that the environment has been in danger for many years.
is

It .... that the environment has been in danger for many years.

30 I went to the barber's for a haircut yesterday.
my

I .... at the barber's yesterday.

31 Traffic can only go one way in that street.
a

That's .... street.

32 Central London will have banned cars within ten years.
been

Cars .... from central London within ten years.

4 Error correction

For questions **33–44**, read the text below and look carefully at each line. Some of the lines are correct, and some have a word which should not be there. If a line is correct, put a tick (✓) next to it. If a line has a word which should not be there, <u>underline</u> the word. There are two examples at the beginning **(0 and 00)**.

PLASTIC FASHION PEOPLE!

0 For years, people have had parts of their bodies reshaped. In the past, ✓
00 <u>the</u> plastic surgery was confined to fashionable, middle-aged people with
33 money to be spare, but nowadays the business of 'body modification'
34 it is booming among the young and not so rich. Teenage girls as well as
35 boys are part of that boom. However, the demand for plastic surgery by
36 young people has been caused concern among parents and teachers.
37 They feel so that teenagers may be harming their health and emotional
38 development by chasing an unrealistic dream of physical perfection,
39 all because of fashion. Even some plastic surgeons have expressed about
40 concerns. It's very hard for teenagers because of they are constantly
41 seeing attractive models and movie stars in the media. The underlying
42 message is that physical appearance is the very most important thing in
43 life. It makes young people want that to change themselves. But it is
44 important to understand that changing the way you look at will not
automatically lead to happiness.

5 Word formation

For questions **45–54**, read the text below. Use the word given in capitals underneath the text to form a word that fits in the space in the text. There is an example at the beginning **(0)**.

POLAR SURVIVAL COURSES

What better method of **(0)** *preparation* for a polar expedition than to take part in our **(45)** .... course situated in Swedish Lapland? Lying about 320 kilometres north of the Arctic Circle, this **(46)** .... area has low temperatures, ideal snow conditions and **(47)** .... landscapes, making it an excellent **(48)** .... to train for your polar adventure. Based in one of the few **(49)** .... wildernesses in Europe, you will learn a range of skills that will prepare you for your expedition, whether it is over **(50)** .... or flat terrain. As your health is so important, **(51)** .... will also be given in first aid, as well as in essential skills for surviving in **(52)** .... regions. This course is not limited to those going on **(53)** .... polar expeditions, as the skills are **(54)** .... useful to anyone who wishes to develop survival techniques.

0 PREPARE	**48** LOCATE	**52** INHABIT
45 CHALLENGE	**49** REMAIN	**53** DANGER
46 GLORY	**50** MOUNTAIN	**54** EQUAL
47 VARY	**51** TRAIN	

17 Celebrations

Speaking: *test your skills*
▶ *Part 2*

1 Photos

Look at the photos of different kinds of celebrations. Match these descriptions to the photos.

A The Millennium Dome, London, welcoming 2000 with fireworks

B Chinese New Year in Singapore: the Lion Dance

C Young people dancing at a High School Prom in the USA

D Bride and groom at a traditional wedding ceremony in New Delhi, India

2  Listen

▶▶ *speaking strategies*

For **Part 2** of the **Speaking test:**

- <u>don't</u> describe the photos in too much detail.

- <u>do</u> give your personal opinion about them.

1 Listen to an exam candidate following this instruction about two of the photos.

'I'd like you to compare and contrast these photographs, which show public celebrations, saying which one looks more enjoyable.'

2 Choose the right answer to these questions.

1 How many parts does the question have? a) One. b) Two.

2 Did the candidate describe the two photos in detail? a) Yes. b) No.

3 Did she give her personal opinion about the subject of the photos? a) Yes. b) No.

4 There was a word she needed to talk about the photos but didn't know. What did she do? a) Stop talking. b) Paraphrase the word.

3 Which of the celebrations would you prefer to attend?

3 💬 Speaking task: *individual long turn*

Look at the photos which show personal celebrations. Take turns to talk about them.

Student A: Compare and contrast the photos and say how much fun you think the people are having.

🕐 Approximately 1 minute

Student B: Compare and contrast the photos and say how important you think celebrations like these are.

🕐 Approximately 1 minute

4 💬 Discussion

Think of a festival or celebration that you really enjoy.

1 What do the participants do?

2 Who enjoys it most, young or elderly people? Why?

3 How do you prepare for it?

4 What do people wear? Do they dress up in special costumes?

▶▶ **WB** p.90

Reading: *test your skills ▶ Part 1*

▶▶ *reading strategies*

Part 1 of the **Reading paper** tests your ability to identify the main idea of a paragraph. Use these strategies:

▶▶ *skimming* Unit 2 p.16

▶▶ *understanding the main idea* Unit 5 p.42

▶▶ *using headings to predict content* Unit 9 p.76

▶▶ *focusing on main points* Unit 13 p.110

1 Understand the task / predict

Read the instructions for the task, the title and the sub-heading of the text.

1 What is the article about?

2 What do you have to do?

3 What do you know about the topic of the text?

2 Read the headings

Read the headings A–H to get an idea of the paragraph topics.

What do you think each paragraph will be about?

3 Skim the text

Answer these questions to check your general understanding.

Paragraph:

0 Why is the Notting Hill Carnival important today?

1 What were the slaves in Trinidad forbidden to do?

2 How did the slaves celebrate their freedom?

3 What happened in the 1950s and 1960s?

4 How similar is the modern carnival to the old carnivals in Trinidad?

5 What are *Static Sound Systems*?

6 What does the festival show about Britain?

4 Multiple-matching task

Read the text again, paragraph by paragraph. Decide which heading summarises the main point. Here are some clues to help you.

Heading:

A talks about *A small beginning*. Which paragraph describes how the tradition of carnival first began?

C talks about *traditional ingredients*. Which paragraph explains what the Carnival is made up of?

G talks about *No freedom*. Which paragraph talks about things people could not do?

┌─ ▶▶ *tip!* ─────────────────

Look for words in the headings that express the same idea as the text.
　　　　　　　　　　　　　　　　　　　　　　◀◀
└──────────────────────────

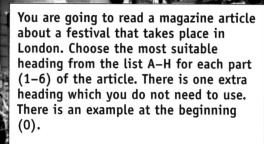

You are going to read a magazine article about a festival that takes place in London. Choose the most suitable heading from the list A–H for each part (1–6) of the article. There is one extra heading which you do not need to use. There is an example at the beginning (0).

A A small beginning

B A reflection of a multi-cultural Britain

C The traditional ingredients of Carnival

D Planning a major festival

E A popular recent development

F The Trinidad Carnival is born

G No freedom of expression

H An unexpected success

5 Vocabulary

▶▶ *guessing meaning from context* Unit 1 p.9

1 Look through the text again. Are there any words you don't know? Try to work out the meaning using context clues.

2 Compare your words with a partner. Then check in your dictionary if you're still not sure.

6 Over to you

How much do you know about the history and background of your most important festivals?

▶▶ WB p.91

The Notting Hill Carnival

Notting Hill is a vibrant, cosmopolitan inner-city area of London. For two days every year, the people of Notting Hill get together to create 'The Greatest Show on Earth'.

0   **H**

The Notting Hill Carnival has been taking place on the last weekend of August for more than 35 years. This great multi-cultural festival was brought to London by immigrants from the West Indies, particularly from the island of Trinidad, where the carnival tradition is very strong. But these immigrants never imagined that it would become one of the biggest festivals in Europe and one of London's most popular tourist attractions.

1

In Trinidad today, the carnival is a festival of Arts which celebrates both the African and European traditions of the island. But it hasn't always been that way. The Black people of Trinidad were taken there from Africa as slaves. Their European masters did not allow them to continue their own traditions of singing and dancing. The only time the slaves were allowed to play musical instruments or wear costumes was during the imported European Carnival, to provide entertainment for their masters. They were even forbidden to be in the streets after dark without their masters.

2

When slavery ended in 1833, the slaves celebrated their freedom by singing and dancing in the streets. They used their artistic skills to create fantastic costumes and masks which made fun of their former masters. Gradually people from all over Trinidad began to take part in these street celebrations. They became experts in the art of costume making and the skills of steel drumming and *calypso* (story telling in song). It was the start of a tradition that would never die out, a tradition that Trinidadians would take with them to other parts of the world.

3

Thousands of people from Trinidad and other West Indian countries emigrated to Britain to work in the 1950s and 60s. Many of them settled in London's Notting Hill area. Remembering their carnivals back home, they dreamed of creating a festival to bring together the people of Notting Hill. In 1964, the first street carnival was organised, with just a few people dressed in costumes, and a steel band. As they had hoped, when the people of Notting Hill heard the first tunes of the band, they came out onto the streets to join in. They didn't want to miss this opportunity to dance and perform in the streets of London.

4

The present-day festival has many of the original elements of the Trinidad Carnival. The most popular of these is the costume parade (also known as the *Mas*, from *Masquerade*), which is a procession of elaborately decorated 'floats' pulled by trucks, and steel bands. Other important elements of the carnival are the *calypso* and *soca* bands, which play the traditional music of carnival. All of these move slowly through the streets, along a route of about five kilometres. The motto of the Notting Hill Carnival is 'Every Spectator is a Participant', so tourists and visitors are invited to join in and dance.

5

As well as the traditional costume parades and live bands, there are also dozens of 'Static Sound Systems' with huge speakers as tall as people pumping out music on every corner. They all have their own DJs, playing a selection of soca, reggae, jazz, soul and many other styles of music. The Sound Systems are relatively new and it is this aspect of the Carnival that most appeals to the young. They have been so successful with the under-20s that they have already become a carnival institution.

6

Over the years the Notting Hill Carnival has been such a success that it now attracts over two million visitors. It is London's biggest outdoor community celebration. And the more it grows, the better it shows the nature of British society, a society made up of many different cultural traditions. As well as celebrating the culture of its founders from the West Indies, the Notting Hill Carnival welcomes participants from all over the world who want to celebrate their own traditions through art, dance and music.

Grammar: *cause and result*
▶ *p.188*

grammar file 21

A *so* and *such*

1 The Carnival has been **so successful that** it attracts two million visitors.

2 The Carnival has been **such a success that** it attracts two million visitors.

3 The band played **so loudly (that)** we couldn't hear each other.

4 It was **such lovely weather (that)** we had a picnic.

B *too* and *enough*

5 The grass was **too wet (for us) to sit** on.

6 My brother's **not old enough** to go to the carnival. (too young)

C *too* or *very*?

7 The tickets were **very** expensive. (cost a lot of money)

8 The tickets were **too** expensive. (for me to buy)

! What's wrong?

1 *The costumes were too expensive to hire them.* X

2 *He was too tired but he didn't fall asleep.* X

3 *She wasn't enough old to walk in the parade.* X

---

1 *so* or *such (a)*?

Fill in the gaps with the correct word(s).

1 I was having .... good fun that I forgot the time!

2 My friend's costume was .... original that he won a prize!

3 The band played .... well that everyone wanted to dance.

4 We were having .... good time that no-one wanted to go home.

---

2 *too ... to*

Rewrite the sentences beginning with the words given.

1 Mum is very busy so she can't make our costumes.
Mum is ....

2 We can't buy the costumes because they are very expensive.
The costumes ....

3 The masks are very heavy so we can't wear them all evening.
The masks ....

4 I can't learn that dance because it's very difficult.
That dance ....

3 *enough*

Use *enough* and a word from the list to fill in the gaps.

fast / big / ~~time~~ / warm / food

1 We didn't have ...*enough time*... to see everything.

2 This costume isn't .... – I need a larger size.

3 Have we got .... for the barbecue?

4 He didn't run .... to win the race.

5 If the weather is .... , we'll have a beach party.

4 Error correction

Read the text below and look carefully at each line 1–15. Some of the lines are correct. Tick them. The other lines each have a word which should not be there. Underline it. There are two examples at the beginning (0 and 00).

CARNIVAL IN BRAZIL

0 Last year we went to Brazil. We spent most of our holiday ✓

00 <u>in</u> exploring the countryside but we left just enough time

1 for to visit Rio, the capital city. We had heard of the Rio

2 Carnival before but we didn't realise that it would be so a

3 spectacular! The day after we arrived, we woke us up early.

4 We were surprised because the streets were already enough

5 packed. In fact, the Rio Carnival it is so famous that

6 people come from all over the world to see it. We rushed

7 to the city centre but it took us so such a long time to get there

8 that we were being too late to see the start of the parade. But it

9 didn't matter. There were such so many people taking part that

10 than the spectacle lasted for hours. There were hundreds of

11 lorries, called *floats*, all decorated with fabulous lights and

12 streamers. They were packed with people dressed in too amazing

13 costumes. Thousands more people walked and danced along the

14 street beside them. And there was such a fantastic music! At times,

15 it seemed loud enough that to make us all deaf.

▶▶ **WB** p.91

Vocabulary building

1 Word formation

Use the word in CAPITALS at the end of each sentence to form a word that fits in the gap. Be careful! You may need a negative or a plural form.

1 New Year's Day is a .... holiday in many countries. NATION

2 At carnival time in Venice, people wear masks so it is .... to see their faces. POSSIBLE

3 The carnival in Brazil is one of the most .... festivals in the world. FAME

4 In Spain, the festival of *Semana Santa* is a popular tourist .... ATTRACT

5 During the Dragon Boat Festival in China, ... compete against each other in boats shaped like dragons. PARTICIPATE

6 During May Day .... in England, children dance round a maypole in some villages. CELEBRATE

2 Phrasal verbs

Fill in the gaps with a phrasal verb from the box in the correct form. The meaning is given in brackets.

dress up (in)   go on   put up   set off   turn out (to be)

In our village, we celebrate May Day with lots of activities. People (1) .... (= *hang*) decorations in the streets and dance round a maypole. Children (2) .... (= *wear*) colourful costumes and take part in a grand parade. The procession (3) .... (= *departs*) from the Village Hall at 10 a.m. and goes right round the village. Everyone comes outside to see what's (4) .... (= *happening*) and join in the fun. Last year we thought the rain would spoil the festival but it (5) .... to be (= *in the end it was*) the best festival we'd ever had!

3 ⬭ Choosing the right word

Underline the right word in each pair. Then ask and answer the questions with a partner.

1 Which festivals do people *celebrate/make* in your country? Do you *illustrate/decorate* your house on this day?

2 Do people organise *processions/queues* through the streets on your national day? Do people wear fancy dress *suits/costumes*?

3 Have you ever *taken part/taken place* in a parade?

4 How old will you be on your next *anniversary/birthday*?

5 What phrases can you use to *say/wish* someone a happy birthday in English?

6 When did someone in your family last *make/have* a party? What was the *occasion/opportunity*?

7 Have you been invited *to/at* a party recently? If so, did you accept or *refuse/deny* the invitation?

4 Open cloze

▶▶ *strategies for the open cloze*

- Read the title and the whole text first for general understanding.
- Decide what kind of word is needed in each gap. The words you need are mainly grammatical, but they may be part of a phrase.

1 Read the text again and think of the word that best fits each space. Use only one word in each space. There is an example at the beginning (0).

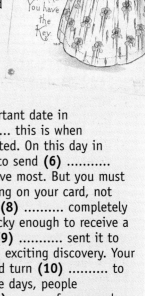

ST. VALENTINES DAY

All over **(0)** ..*the*.... world, people come together to celebrate local customs and festivals. Some dress up **(1)** .... costumes and take **(2)** .... in parades. Others put **(3)** .... decorations in the streets or **(4)** .... parties in their houses.

14th February is an important date in many countries **(5)** .... this is when Valentine's Day is celebrated. On this day in Britain, it is the custom to send **(6)** .... card to the person you love most. But you must **(7)** .... write anything on your card, not even your name! It must **(8)** .... completely anonymous. If you are lucky enough to receive a card, you have to guess **(9)** .... sent it to you! This can be quite an exciting discovery. Your next-door neighbour could turn **(10)** .... to be a secret admirer! These days, people sometimes send each **(11)** .... funny cards. Most Valentine cards, **(12)** .... , are still extremely romantic! Men who really want to impress **(13)** .... wives or girlfriends buy them red roses **(14)** .... Valentine's Day. But flowers are **(15)** .... expensive at this time of year that some wives have to make do with a card – or just a kiss!

2 What types of words were tested? Tick them.

- phrasal verbs
- fixed expressions
- prepositions
- pronouns/relative pronouns
- articles/determiners
- linking words
- verbs
- adverbs

 WB p.93

Listening: *test your skills*
▶ Part 1

▶▶ *listening strategies*

Part 1 of the **Listening paper** tests your ability:

• to understand specific information.

• to identify the speaker's feelings or opinions.

• to work out what the speaker is saying or doing.

Use these strategies:

▶▶ *listening for a purpose* Unit 1 p.12

▶▶ *listening for linking words* Unit 5 p.46

▶▶ *working out the main idea from details* Unit 11 p.96

1 Understand the task

1 Look at the task. Read questions 1–8 and underline key words so you know exactly what you are listening for.

2 Think about what you might hear. Here are some clues.

Question:

1 What could the boy say about each thing? Was the food bad? Wasn't the music good?

2 Were there not enough/too many performances? Were the plays good or bad? Was there not enough variety?

3 What words and phrases could someone use to talk about a holiday? a party? shopping?

2 🔲 Listening task

1 Listen to the extracts and answer the questions. You will hear each extract once.

▶▶ *tip!*
- Choose the best answer the first time you listen.
- Check your answers the second time you listen. ◀◀

2 Compare your answers. What phrases made you choose?

3 💬 Over to you

1 How do you celebrate the end of exams? your birthday? other important occasions in your life?

2 Describe a typical wedding in your country.

Listening task

You will hear people talking in eight different situations. For questions 1–8, choose the best answer A, B or C.

1 You hear two friends talking about a school party they went to.
What is the boy complaining about?
A the food
B the music
C the lighting
| 1 |

2 You hear a girl talking about a theatre festival she went to.
What disappointed her about the festival?
A the number of performances she saw
B the quality of the plays she went to
C the variety of things on the programme
| 2 |

3 You hear two girls talking about how they will celebrate passing their exams.
What do they decide to do?
A have a holiday
B throw a party
C go shopping
| 3 |

4 You hear this announcement on the radio.
What does the presenter want listeners to do?
A join a club
B buy a product
C enter a competition
| 4 |

5 You hear a girl and a boy talking about a present the girl received.
How does she feel about the present?
A worried
B sad
C amused
| 5 |

6 You hear a boy talking to a friend about a mistake he made.
What is he doing when he speaks?
A suggesting a course of action
B apologising for his behaviour
C asking for his friend's advice
| 6 |

7 You hear a young man talking about a wedding party.
What does he say about the party?
A It was more enjoyable than he'd expected.
B It was held in an unusual place.
C It started later than had been planned.
| 7 |

8 You hear a girl talking about some people she met at a party.
What is her opinion of them?
A They were polite.
B They were talkative.
C They were entertaining.
| 8 |

Writing: *test your skills* ▶ Part 2

1 Sample writing task

Read the task.

1 Who is the main character?
2 Where should the prompt sentence appear in the story?

Writing task

You have seen this notice in your classroom.

> # Calling all students!
> **Could you write a story for the school magazine? The first line or the last line of your story should be:**
>
> *'This is definitely my lucky day,' Kate told herself happily.*
>
> **The best stories will be published next month.**

Write your story, describing what happened in 120–180 words.

2 Compare two sample answers

Look at the list of features which a good story should have. Then read the two stories. Tick the features that each story has. Which story is better?

A good story:	Story A	Story B
1 has a clear beginning, middle and end.	✓	✓
2 is organised into 3–4 paragraphs.		
3 has interesting details.		
4 uses linking expressions to connect sentences and paragraphs.		
5 uses a range of vocabulary, not just basic words.		
6 contains some direct speech.		
7 uses a range of past tenses.		
8 has correct punctuation and spelling.		
9 has very few grammar mistakes.		

Story A

It was carnival day in Kate's town and she and her friends went to join the fun. The streets were full with people and everyone was having a good time. After a while, the parade started and a procession of floats made the way through the town.

A short time later, Kate was busy taking a photo when suddenly someone pushed her. She turned round quickly and saw a young man. She realised that he had taken her bag and he was running away with it. 'Help!' she shouted. 'That man has just robbed me!' People turned round, but the man had disappeared completely.

After the parade had finished, Kate set off home with her friends. She was walking slowly after them because she was still upset about what happened. Suddenly, one of her friends ran and picked something up from the road. It was Kate's bag! To her surprise, everything was in it, even her money. 'This is definitely my lucky day,' Kate told herself happily.

Story B

This happened on the New Year's Day. It was a special day for Kate. She loved the music so she played in her school band. The band allways played in a big parade on the New Year's Day.

In the morning. Kate was running to catch the bus to go to the town centre. Her friends were on the bus too. Everyone was on a good mood. They were talking and laughing because they had holiday from school!

They arrived on the centre of the city and everyone got out the bus. Kate talked with her friends and the bus drove away.

Kate sudenly had a shock. Her trumpet was on the bus! she forgot it! It was too late. Kate could not do anything.

The parade began and Kate walked between all the other students. Luckily nobody noticed she does not have a trumpet!

They had a realy nice time.

This is definitly my lucky day. Kate told herself happily.

3 What does the examiner want?

1 Read these comments by the examiner about one of the stories on p.149. Which story do they refer to?

CONTENT: quite interesting storyline, but not well developed

ACCURACY: errors in tenses, spelling and punctuation

RANGE: limited range of vocabulary and grammar

ORGANISATION: too many paragraphs; sentences and paragraphs not well linked together

---

2 Find and correct the following mistakes in the story:

- three mistakes with articles
- three mistakes with prepositions
- three tense mistakes
- two punctuation mistakes
- four spelling mistakes

3 Improve the organisation.

1 How many paragraphs should the story have?
2 Which sentences could you combine using a range of linking words?

Over to you

4 Writing task

Read the task.

1 Who is going to read your story?
2 How must you begin or end your story?

Writing task

An international students' magazine is holding a competition for interesting stories. The winners will win a prize of £250. The rules of the competition say that the story must use the following sentences as the first OR the last line:

John didn't think he'd ever been so happy.

Write your story in 120–180 words.

---

5 Brainstorm ideas

Think about these questions.

1 Who was John?
2 Why was he happy?
3 What happened to him?
4 Who else was involved?

6 Plan your story

1 Decide if the sentences given in the writing task go best at the beginning or at the end of your story.

2 Choose the best ideas from your notes in Exercise 5.

3 Make a plan.

Para. 1 (Introduction)
Topic: The situation / background information. (Who? Where? When?)
Sentence from writing task?
Para. 2
Topic: What happened? More background? (Why? How?)
Details: ....
Paras. 3 / 4
Topic: What happened next?
Details: ....
Final para. (Conclusion)
Topic: What happened at the end?
Sentence from writing task?

7 Write

Write your story. Remember to include the prompt sentences as the first or last line of the story.

8 Check your work

Look at the list of features in Exercise 2 on p.149. How many does your story contain?

▶▶ **WB** p.94

18 | Getting around

Speaking: *test your skills*
► *Part 2*

1 Vocabulary

Look at the photos.

1 Which photos show a person/people:
   a) on a business trip?   b) on an adventure holiday?
   c) on a train journey?   d) on a guided tour?

2 How do you prefer to travel:
   a) every day?   b) when you go on holiday?

2 Listen

▶▶ *speaking strategies*

In **Part 2** of the **Speaking test**, when Candidate A has finished talking about his/her photos, the examiner asks Candidate B to make a short comment.

Make sure your answer is very brief – no more than 20 seconds.

1 Look at photos 1 and 2. Listen to two exam candidates doing a Part 2 task.

1 What does the examiner ask Candidate A to do?

2 What does he ask Candidate B?

3 How long does Candidate B speak for?
   a) About 1 minute.   b) About 20 seconds.

4 Candidate B didn't understand the examiner's question at first. What did she say?

2 How would <u>you</u> answer the questions on the recording?

3 Speaking task: *individual long turn*

Look at photos 3 and 4, which show different types of holiday travel. Take turns to talk about them.

Student A: Compare and contrast the photos and say which form of holiday travel you would prefer and why.
   Approximately 1 minute

Student B: How do you usually travel on holiday?
   Approximately 20 seconds

Student B: Compare and contrast the photos and say why you think the people chose to go on these holidays.
   Approximately 1 minute

Student A: Which type of holiday would you like to go on?
   Approximately 20 seconds

4 Discussion

1 What are the most popular holiday destinations in your country?

2 If you could travel anywhere in the world, where would you choose to go?

▶▶ WB p.95

151

Reading: *test your skills ▶ Part 2*

▶▶ *reading strategies*

Part 2 of the **Reading paper** tests your ability to understand the main idea and details; the writer's opinions; the overall message. Use these strategies:

▶▶ *understanding details* Unit 6 p.50
▶▶ *multiple-choice questions* Unit 10 p.85

There may be questions testing reference links and your ability to work out the meaning of a word from context. Use these strategies:

▶▶ *guessing meaning from context* Unit 1 p.9
▶▶ *grammatical reference links* Unit 3 p.25

1 Understand the task

Read the instructions for the task, the title and the introduction to the text.

1 What are you going to read?

2 What kind of experiences do you think the text will describe?

2 Read for general understanding

Read the text quite quickly.

Paragraph:

1 How was the experience different from what Bryson had expected? Was it a problem?

2 Did he worry about getting lost?

3 What did he worry about most?

4 Did he walk the whole length of the trail?

5 Did he enjoy the experience? Why was it *worth it in the end*?

3 Multiple-choice questions

1 Look at the multiple-choice questions and read the text carefully to find the answers. Underline the parts of the text which give the answers.

2 Now look at the answers A–D and choose the one that is closest to your own answer.

▶▶ *tip!*

Look for words and phrases with similar meanings in the options **A–D** and in the text. ◀◀

4 Vocabulary

▶▶ *guessing meaning from context* Unit 1 p.9

1 Look through the text again. Are there any words you don't know? Try to work out the meaning using context clues.

2 ⬭ Compare your words with a partner. Then check in your dictionary if you're still not sure.

5 ⬭ Over to you

How has travelling by car, train and plane changed the way we live and see the world?

▶▶ **WB** p.95

You are going to read an interview with a famous travel writer. For questions 1–7, choose the answer A, B, C or D which you think fits best according to the text.

The Longest Hike

The Appalachian Trail stretches for 2,200 miles along the east coast of the United States, across remote mountain wilderness and woods. The travel writer BILL BRYSON spent months hiking the trail with a childhood friend he had not seen for 20 years. His book *A Walk in the Woods* is a humorous account of his experiences. Don George interviewed him.

When they set off on the Trail, Bill Bryson realised very quickly that the hiking experience was going to be very
5 different from how he had imagined it. First of all, he and his companion didn't meet many other people on the trail. Secondly, his companion was a lot less talkative than he had expected. 'I
10 thought he was going to have great stories of what he'd been doing for the last 20 years, but he didn't,' said Bryson. Nevertheless, their relations were very **congenial** throughout. There
15 was no stress or tension between them, though there wasn't much conversation either.

Bryson soon realised that they would have no trouble finding their way along
20 the trail. The Appalachian Trail is the most clearly defined footpath imaginable. Where there might be any doubt at all – where a side trail enters the main path or where the
25 Appalachian Trail crosses a road – there are always signs. Incredibly, a few people still manage to get lost. Bryson met one man on the trail who had been lost for three days. The man could not
30 remember clearly how that had happened. Maybe he got off the trail without realising what he was doing, or he may have wanted to find a short-cut.

A WALK in the WOODS

Bryson's biggest fear during the hike was not getting
35 lost: it was bear attacks. 'They are extremely rare, but if
you are going to get hurt by a big animal on the
Appalachian Trail, **that**'s the one that will hurt you,'
says Bryson. He knew that his fear was irrational or
exaggerated, but he couldn't quite shake it off, especially
40 as he was often alone. When they were walking, he and
his companion were several minutes apart and not
within sight of each other. 'There are those times when
you come around a bend, and you hear crashing in the
undergrowth. Immediately you think: "Is that a bear?"
45 Later you realise it was probably just a deer, but it's
always at the back of your mind.'

Bryson walked 1,400 kilometres, a third of the total
length of the trail. 'I am filled with admiration for those
who see it through. But 1,400 is still a lot of kilometres,'
50 he says. The most important lesson he got from the trip
was just how big the world is. 'When you get on the trail,
you are approaching the world in a way that you've
never approached it before, that is, on foot. You think
you know what to expect, but you just don't. When you
55 say 3,520 kilometres, it's difficult to understand that
length of journey. You can only imagine travelling that
far in a car or a plane. It's a long way.'

Bryson admits that he hated 98.8 per cent of the
journey, but says it was worth it in the end. 'There were
60 moments of great happiness when the sun came out and
we reached a mountain top with a great view. But most
of the time it's either just boring, or you're cold or wet
or uncomfortable. Most of the
time if you're honest, you
65 don't want to be there. You
want to be somewhere else
where you are more
comfortable. You tell yourself
that you will never take
70 running water for granted
again, or flush toilets or hot
meals. However, it's worth it
just for those moments of
happiness and for what you
75 learn about the landscape
and about yourself.'

1 How did Bryson feel about his companion's
silence?
A angry
B disappointed
C offended
D confused

2 What does the word *congenial* mean in line
14?
A agreeable
B special
C unfriendly
D interesting

3 According to Bryson, getting lost in the
Appalachian Trail is
A the result of unclear signs.
B a problem for hikers on their own.
C part of the hiking adventure.
D unlikely to happen to most people.

4 What does the word *that* in line 37 refer to?
A trail
B food
C fear
D bear

5 What does Bryson say about his fear of
bears?
A He thought his fears were justified.
B He was ashamed of his fears.
C He could not get rid of his fears.
D He believed nobody else shared
his fears.

6 The trip made Bryson realise the true
meaning of
A distances.
B friendship.
C transport.
D nature.

7 What does Bryson say about most of the time
he spent on the Appalachian Trail?
A It was thrilling.
B It was unpleasant.
C It was frightening.
D It was uninteresting.

Grammar: *modals (obligation, advice)* ▶ *p.187*

grammar file 18

A Obligation

1 *The stewardess says we **must/mustn't** sit here.* (obligation imposed by speaker)

2 *You **have to** get a visa to enter the USA.* (a rule/law)

3 *We **had to** pay a deposit on our holiday.* (past time)

B Lack of Obligation

4 *You **can** come on holiday with us if you like.* (you're free to choose)

5 *You **don't have to** come if you don't want to.* (not necessary)

6 *You **don't need** a visa to come to my country.* (not necessary)

7 *We didn't **have to/need to** pay for our tickets.* (so we didn't)

8 *We **needn't have** reserved seats.* (but we did)

C Advice/criticism

9 *You **should/ought to** wear a seat belt.* (present time)

10 *You **oughtn't to/shouldn't have crossed** the road without looking!* (past time)

! What's wrong?

1 *My brother drove me all the way so I needn't have taken a taxi.* ✗

2 *We mustn't listen to the guide if we don't want to.* ✗

3 *You should listen to your teacher last year.* ✗

1 *must, have to, mustn't* or *don't have to*?

Fill in the gaps with the correct verb.

1 The law says you .... have a passport if you're going abroad.

2 You .... drink a lot of alcohol and then drive a car.

3 Do we .... wear seat belts all the time we're on the plane?

4 You .... tell us where you're going if you don't want to.

5 Stewardess: 'I'm sorry, sir, but you .... put out your cigarette!'

6 I'm glad we .... go out tonight – there's a good film on TV!

2 *must, mustn't, don't have to, should, need*

Finish these sentences in your own way.

1 Before you get on a plane, you must ....

2 When you travel by train, you don't have to ....

3 If the traffic lights are red, you mustn't ....

4 Before you go on holiday, you should ....

5 If you're in a foreign country, you shouldn't ....

6 You don't need to .... if you're going camping.

3 Criticising past actions

John Taylor isn't a very good traveller. Read what he says below and make comments. Use:

should/shouldn't have   ought to/ought not to have

1 I started to pack my suitcase 10 minutes before I left for the airport.
He shouldn't have packed his case just before he left.
He ought to have ...

2 I kept my passport and wallet in the back pocket of my jeans.

3 I used my mobile phone during the flight even though it's forbidden.

4 I put the glasses I'd bought for my mother at the bottom of my case.

4 Transformations

Complete the second sentence so that it has a similar meaning to the first, using the word given. Do not change the word given. Use between two and five words.

1 It's advisable to take traveller's cheques when you go abroad. **should**
You .... traveller's cheques when you go abroad.

2 It isn't necessary to pack so many clothes. **need**
You .... so many clothes.

3 You played loud music on the plane, which was wrong. **have**
You .... loud music on the plane.

4 The law makes car drivers wear seat belts in town. **to**
Car drivers .... seat belts in town.

5 The guide says we're forbidden to walk on the grass. **not**
The guide says we .... on the grass.

6 It was wrong of the passenger to tell lies. **should**
The passenger .... the truth.

7 Booking in advance wasn't necessary. **need**
We .... in advance.

8 Travelling without a ticket was wrong. **bought**
You .... a ticket.

9 It wasn't necessary to take our passports, but we did. **have**
We .... our passports, but we did.

10 It was wrong of him to ride his bike without wearing his helmet. **ought**
He .... his helmet when riding his bike.

▶▶ **WB** p.96

Vocabulary building

1 ⟲ Choosing the right word

Underline the correct word in each pair. Then ask and answer the questions with a partner.

1 Do your parents ever go away on business *trips/voyages*?
2 Are you going *in/on* a trip with your school this year?
3 How often have you travelled *by/with* plane?
4 Have you ever *missed/lost* a plane? Why?
5 When tourists visit your region, which airport do they land *at/on*?
6 Which *strange/foreign* countries would you like to visit?
7 Would you like to go *at/on* a cruise? Where?
8 Describe the most exciting *travel/journey* you have ever been on.

2 At the airport

What do you do at the start and the end of a plane journey? Read the instructions below and fill in the gaps with words from the box. Then put the instructions in the right order.

seat belt	hand luggage	arrivals lounge	get off
passport	departure lounge	lands	boarding card
takes off	passport control	check-in desk	

☐ a) Give the clerk your ticket (and your .... if you are going abroad) and check in your luggage.

☐ b) When you get on the plane, put your .... in the locker over your head.

☐ c) After the plane ...... , stay in your seat until the plane stops moving.

☐ d) When you .... the plane, go to the .... and wait while your luggage is unloaded.

☐ e) The clerk will give you a .... with your seat number on it.

☐ f) Then put your .... on and keep it on while the plane ....

[1] g) As soon as you arrive at the airport, go straight to the ....

☐ h) Then go through .... Wait in the .... until they announce that your flight is ready to depart.

3 Lexical cloze

▶▶ *strategies for the lexical cloze*

- Read the whole text for general understanding.
- Look at the words each side of the gap. Which option fits best?

Decide which answer A, B, C or D best fits each space. There is an example at the beginning (0).

0 A packed   **B** package   **C** company   **D** grouped

A DIFFERENT SORT OF HOLIDAY!

Have you ever been on a **(0)** *B.* holiday? Just in case you haven't, let me describe a typical holiday. First of all, you and your family look through dozens of holiday **(1)** .... . Eventually, you find the holiday of your dreams! You all rush down **(2)** .... your nearest travel **(3)** .... . You are so excited you can hardly wait to pay the deposit and **(4)** .... your holiday.

When the big day comes, you **(5)** .... your suitcases. You **(6)** .... off at dawn and **(7)** .... at the airport far too early because you're scared of **(8)** .... your plane. After long **(9)** .... at the airport, your flight is called and the plane takes **(10)** .... at last. You finally **(11)** .... your holiday resort after hours of travelling.

But the holiday is a disaster! You're staying **(12)** .... a foreign country but you don't speak the language so you can't **(13)** .... anything about the local people or their culture. Instead, you **(14)** .... the holiday with people exactly like yourself, and you all do exactly the same things, **(15)** .... exactly the same times.

Choose a 'COME ALIVE' adventure holiday this year and experience the difference!

	A	B	C	D
1	leaflets	programmes	propaganda	brochures
2	at	in	to	through
3	agent's	office	bureau	shop
4	hire	book	preserve	rent
5	make	pack	stuff	load
6	put	get	make	set
7	get	go	reach	arrive
8	losing	catching	missing	failing
9	times	stays	stops	delays
10	off	up	out	away
11	arrive	reach	travel	land
12	at	on	inside	in
13	make out	find out	bring out	get out
14	spend	use	occupy	last
15	at	in	on	with

▶▶ **WB** p.98

Listening: *test your skills* ▶ *Part 3*

▶▶ *listening strategies*

Part 3 of the **Listening paper**, multiple matching, tests your ability to understand the main point each speaker makes. Use these strategies:

▶▶ *identifying the main points* Unit 3 p.28

▶▶ *predicting what you will hear* Unit 7 p.62

▶▶ *making use of the second listening* Unit 13 p.114

1 **Understand the task**

Read the instructions for the task.

What topic will the speakers talk about?

2 **Predict**

Read the statements A–F.

What do you think each speaker might say? Think of phrases that each speaker could use.

3 🔲 **Listening task**

1 Listen to the recording and do the task.

▶▶ *tip!*

Remember some speakers may mention the same topics, but the main point they are making is different.

2 Listen again and check your answers.

4 💬 **Over to you**

1 You heard about several different kinds of holiday in the recording. Which one would <u>you</u> enjoy most?

2 What makes a good holiday for you?

3 What was <u>your</u> most memorable holiday. Why was it memorable?

Listening task

You will hear five young people talking about holidays they will never forget. For questions 1–5, choose from the list A–F what each speaker says about his or her holiday. Use the letters only once. There is one extra letter which you do not need to use.

A I made a new friend.

B I travelled on my own.

C I met some old friends.

D I did various social activities.

E I had to face an unexpected problem.

F I did something to help others.

Speaker 1 [**1**]

Speaker 2 [**2**]

Speaker 3 [**3**]

Speaker 4 [**4**]

Speaker 5 [**5**]

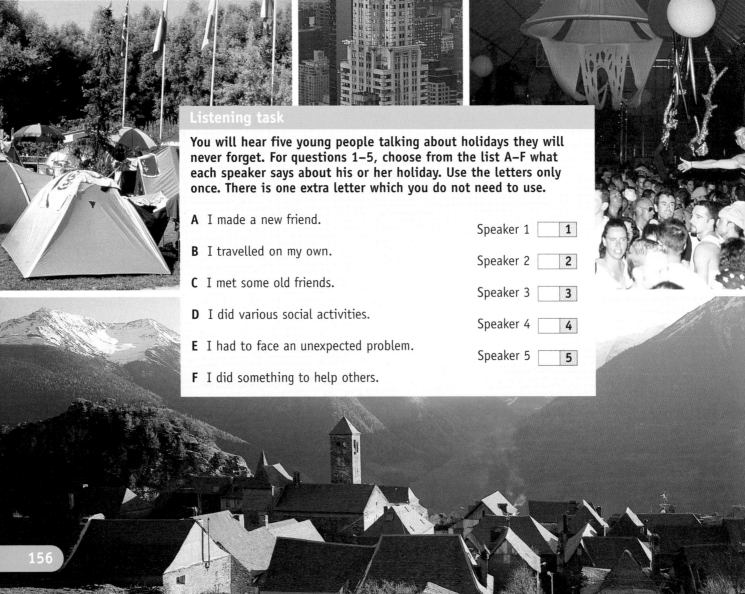

Writing: *test your skills*
▶ *Part 2*

1 Sample writing task
Read the task.

1 Who is going to read your article?
2 Should your style be a) informal?
 b) neutral? c) very formal?

Writing task

An international students' magazine is running a travel-writing competition. Write an article, describing the most interesting place you have ever visited and explaining why readers should go there. The prize is a two-week holiday in the USA.

Write your article in 120–180 words.

Article A

AN INTERESTING PLACE TO VISIT

Last year my family decided to go to France for a trip. The most interesting place we have been to was Paris.

Paris is the capitol of France and it is very big and crowded. There are many interesting places there and we made the most of our time sightseeing. We visited the Louvre and saw the famous painting of Mona Lisa. Then we went to the palace of Versailles. After that we went to Disneyland. We spent the whole day there and had a lot of fun. I was very exciting.

We went shopping as well. Many shops sell famous designer clothes, but there prices are very expensive. There is also a nice market next to the river Seine. You can find many different things in this market.

In my opinion, Paris is very intresting for everyone. I would recomend it for a good family holiday.

2 Compare two sample answers

Look at the list of features which a good article should have. Then read the two articles. Tick the features that each article has. Which article is better?

A good article:	Article A	Article B
1 has an interesting title.		✓
2 is organised into three or four paragraphs.		
3 addresses the reader directly.		
4 may use questions to involve the reader.		
5 uses a range of vivid and imaginative vocabulary.		

Article B

The Magic of Kenya

Close your eyes and imagine you are in a different world. In front of you, there are open plains, wide sky, and jungle. There are large herds of animals like zebra, elephant and wildebeest. Can you guess where you are? You're in Africa, of course, the most fabulous place on earth!

What makes Africa a such special place? It's the countryside and the fabulous wildlife, of course. Just imagine how it feels to go on safari and to see lions, leopards and cheetahs really close to you!

Have you heard of the Masai Mara? It's a huge nature reserve in Kenya. The only people who live there are a tribe called the Masai. They are amazing – they wear long cloaks and lots of jewels and decorations. They live on the land and keep sheep and goats. You can visit a Masai village and learn all about their traditions and how they live. I promise you won't feel dissapointed.

Kenya is a fascinating place. If you want adventure and excitement, you couldn't find anywhere better. I really recommend it!

3 What does the examiner want?

1 Read these comments by the examiner about one of the articles on p.157. Which article do they refer to?

CONTENT: has answered the question.

ACCURACY: several basic grammar and spelling mistakes; some words used wrongly.

RANGE: rather simple vocabulary and grammatical structures.

ORGANISATION: paragraphs not well developed.

READER: would probably not find the description very interesting.

2 Find and correct the following mistakes in the article:

- one tense mistake
- one word used wrongly
- four spelling mistakes

3 Where could you add extra details to make the article more interesting?

Over to you

4 Writing task

1 Read the task. Underline the important points you have to write about.
2 Who is going to read the article?
3 What style should you use?

Writing task

Your school magazine is looking for articles. Write an article describing the most exciting day you have ever spent on holiday outside your country and what you did that made the day so special.

The best article will win a holiday of your choice.

Write your article in 120–180 words.

5 ○ Brainstorm ideas

Answer these questions and note down your ideas. You can use your imagination!

1 Which country were you in? Who were you with? Where were you staying?
2 What happened on this exciting day? List all the things you did that made it so exciting.
3 How did you feel at the time? How do you feel now when you remember everything that happened?

Example:

- *was on 3-day camping holiday with youth club in Germany*
- *spent one day at an adventure centre*
- *went white-water rafting in the morning – fell out twice!*
- *went rock-climbing in afternoon*
- *finished off by bungee-jumping from high bridge – really scary but great!*

6 Plan your article

Choose the best ideas from your notes in Exercise 5 and make a plan like this one.

Para. 1 (Introduction)
Topic: Where I was/why/who I was with.

Useful phrases: Have you ever …? What's the most exciting way you can imagine to spend a day abroad?

Para. 2
Topic: How I spent the morning. Why it was exciting.
Topic sentence: ....
Details: ....

Useful phrases: Just close your eyes and imagine …

Para. 3
Topic: How I spent the second half of the day. How I felt.
Topic sentence: ....
Details: ....

Useful phrases: Can you imagine what happened that afternoon?

Final para. (Conclusion)
Topic: How I felt at the end of that day. Why I still think it was such an exciting time.

7 Write

Write your article.

8 Check your work

Look at the list of features in Exercise 2 on p.157. How many does your article have?

▶▶ **WB** p.99

19 The age of TV

Speaking: *test your skills ▶ Parts 3 and 4*

1 About you

1 How much TV do you watch every week?
2 Who decides what to watch in your house?
3 Look at the types of programme in the box. Which ones do you watch most often? Why?

soap opera	documentary	wildlife programme
comedy show	historical drama	quiz show
science fiction	news and weather	game show
drama series	chat show	film	cartoons
medical drama	music video	sport	adventure

2 Listen

▶▶ *speaking strategies*

In **Part 3** of the **Speaking test**:
- <u>do</u> listen carefully to the instructions for the task.
- <u>do</u> make sure you take an equal part in the discussion.

1 Listen to two exam candidates doing a Part 3 task.

1 What task does the examiner give them?
2 One candidate doesn't understand the task at first. What does she say?
3 Below are some things you should do in a Part 3 task. Which ones do the candidates do? Tick them.

a) express your own opinions
b) ask your partner for his/her opinions
c) react to your partner's ideas
d) say if you agree or disagree with your partner
e) try to come to a conclusion together

2 Listen again. What expressions did the speakers use for a)–e) above?

3 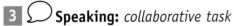 Speaking: *collaborative task*

1 Work together to do the task in Exercise 2. Talk about the programmes in Exercise 1.

⏱ Approximately 3 minutes

2 Tell the rest of the class what you have decided.

4 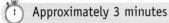 Discussion

1 What are the points for and against having a TV in your bedroom?
2 How much time do you spend talking with friends about the programmes you watch?
3 Do you think TV is becoming more or less important to people your age?

▶▶ **WB** p.100

Reading: *test your skills* ▶ *Part 3*

▶▶ *reading strategies*

Part 3 of the **Reading paper** tests your ability to understand how the different parts of a text are connected. For this task, you need to be able to recognise grammatical and lexical links between sentences and paragraphs. Use these strategies:

▶▶ *understanding a sequence of events* Unit 3 p.24

▶▶ *grammatical reference links* Unit 3 p.25

▶▶ *related words* Unit 7 p.58

▶▶ *linking expressions* Unit 11 p.92

▶▶ *predicting what comes next* Unit 15 p.126

1 Understand the task / predict

Read the instructions for the task and the title of the text.

1 What are you going to read about?

2 What do you have to do?

3 How would you answer the question in the title? What answers do you think the text will give?

2 Read the text

Read the text once all the way through, ignoring the gaps for the moment. Check your understanding of the main points.

Paragraph:

0 How did soap operas begin?

1 Is everyone in favour of soap operas?

2 What is the main reason for their popularity?

3 How seriously do the viewers take soaps?

4 Why are soaps easy to follow from episode to episode?

5 What makes viewers look forward to the next episode of a soap?

6 What do viewers discuss between episodes?

3 Gapped text

Read the text again, looking carefully at each gap, and do the reading task.

▶▶ *tip!*

Read the sentence(s) before and after the gap to help you decide what information is missing. ◀◀

You are going to read a magazine article about soap operas. Seven sentences have been removed from the article. Choose from the sentences A–H the one which fits each gap 1–6. There is one extra sentence which you do not need to use. There is an example at the beginning (0).

Why are we addicted to soaps?

Merris Griffiths explains.

Soap opera is the most popular form of television programming in the world today. But the very first soaps were broadcast on US daytime radio back in the 1930s and 40s and were aimed mainly at housewives. Where did the name *soap opera* come from? **0 H**
Opera refers to the fact that soap operas are often 'larger than life' and full of sensational events, just like Italian opera. As television became more and more popular, it wasn't long before soap operas became established on the small screen as well.

Over the years, there have been endless arguments about the value of soaps. **1** Others believe they are the only programmes that tell the truth and show society as it really is. Whatever the critics say, the fact remains that millions of people tune in eagerly to their favourite serial every day. The soap opera has succeeded in capturing the imagination of the entire world.

Why are soaps so popular? The most important reason is that they are about the daily activities of ordinary people, and they usually centre around a small community or a large family. **2** It allows the scriptwriter to create a complicated plot, with five or six different storylines all running at the same time. The stories are usually based on problems within personal relationships and family life, so the viewers can easily identify with the feelings and opinions of the characters. They can see that the lives of the people on the screen are not so very different from their own.

3 They write letters to their favourites, giving them advice and offering their own opinions, and sometimes copy their styles of dress and behaviour. Events like births, weddings or deaths in soaps are always followed with great interest. If a favourite character is unfairly

40 treated, this usually provokes strong reactions. In one famous
soap, a woman was sent to prison, and viewers started a national
campaign to have her set free.

Soaps may also be popular because they offer easy,
undemanding entertainment. Viewers don't have to concentrate
45 very hard to follow the story. The same characters are seen every
day, and the stories move along quite slowly. If viewers are forced
to miss their favourite soap for a couple of weeks, there's no need
to worry. **4** ⬚ This is because the script constantly refers back
to past events, and because each storyline takes a long time to
50 develop.

Another important reason why soaps attract large audiences is
the use of a technique called the 'cliff-hanger' ending. This means
that each episode always ends at a critical point in the story. **5** ⬚
This technique almost guarantees that thousands of viewers will
55 tune in to the next episode to find out what happens next.

In between episodes, viewers can speculate with their friends
about the direction that the plot may take. **6** ⬚ Some viewers
say they enjoy gossiping about the soap as much as they enjoy
watching the actual programme. As well as trying to predict what
60 is going to happen, they like to analyse the behaviour and
motives of the characters, and make comparisons with their own
lives.

According to their fans, soaps are good for you. They are good
entertainment, but they also provide 'food for thought', allowing
65 viewers to think about a range of issues and problems of everyday
life and relationships.

A Some viewers even start to think of the TV characters as real
friends and family.

B A dramatic incident such as an argument is deliberately cut short
by the closing title sequence.

C For some critics, they are no more than mindless entertainment.

D They only need to watch one or two episodes to catch up again.

E However, soap operas are much more dramatic than real life.

F This focus on local and domestic events is very important.

G The only way to find out if they are right or wrong is by
watching the next episode.

H The word *soap* was used because soap powder manufacturers
advertised their products on these programmes.

4 Vocabulary

▶▶ *guessing meaning from context* Unit 1 p.9

**1 Look through the text again.
Are there any words you don't
know? Try to work out the
meaning using context clues.**

2 💬 **Compare your words with a
partner. Then check in your
dictionary if you're still not sure.**

5 💬 Over to you

1 What are the most popular soaps
in your country?

2 Do you know the names of the
characters in a) one soap b) two
soaps c) more than two d) none
at all?

3 Do you and your friends ever
discuss what the characters
should do?

Grammar: *-ing forms and infinitives (2)* ▶ *p.184*

grammar file 10

A -*ing* forms
- **as the subject of a sentence:**
1 ***Watching*** too much TV is bad for you.
- **after certain nouns and phrases:**
2 **It's a waste of time** borrowing that video.
3 It's **no good** switching on the TV; it's not working.

B verb + *to*-infinitive after certain adjectives and nouns:
4 It was a real **surprise to hear** the news.
5 It's **bad** (for you) **to watch** too much TV.
6 It was **silly** (of me / you / him) **to lose** the tickets for the concert.

! What's wrong?
1 *It's no use to go to see that film.* X
2 *To act in a soap opera it must be great fun.* X
3 *It's impossible getting tickets for that TV show.* X

1 *-ing* form or *to*-infinitive?

Combine the sentences, beginning with the words given.

1 My friend bought me a ticket. It was kind of him.

It was kind *of my friend to buy me a ticket.*

2 We queued for seats. It was a waste of time.

It was a waste of time ....

3 I saw Keanu Reeves in the café. I was amazed.

I was amazed ....

4 After the show, we went backstage and met the cast. It was great fun.

It was great fun ....

5 My sister lost the video we bought. It was careless of her.

It was careless ....

2 Find the mistakes

Two of the sentences below are correct. Tick them. Correct the mistakes in the other sentences.

1 To go to the cinema is really expensive these days.
2 It was really silly of you missing your favourite programme.
3 Seeing the actors film that scene was an amazing experience.
4 I was surprised hearing that my favourite actor had got married.
5 It's not worth to waste money on that CD.
6 I can't help screaming when I watch really scary horror films.

3 💬 Questions

Put the verbs in brackets into the correct form. Then ask and answer the questions with a partner

1 Is .... (go) to the cinema your favourite activity? If not, what is?
2 It's a waste of time .... (go) to the cinema when you have a TV at home. Do you agree?
3 Would it be hard for you .... (give up) watching TV? Why?
4 Have you got a video machine at home? Is it difficult .... (operate)?
5 Is it easy or difficult .... (persuade) your family to watch the TV programmes you want to watch?
6 Would you be sad .... (hear) your favourite TV soap opera was going to end?

4 Open cloze

▶▶ *strategies for the open cloze* Unit 17 p.147

1 Read the text and think of the word that best fits each space. Use only one word in each space. There is an example at the beginning (0).

A VISIT TO A TV STUDIO

Last week I went **(0)**...*on*... a trip with my drama class. We went to a TV studio to find **(1)** .... how TV shows **(2)** .... made. I was amazed **(3)** .... hear that they were filming **(4)** .... latest episode of *Coronation Street*, **(5)** .... is my favourite soap opera!

When we got to the studio, the producer took us backstage and let **(6)** .... talk to the cast. I was surprised **(7)** .... discover how friendly the actors were. **(8)** .... was great fun talking to them and discovering what life as a TV star **(9)** .... really like. After a while, we took **(10)** .... seats and the filming started. I was surprised **(11)** .... discover how hard the actors worked. The show goes out four times **(12)** .... week and it's amazing **(13)** .... think how little time there is to rehearse. It can't be easy **(14)** .... any actor to learn a scene in such a short time – but they do it! The cast carried on filming until midnight but it wasn't possible for us to stay **(15)** .... long. We crept out of the studio, really impressed by what we had seen.

2 What types of words were tested?

▶▶ **WB** p.101

Vocabulary building

1  Word sets: *film quiz*

1 Work in groups to answer these questions. Which group finished first?

1 What do we call all the actors in a film – the *cast* or the *crew*?

2 Which famous film *character* is a British spy and likes Martini, beautiful women and fast cars?

3 In films and plays, is the *villain* a good or a bad guy?

4 Who is the *hero* of the *Star Wars* films?

5 In one sentence, what is the *plot* of the film *Titanic*?

6 Which American producer made *cartoons* like *Pinocchio*, *Bambi*, and *Snow White and the Seven Dwarfs*?

7 Why does an actor need a *script*?

8 Are *science-fiction* films usually set in the present, past or future?

2 Now ask and answer these questions.

1 Who's your favourite film star? Does he/she usually play heroes or villains?

2 What's your favourite film? What's it about? Describe the plot.

2 Prepositions

Fill in the gaps with the correct preposition: *in*, *on* or *for*. Underline the prepositional phrases. Then ask and answer the questions with a partner.

1 What do you do if there's nothing ..... TV?

2 How much TV do you watch every week, ... average?

3 Which films do you know that are set ..... the future?

4 Do you know which sort of films Steven Spielberg is famous ..... directing?

5 When you go to the cinema, do you book seats ..... advance?

6 Can you name a film that is based ..... a novel?

3 Word formation: *find the mistakes*

1 Read the answers which one student wrote in this exercise. Three answers are wrong. Correct them and say why they are wrong.

1 Watching TV is good family *...entertaining...* . ENTERTAIN

2 The film wasn't supposed to be a comedy but I found it very *...amusing...* . AMUSE

3 Soap operas have become *...amazing...* popular these days. AMAZE

4 TV is a cheap and really *...enjoying...* way of relaxing. ENJOY

5 Nobody could deny the increasing *...popularity...* of soap operas. POPULAR

2 In sentences 6–10, the form of the word is correct, but the spelling is wrong. Correct the mistakes.

6 I like really *...scarey...* horror films. SCARE

7 The plot of the film was *...unbelievible...* . BELIEVE

8 I watch adventure films whenever I get the *...oportunity...* . OPPORTUNE

9 The film I saw last night was *...extremly...* funny. EXTREME

10 The producer has to accept *responsability* if a film is a box office disaster. RESPONSIBLE

4 Word-formation task

▶▶ *strategies for word formation*

• Read the whole text first.

• For each gap, decide what kind of word you need (noun, adjective, etc.).

• Check your spelling when you have finished.

Read the text below. Use the word given in capitals underneath the text to form a word that fits in the space in the text. There is an example at the beginning (0).

TV VIEWING HABITS

British TV **(0)** *viewers* have noticed a lot of changes over recent years. In the past, there was a wide **(1)** .... of programmes on TV. There were **(2)** .... documentaries and serious news stories, as well as films and plays. But there are fewer **(3)** .... programmes on TV these days. Look at the TV guide – you will have **(4)** .... finding anything to watch that isn't a quiz show or a soap opera! Some people are **(5)** .... annoyed at these changes. They say that today's viewers seem more interested in **(6)** .... characters than in real people. Incredibly, some people find it **(7)** .... to distinguish between soap opera and real life! But TV producers refuse to listen to all this **(8)** .... They complain that viewers get **(9)** .... very easily these days. And if viewers are **(10)** .... to concentrate on serious programmes, what is the point of putting them on?

0 VIEW	**4** DIFFICULT	**8** CRITIC
1 VARY	**5** EXTREME	**9** BORE
2 INTEREST	**6** FICTION	**10** ABLE
3 CULTURE	**7** POSSIBLE	

▶▶ **WB** p.102

Listening: *test your skills* ▶ *Part 2*

▶▶ *listening strategies*

Part 2 of the **Listening paper** tests your ability to understand specific information. Use these strategies:

▶▶ *predicting the information you need* Unit 8 p.70
▶▶ *listening for parallel ideas* Unit 9 p.80
▶▶ *dealing with unknown words* Unit 12 p.104

1 Understand the task

Read the instructions for the Listening task.

1 What are you going to hear?

2 How many sentences do you have to complete?

3 Will you hear exactly the same sentences on the recording?

4 Will you hear the words which go in the gaps on the recording?

5 What is the maximum number of words you should write in each gap?

2 Predict

Read the statements 1–10 carefully. What kind of information do you need to listen for to fill in the gaps? For example:

Question:

1 another name for *special effects*

2 a date

4 the name of a film

7 a length of time

3 🎞 Listening task

1 Listen to the recording and do the task. Remember, the sentences in the Listening task summarise the main points of the recording, so you won't hear exactly the same words.

▶▶ *tip!*

While you listen the first time, fill in as many gaps as you can, but don't stop if you miss a gap. You can fill it in the second time you listen. ◀◀

2 Check and complete your answers the second time you listen.

4 💬 Over to you

1 What is your favourite special effects film? Why?

2 Think of advertisements you like on TV. Do any of them use special effects?

Listening task

You will hear a radio interview with a man who has written a book about the use of special effects in films. For questions 1–10, complete the sentences.

In the early days of the cinema, what we now call *special effects* were known as [___ **1**]

Special effects were first used on film by a French magician in the year [___ **2**]

Nowadays, film makers can make buildings and even [___ **3**] seem to disappear on film.

The film called [___ **4**] was very influential for its use of special effects.

With digital technology, it is easy to move both [___ and ___ **5**] in a film.

Artists who work in computer graphics often need to study the [___ **6**] of animals in detail.

The model of The White House used in the film *Independence Day* took a total of [___ **7**] to build.

Specialist technicians are responsible for certain effects, such as [___ **8**]

At present, the most difficult job for special-effects artists is to produce synthetic [___ **9**]

Nowadays, special-effects artists must have both technical knowledge and [___ **10**]

Writing: *test your skills* ▶ *Part 2*

1 Sample writing task

Read the task.

1 Who is going to read your composition?
2 Do you have to a) write in favour of the statement b) write against the statement c) consider arguments for <u>and</u> against?

Writing task

You have just been reading an article in class about the quality of television programmes. Your teacher would like you to write a composition, giving your opinion on the statement:

Most TV programmes are not worth watching.

Write your composition in 120–180 words.

2 Compare two sample answers

Look at the list of features which a good discussion composition should contain. Then, read the two compositions. Tick the features that each composition contains. Which composition is better?

A good composition:	Composition A	Composition B
1 is well argued and easy to follow.		✓
2 is organised into 3–4 clear paragraphs.		
3 has a well-developed introduction and conclusion (more than one sentence).		
4 supports the main arguments with details and examples.		
5 uses linking expressions to connect sentences and paragraphs.		
6 summarises the writer's opinion in the conclusion.		

Composition A

I do not agree with this opinion.

Some shows are not very good, it is true. But TV is a good way to learn about the world, and you can see many films and other shows. One of my favourite programmes it is a natur documentary called 'Wild Earth'. The photography is very good and I can to see things that I would never be able to see by myself, I like sports programmes too.

On the other hand, there are too much old films on TV. And I do not think the comedy shows are very good. They are too boreing.

In my opinion, some TV programmes are good, but some are very bad.

Composition B

We have more than 10 channels in our country. However, only a few programmes are really good. Most of the others are definitely not worth watching.

One big problem is that a lot of programmes are repeated many times. For example, the same films are shown a dozen times in one year, and most of them are very old. Soap operas and other shows are also repeated, so it is very boring.

Another problem is that many programmes are really bad. For example, there are many game shows, where contestants have to answer silly questions to win a fantastic prize. These shows are awful but we get them several times per week. Then there are the chat shows where ordinary people discuss their problems. These are the worst! The people usually end up fighting with each other in public and it is really embarrassing.

As far as I'm concerned, owning a TV is a waste of time because of the bad standard of programmes. It is better to watch videos or go to the cinema. That way you see things you really want to see.

3 What does the examiner want?

1 Read these comments by the examiner about one of the compositions on p.165. Which composition do they refer to?

CONTENT: weak attempt to answer the task set.

ACCURACY: some basic grammar, punctuation and spelling mistakes.

RANGE: limited range of structure and vocabulary.

ORGANISATION: some paragraphs are too short/not well developed.

READER: would not have enough information.

---

2 There are grammar, spelling and punctuation mistakes in the composition. Find and correct them.

3 Improve the organisation

Which paragraph needs a topic sentence and more supporting details?

Over to you

4 Writing task

Read the task.

1 What topic do you have to write about?
2 Who is going to read the composition?
3 What style should you use, neutral/formal or informal?

Writing task

You have had a discussion in class about the following statement:

Television has a bad effect on family life.

Your teacher would like you to write a composition, giving your own views on the statement.

Write your composition in 120–180 words.

---

5 ◯ Brainstorm ideas

Look at these statements. Do you agree or disagree with them? What other statements could you make about TV and family life?

1 Families don't talk when the TV is on.
2 Children who have a TV in their rooms don't have enough contact with their family.
3 It's good for families to relax together in front of the TV after a busy day.
4 Families can find out interesting things from the TV and talk about what they see.

6 Plan your composition

1 Think again about the statement in the exam task. Decide if you want to:

a) agree b) disagree c) look at both sides of the question.

2 Now make a plan. Choose from Plan A or Plan B:

A

Para. 1 (Introduction)
State the problem and give my opinion, in brief.
Useful phrases: People often argue that ... , and/but I completely agree/disagree. I think ...

Para. 2 My first argument(s)
Useful phrases: In the first place, ... It seems to me that ...

Paras. 3/4 My next arguments
Useful phrases: Another point to consider is ...

Final para. (Conclusion)
Summary of my opinion and why I hold it. Closing remarks.
Useful phrases: To sum up, I believe that ... . This is because ...

B

Para. 1 (Introduction)
State the problem and say that there are two sides to the argument
Useful phrases: Some people believe that ... , but others disagree. Let us look at both sides of the question.

Para. 2 Why TV may sometimes have a bad effect on the family.
Useful phrases: On the one hand, ...

Para. 3 Why TV may sometimes have a good effect on family life.
Useful phrases: However, there is another side to the question.

Final para. (Conclusion)
Summary of what I think and why. Closing remarks.

7 Write

Write your composition.

8 Check your work

Look at the list of features in Exercise 2 on p.165. How many does your composition have?

▶▶ WB p.104

20 Testing, testing

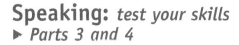

Speaking: *test your skills*
▶ *Parts 3 and 4*

1 Vocabulary

Look at the photos, which show different school subjects.

1 Which of the subjects in the box are illustrated?

2 Are there any subjects in the box which you don't study at your school? Can you add any more?

Sports / Physical Education   Information Technology
Religious Studies   Biology   Chemistry   Physics
Music   Art   Psychology   History   Drama
Modern Languages   Design Technology   Geography
Environmental Studies   Maths   Business Studies

2 💬 Speaking: *collaborative task*

1 Imagine that you have the chance to plan the curriculum for a new school. Talk together and decide which subjects in Exercise 1 to include. Then decide which <u>three</u> should be compulsory.

⏱ Approximately 3 minutes

2 Compare your choices with the class.

3 📼 Listen

▶▶ *speaking strategies*

In **Part 4** of the **Speaking test**, the examiner asks you some questions which develop your discussion in Part 3.

<u>Do</u> express your own opinions <u>and</u> react to the other candidate's opinions.

1 Here are some questions which the examiner might ask after the task in Exercise 2.

1 Do school subjects prepare you for a job when you leave school?

2 Do you think students today have too much homework?

3 What is more important – getting good marks, or learning something interesting?

4 Should boys and girls be educated in different schools?

5 Should students wear uniforms to school?

2 Listen to the examiner and two exam candidates doing Part 4.

1 Which questions does the examiner ask?

2 Below are some things you should do in Part 4. Which ones do the candidates do? Tick them.
   a) give your opinions
   b) justify your opinions with reasons
   c) find out what your partner thinks
   d) react to your partner's ideas
   e) agree or disagree with your partner

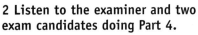

3 Listen again. What expressions did the speakers use for a)–e) above?

4 💬 Speaking task: *discussion*

1 In groups of three, choose two or three of the questions in Exercise 3.1 and discuss them. One student should be the examiner and ask the questions.

⏱ Approximately 4 minutes

2 Compare your ideas with the rest of the class.

▶▶ WB p.105

Reading: *test your skills ▶ Part 4*

▶▶ *reading strategies*

Part 4 of the **Reading paper** tests your ability to scan several texts for specific information. Use these strategies:

▶▶ *scanning for specific information* Unit 4 p.32

▶▶ *scanning for parallel expressions* Unit 8 p.66

▶▶ *predicting where to find information* Unit 12 p.100

1 Understand the task / predict

Read the instructions for the task, the title and the sub-heading of the text.

1 What is the article about?

2 What do you think the six students will suggest?

2 Multiple-matching task

1 Read questions 1–14. For each question, underline the key words. Decide which section probably has the answer. Then scan the texts, using the underlined words to help you find parallel expressions.

Example:

Find the expression in text E that matches the key words in the example, (0).

2 Read that part of the text more carefully to check your answer is correct. Here are some clues:

9 Which two texts mention *coffee*? Which text contains the correct answer?

12/13 Which three texts mention *the night before*? Which **two** are the correct answers?

▶▶ *tip!*

If you don't know a word you need, use a guessing strategy that you have learnt. If you don't need the word to answer a question, just ignore it!

You are going to read a magazine article in which six students say how they cope with exams. For questions 1–14, choose from the people A–F. The people may be chosen more than once. When more than one answer is required, these may be given in any order. There is an example at the beginning (0).

Which of the students

thinks you should keep a <u>sense of humour</u>? `0` `E`

discusses his/her worries with more experienced people? `1` `☐`

stops and thinks before answering a question in the exam? `2` `☐`

likes to be with people who have a positive attitude? `3` `☐`

takes short breaks while he/she is revising? `4` `☐`

thinks it is important to continue with a social life? `5` `☐` `6` `☐`

relaxes with music? `7` `☐`

has not always done as well as he/she could in exams? `8` `☐`

finds that coffee makes him/her feel more anxious? `9` `☐`

believes that lots of physical activity is good during exams? `10` `☐`

finds that other students in the exam room make him/her nervous? `11` `☐`

believes that a lot of studying the night before is not helpful? `12` `☐` `13` `☐`

thinks that the time for revision always seems too short? `14` `☐`

3 Vocabulary

▶▶ *guessing meaning from context* Unit 1 p.9

1 Look through the text again. Are there any words you don't know? Try to work out the meaning using context clues.

2 💬 **Compare your words with a partner. Then check in your dictionary if you're still not sure.**

4 💬 Over to you

1 Whose advice do you think is best?

2 Do you think students have to take too many exams?

3 Can you think of any other ways teachers could find out what students know?

▶▶ **WB** p.105

How to cope with exams

For many students, the run-up to important exams is a stressful time.
Six students explain how they cope.

A Kelly Marsden

Revising for exams can be really tiring, so I try to stay alert by drinking cups of coffee while I'm studying. But the most important thing for me is to make sure I sleep well
5 the night before an exam. I need at least eight hours a night to feel really awake the next day. Before I go to sleep, I put on a CD of my favourite singer, or read a book or magazine – nothing to do with the exam. It
10 really wouldn't help if I stayed up late studying because I would be too tired the next day to do my best.

B John Nott

For me the best way to stay on top of things during exams is not to worry too
15 much and to take time off from revision. Some people give up everything to spend their time studying, but I don't actually think this helps you to do any better. I still meet up with my friends while exams are
20 on. As well as that, I do a lot of exercise and I make sure I have a good work-out the night before an exam. I just know that my brain will function better if I feel in good shape.

C Alina Taylor

25 I tend to panic in exams, so I have learnt that the best way to cope is to watch the time carefully throughout the exam. I plan how much time I will need for each question, and keep an eye on the clock to
30 see how I am doing. I never tackle a question until I have thought about it, and made some rough notes on the answer. I try hard to ignore all those people around me who are writing really fast, as if they
35 were crazy! They really put me off. When I see them, I think, 'It's time I started writing too!' and that's when I start to panic.

D Richard Brook

I get very stressed about exams a long time before they happen, and I have
40 always wished I had more time to study. In the past, I have found that I got lower marks than I could have got because I spent time worrying, not studying. So now, I talk things over with my parents
45 and teachers. They often give very good advice, as they have been through it all before, and it helps to get all my anxieties into the open. I'd rather do this than waste a lot of valuable revision time
50 worrying about everything.

E Helena Davies

During exams, I avoid all those negative people who are completely stressed out and wish they had done more work. The night before an exam, I go out with my
55 friends – I don't believe in last-minute revision. We usually go for a walk, or go round to someone's house, order a pizza and watch a good video, preferably a comedy. It's important to laugh a lot, and
60 see the funny side of things when there is so much hard work to do the next day. When I go to bed, I simply glance through my notes one more time, and this helps me to feel ready for anything the next day!

F Bill Parson

65 I know that I can only concentrate for a limited time, so I stop every hour or so for 10 minutes during my revision sessions. Even if I was the world's greatest genius, I would start getting tired after an hour or
70 so. I may go for a walk around the block to clear my head, or just sit and think about something else to take my mind off the exams. After that, it's much easier to go back to my books. I think it's also
75 important to avoid drinking lots of strong coffee, because it tends to increase my anxiety, so I drink lots of fruit juice or mineral water.

Grammar: *modals (deductions)*
▶ *p.187*

grammar file 19

A Deductions about the present
- *must/can't/might/could* + bare infinitive
1 *That man* **must be** *the new sports teacher.* (my assumption)
2 *He* **can't** (NOT ~~mustn't~~) *be the new teacher.* (it's not possible)
3 *He* **may/might/could** (NOT ~~can~~) *be a journalist.* (perhaps he is, perhaps he isn't)
- **continuous form:** *must, etc. + be + -ing*
4 *He* **must/might be** *making a video of the school.* (at the moment)

B Deductions about the past
- *must/can't/might/could* + have + past participle
5 *The boy looks upset. He* **must have had** *some bad news.*
6 *He* **can't/couldn't have passed** *his exams.*
7 *He* **may/might have lost** *something important.*
- **continuous form:** *must, etc. + have been + -ing*
8 *The headmaster* **might have been telling** *him off!*

! What's wrong?

1 *Bob came first in the exam! He can have cheated!* X
2 *Stella's been here with me. You mustn't have seen her in the shop.* X

---

1 Deductions about the present
Fill in the gaps with a modal and a verb from the list in the correct form. Don't use the same verb twice.

win / ~~have~~ / concentrate / hate / be / pass

1 Tom's spent all evening revising. He .*must have*... an exam tomorrow.
2 Maria .... her exam if she works hard, but I'm not sure.
3 Peter's hands are shaking. He .... nervous.
4 Tessa .... very hard because she's got her stereo on really loud!
5 I can hear cheers. Our team ....!
6 Tim .... doing sport – he's always ill before sports lessons!

2 Present and past deductions
Underline the correct option.

1 **A:** Chris has a new computer!
  B: He must *get/have got* it for his birthday.
2 **A:** Where's Steve?
  B: I'm not sure. He *may/can* be in the park.
3 **A:** Conrad didn't hear what the examiner said.
  B: He couldn't have been *listening/listened*.
4 **A:** Celia seems very shy.
  B: She *mustn't/can't* be shy. She's in a rock group!
5 **A:** Why is Fiona late?
  B: She might *oversleep/have overslept*.
6 **A:** I saw Mike in the town centre last night.
  B: It *mightn't/couldn't* have been Mike – he was here.
7 **A:** Are you coming to the disco tonight?
  B: You *must/might* be joking! I've got to revise for the exams.

3 Transformations
Complete the second sentence so that it has a similar meaning to the first sentence, using the word given. Do not change the word given. Use between two and five words

1 I'm sure you are tired. **must**
  You .... tired.
2 Perhaps John is in the library. **gone**
  John .... the library.
3 I'm certain Mary isn't in Paris! **be**
  Mary .... Paris!
4 Maybe Peter went home early. **might**
  Peter .... home early.
5 I'm certain Sarah isn't telling the truth! **must**
  Sarah .... lies!
6 I don't think I got the answer right. **must**
  I .... a mistake in the answer.
7 Maybe Peter was waiting for us outside. **could**
  Peter .... for us outside.
8 It's possible that I failed the exam. **may**
  I .... passed the exam.
9 I'm certain Bob hasn't left because his bike is here. **have**
  Bob .... because his bike is here.
10 I'm sure my friend wanted to be in the school team. **must**
  My friend .... to be in the school team.

▶▶ **WB** p.106

Vocabulary building

1 Word formation

1 Complete the table. Use your dictionary to help you. How do you pronounce the words?

Subject	Person	Adjective
1 psychology	psychologist	psychological
2 chemistry	....	....
3 art	....	....
4 music	....	....
5 history	....	....
6 politics	....	....

2 Now fill in the gaps with a word from the box in the correct form. Don't use the same word twice.

1 John F Kennedy was a famous .... figure in the USA.

2 A guitar is a .... instrument.

3 Picasso is my favourite ....

4 If you mix various acids together, you get a .... reaction.

5 My History teacher is a well-known local ....

2 Phrasal verbs

Replace the words and phrases in *italics* with a phrasal verb from the box in the correct form. Then say if the sentences are true or false for you.

let sb. off	make up sth.	tell sb. off
work sth. out	rub sth. out	look sth. up

1 If I don't know the meaning of a word, I usually *find* it in the dictionary.

2 If I'm late for class, I always *invent* an excuse.

3 If I can't *calculate* the solution to a problem in my homework, I normally ask my parents for help.

4 The teacher sometimes has to *reprimand* me for not paying attention in class.

5 When I do a test, I write my answers in pencil first so I can *erase* them if I need to.

6 Our teacher always *lets us escape without punishment* if we forget to do our homework.

3 Lexical cloze

▶▶ *strategies for the lexical cloze* Unit 18 p.155

Read the text below and decide which answer A, B, C or D best fits each space. There is an example at the beginning (0).

0   **A** <u>pass</u>   **B** take   **C** make   **D** write

A DETERMINED STUDENT

It isn't always easy to **(0)** ..A.. an exam. But you should never **(1)** .... up trying! When Paula Morrison decided to learn to drive, she didn't **(2)** .... how difficult it would be.

She looked **(3)** .... the phone number of her nearest driving school and enrolled on a six-week **(4)** .... . She wanted to **(5)** .... her test in the summer. If she **(6)** .... in passing it, she would buy a car. Unfortunately, Paula was very bad **(7)** .... driving! The instructor was patient when she **(8)** .... mistakes. But he knew she had **(9)** .... chance of success. After a while, he tried to **(10)** .... her from learning to drive.

But Paula went on trying. Eventually, her husband **(11)** .... to give her lessons. It was a disaster! Paula couldn't **(12)** .... how to steer the car or how to reverse safely. When her husband said anything, she told him **(13)** .... for shouting at her. When the day of her test came, Paula still couldn't drive. She **(14)** .... the test, of course.

That was two years ago but Paula is **(15)** .... learning! She has taken the test 26 times since then. One day, she says, she will succeed!

1	**A** send	**B** pick	**C** give	**D** get
2	**A** recognise	**B** realise	**C** notice	**D** think
3	**A** through	**B** into	**C** up	**D** in
4	**A** course	**B** school	**C** degree	**D** diploma
5	**A** make	**B** take	**C** try	**D** attempt
6	**A** managed	**B** won	**C** achieved	**D** succeeded
7	**A** at	**B** in	**C** on	**D** with
8	**A** did	**B** got	**C** made	**D** gave
9	**A** a little	**B** little	**C** few	**D** a few
10	**A** persuade	**B** urge	**C** warn	**D** discourage
11	**A** agreed	**B** accepted	**C** forced	**D** allowed
12	**A** work up	**B** work over	**C** work through	**D** work out
13	**A** out	**B** down	**C** off	**D** by
14	**A** dropped	**B** failed	**C** lost	**D** mistook
15	**A** yet	**B** still	**C** also	**D** ever

▶▶ **WB** p.108

Listening: *test your skills* ▶ Part 4

▶▶ *listening strategies*

Part 4 of the **Listening paper** may test your ability to understand gist, main idea, detail, opinion and attitude. Use these strategies:

▶▶ *listening for a purpose* Unit 1 p.12

▶▶ *focusing on the information you need* Unit 14 p.122

1 Understand the task
Read the instructions for the task.

What are you going to hear?

2 Identify what to listen for
1 Read questions 1–7 and underline the key words. (Don't look at the options yet.) What do you need to listen for? For example:

Question:

1 the reason Sarah gives for going on an exchange

2 the greatest benefit Sarah got from the trip

2 Think about what Sarah might say.

3 🎞 Listening task
1 The first time you hear the recording, listen for the answers. Don't worry about the options.

2 Listen again and tick the best option.

4 💬 Over to you
Your teacher is planning to take your class to Britain to study for one month.

1 How do you feel about the idea of spending a month in Britain?

2 What can you do to prepare yourselves for it?

Listening task

You will hear an interview with Sarah Gooch, an English schoolgirl who spent six months studying abroad. For questions 1–7, choose the best answer A, B or C.

1 Why did Sarah decide to go on a student exchange trip to Spain?

  A She had friends in the country.

  B She wanted to speak the language well.   ☐ 1

  C She was interested in travelling.

2 For Sarah, the greatest benefit of the trip was

  A getting to know a different culture.

  B having the chance to meet new people.   ☐ 2

  C learning to be more independent.

3 Sarah says that her classmates in Spain were

  A keen to help her understand.

  B impressed by her performance.   ☐ 3

  C amused by her weak Spanish.

4 What does Sarah say about her exam results abroad?

  A She was disappointed by them.

  B She regrets not doing better.   ☐ 4

  C She doesn't see them as important.

5 What surprised Sarah most about Spain?

  A the quality of the food

  B the varied landscape   ☐ 5

  C the attitude of the people

6 Of the people she met in Spain, who does Sarah miss the most?

  A her teachers

  B her host family   ☐ 6

  C her school friends

7 Sarah feels that before students go to study in another country, they should

  A learn the country's language.

  B find out about the country's customs.   ☐ 7

  C study the country's geography.

Writing: *test your skills* ▶ *Paper 2*

exam file

In **Paper 2**, you have to do two pieces of writing.
You **must** answer the question in **Part 1**.

In **Part 2**, you are given four options and you must choose <u>one</u>. (One of the options is a question on a set book.)

The questions test your ability to write for a specific purpose and for a specific reader, using an appropriate format and style.

▶▶ *writing strategies: Part 1*

Part 1 tests your ability to understand the information provided, and to write a letter including the essential points in the information. Use the strategies you have learned in this course.

▶▶ *transactional letters* Units 6, 9, 16

Part 1

You **must** answer this question.

1 You recently entered a competition in an English language magazine. You have just received this letter from the organisers, and have made some notes on it. Read the letter and the notes you have made. Then, using all the information in your notes, write a suitable reply.

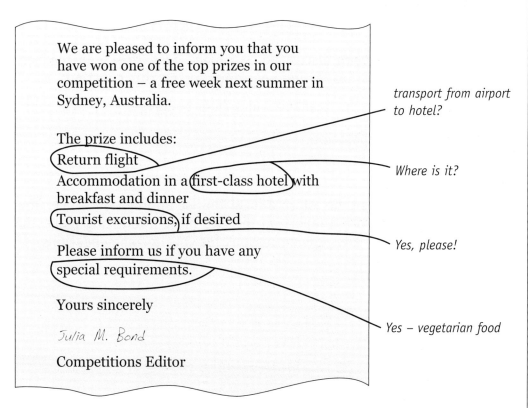

We are pleased to inform you that you have won one of the top prizes in our competition – a free week next summer in Sydney, Australia.

The prize includes:
Return flight — *transport from airport to hotel?*
Accommodation in a first-class hotel with breakfast and dinner — *Where is it?*
Tourist excursions, if desired — *Yes, please!*

Please inform us if you have any special requirements. — *Yes – vegetarian food*

Yours sincerely

Julia M. Bond

Competitions Editor

Write a **letter** of between **120 and 180** words in an appropriate style. Do not write any addresses.

▶▶ *writing strategies: Part 2*

Try to choose a task that you know something about. Use the strategies you have learned for each type of writing.

▶▶ *stories* Units 10, 13

▶▶ *compositions* Units 11, 15

▶▶ *reports* Units 7, 12

Part 2

Write an answer to **one** of the questions **2–4** in this part. Write your answer in **120–180** words in an appropriate style.

2 You have decided to enter a short story competition. The competition rules say that the story must **begin** or **end** with these words:

Harry ran to the telephone and dialled the number as fast as he could.

Write your **story**.

3 Your class has been discussing teenagers' lives. Now your teacher would like you to write a composition, giving your opinions on this question:

Is it a good idea for teenagers at school to have a part-time job?

Write your **composition**.

4 You have a part-time job in a local tourist information office. Your manager has asked you to write a report on the **two** most interesting places for foreign tourists to visit in your area, giving reasons for your recommendations.

Write your **report**.

▶▶ **WB** p.109

Progress test 5

1 Lexical cloze

For questions **1–15**, read the text below and decide which answer **A, B, C** or **D** best fits each space. There is an example at the beginning **(0)**.

Example:

0 A a   **B** the   **C** some   **D** any

THE FOURTH OF JULY

The fourth of July is **(0)** _B._ day when the American Declaration of Independence was signed in 1776. It was the time of colonies **(1)** ... empires, when soldiers were **(2)** ... wars all over the world. As a result of the wars, the British ended **(3)** ... with an enormous national debt because they had been **(4)** ... expensive. To pay off this debt, Britain **(5)** ... taxes in her 13 North American colonies to **(6)** ... levels than they had ever been before.

The people who were living in the colonies were **(7)** ... unhappy about this because they had to pay a lot of money to a parliament in Britain **(8)** ... they had no representatives. In 1774, all the colonies **(9)** ... delegates to the first North American Continental Congress and they **(10)** ... to start a revolutionary war against British rule in the Colonies. One **(11)** ... the delegates, Thomas Jefferson, **(12)** ... the Declaration of Independence and on 4th July 1776 nine of the 13 colonies **(13)** ... it. In Independence Hall in Philadelphia, the 'Liberty Bell' was rung to **(14)** ... the birth of the United States of America, and a new feeling of **(15)** ... began.

1 A and	**B** or	**C** either	**D** but
2 A having	**B** fighting	**C** doing	**D** making
3 A up	**B** in	**C** out	**D** by
4 A much	**B** far	**C** more	**D** so
5 A rose	**B** grew	**C** raised	**D** lifted
6 A taller	**B** bigger	**C** higher	**D** larger
7 A too	**B** very	**C** such	**D** enough
8 A where	**B** that	**C** which	**D** who
9 A made	**B** had	**C** delivered	**D** sent
10 A resulted	**B** offered	**C** thought	**D** decided
11 A for	**B** by	**C** of	**D** from
12 A wrote	**B** did	**C** said	**D** spoke
13 A praised	**B** approved	**C** thanked	**D** congratulated
14 A celebrate	**B** illustrate	**C** decorate	**D** wish
15 A satisfaction	**B** pleasure	**C** chance	**D** optimism

2 Open cloze

For questions **16–30**, read the text below and think of the word which best fits each space. Use only one word in each space. There is an example at the beginning **(0)**.

TV FACTS

John Logie Baird is famous for inventing the television, **(0)** _but_ in fact he was not the inventor. He followed a design produced by **(16)** .... engineer, Paul Nipkow. However, Baird **(17)** .... the first person to make Nipkow's ideas work, and he managed **(18)** .... produce the first television picture as long **(19)** .... as 1932.

If you **(20)** .... able to slow down your television set, you could see the way **(21)** .... makes a picture on the screen. Your television screen is made up **(22)** .... about 600 separate horizontal lines. A small beam moves down and across the screen **(23)** .... the same time. This beam is made up of billions of tiny particles called electrons. The TV screen **(24)** .... covered in a material that is sensitive to them. When the electrons hit the screen, **(25)** .... make it light up. Our brains put all the glowing parts of the screen together **(26)** .... we see a complete picture.

Television signals move **(27)** .... space all the time. They take **(28)** .... years to reach other solar systems. Live pictures of the football World Cup in 1990 will soon **(29)** .... reaching Sirius, a star more **(30)** .... eight billion kilometres away.

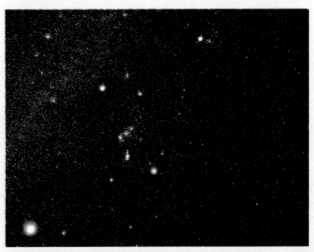

At lower left is the star Sirius, the brightest star in the sky.

3 Key word transformations

For questions **31–40**, complete the second sentence so that it has a similar meaning to the first sentence, using the word given. **Do not change the word given.** You must use between two and five words, including the word given. There is an example at the beginning (0).

Example:

0 You mustn't spend so much money.
stop

You must ...*stop spending*... so much money.

31 The festival was so successful that they decided to organise another one.
such

The festival was .... that they decided to organise another one.

32 The new dress wasn't big enough for her. **too**

The new dress .... for her.

33 Eating and drinking is not allowed in the classroom. **must**

Students .... in the classroom.

34 He is such a good runner that he's going to enter a competition. **so**

He .... that he's going to enter a competition

35 We'd be very happy if you stayed with us for a few days. **up**

We'd be very happy to .... for a few days.

36 It was wrong to do what you did.
should

You .... what you did.

37 You ought to go to the doctor about your cold. **had**

You .... go to the doctor about your cold.

38 I was surprised when I saw my exam results. **see**

It was a .... my exam results.

39 You can't see the island from here.
possible

It's .... the island from here.

40 It's not necessary to wear fancy dress if you don't want to. **have**

You .... fancy dress if you don't want to.

4 Error correction

For questions **41–55**, read the text below and look carefully at each line. Some of the lines are correct, and some have a word which should not be there. If a line is correct, put a tick (✓) next to it. If a line has a word which should not be there, underline the word. There are two examples at the beginning (**0** and **00**).

EXAM SURVIVAL GUIDE

0 The exam season comes round every year. Students start revising ✓
00 and <u>are</u> begin the countdown to the first day of the exams. Good exam
41 grades will be open doors to more jobs and education opportunities,
42 and in time for to higher earnings. Many parents find exams so worrying
43 that it affects their children, but being well-organised and planning ahead
44 these are the keys to success in those last few weeks before the exams
45 they begin. Parents need to provide a quiet space for their children to
46 study in, and this should not be where the TV can to disturb them.
47 Having a revision timetable of work, and checklists of areas have to be
48 revised, will certainly help children to cope with the workload. If so
49 children need to revise facts, such as for the history, they should use
50 cards for writing down notes. They must not try to do too much. The
51 timetable should also include time for relaxing – as watching TV or
52 having a game of tennis, for example. It is also very important to go
53 to bed at a reasonable time in the night before an exam. Having a
54 proper breakfast before setting off for a school is absolutely essential.
55 A full stomach which will help students to concentrate better in the exam.

5 Word formation

For questions **56–65**, read the text below. Use the word given in capitals underneath the text to form a word that fits in the space in the text. There is an example at the beginning (0).

DESIGNER UNIFORMS

The **(0)** *designer* Sir Paul Smith has designed the new uniform for a school in Nottingham. In front of his jealous classmates, the now **(56)** .... Adam Grice, aged 15, modelled the **(57)** .... uniform, which is based on the students' own demands. When these **(58)** .... students were asked what they wanted, they said that a simple design would be the most **(59)** .... The new uniforms include a **(60)** .... short-sleeved shirt with a modern square hem for the boys, and an **(61)** .... designed open-necked shirt for the girls. The school's logo is **(62)** .... situated on the collar of the girls' shirts and on the pocket of the boys'. The **(63)** .... aspect of the design, according to the students, is the **(64)** .... tape running down the boys' shirts and across the left pocket of the girls'. The **(65)** .... tape is decorated with Paul Smith's characteristic stripes in the school's colours.

0 DESIGN	**59** SUCCESS	**63** GOOD
56 FAME	**60** TRADITION	**64** PATTERN
57 FASHION	**61** ELEGANT	**65** TREND
58 SECOND	**62** ATTRACTIVE	

Communication tasks and answers

Extracts from LONGMAN *Active Study* DICTIONARY

have ²*v* [T not in passive] **had, had, having**
1 also **have got** used to say what someone or something looks like, or what features they possess: *He's got brown eyes and dark hair.* | *Japan has a population of over 120 million.* **2** also **have got** to own something, or be able to use something: *Kurt had a nice bike, but it got stolen.* | *Does she have a CD player?* | **have the money/time etc** (= have enough money, time etc): *I'd like to help, but I don't have the time.* **3** to eat, drink, or smoke something: *Let's go and have a beer.* | *We're having steak tonight.* | **have lunch/breakfast/dinner etc** *What time do you usually have lunch?* **4** to experience or do something: **have problems/trouble etc** *I'm having problem using this fax machine.* | **have fun** *The kids had great fun at the theme park.* | **have a meeting/party** *Let's have a party!* | **have a holiday/bath/wash etc** *I'll just have a quick wash before we leave.* **5** *BrE* also **have got** to receive something such as a letter, information, or advice: *Have you had any news from Michael?*

trav·el ¹ / ˈtrævəl / *v* **–lled, -lling** *BrE*, **-led, -ling** *AmE* **1** [I, T] to make a journey from one place to another: *Jack spent the summer travelling around Europe.* | *I usually travel to work by car.* | *They travelled over 400 miles on the first day.* **2** [I] to move from one place or person to another: *News travels fast in a small town like this.*
travel² *n* [U] the activity of travelling: *Heavy rain is making road travel difficult.*

> **USAGE NOTE: travel, travels, journey, voyage, and trip**
>
> **Travel** is the general activity of moving from place to place: *He returned after years of foreign travel.* Use **travels** when someone goes to different places over a period of time; *Did you go to LA during your travels around the US?* Use **journey** especially to talk about the time spent or distance travelled going from one place to another: *a 60-hour journey by train.* A **voyage** is a journey by sea: *the voyage from England to Australia.* A **trip** is used especially about a short journey, or when you spend only a short time in another place: *a week-long trip to Barcelona* | *I hope you enjoy your trip.*

o·be·di·ence / əˈbiːdiəns / *n* [U] when someone does what a person, law, or rule tells them to do: **+ to** *obedience to her father's wishes*
o·be·di·ent / əˈbiːdiənt / *adj* someone who is obedient does what a person, law, or rule tells them to do: *a quiet and obedient child* - **obediently** *adv* ►opposite DISOBEDIENT

o·bey / əʊˈbeɪ, ə-ǁoʊ-, ə- / *v* [I,T] to do what a person, law, or rule tells you to do: *Most dogs will obey simple commands* ►opposite DISOBEY

go into sth *phr v* [T] **1** to start working in a particular profession: *Vivian wants to go into teaching.* **2** to describe or explain something thoroughly: *I don't want to go into details right now, but it was horrible.*
go off *phr v* **1** [I] to explode: *The bomb went off without warning.* **2** [I] to make a loud noise: *My alarm clock didn't go off!* **3 go off well/badly etc** to happen in a particular way: *The ceremony went off perfectly* **4** *BrE* [I] if food goes off, it goes bad **5** [I] *BrE informal* to stop liking someone or something: *I've gone off coffee.*
go off with sth *phr v* [T] to take away something that belongs to someone else: *She's gone off with my pen.*
go on *phr v* [I] **1** to continue without stopping or changing: *We can't go on fighting like this!* | *The meeting went on longer than I expected.* **2** to happen: *What's going on down there?* **3** to do something new when you have finished something else: *Shall we go on to the next item on the agenda?* **4** to continue speaking, after you have stopped for a while: **+ with** *After a short pause, Maria went on with her story.* **5** if time goes on, it passes: *As time went on, he became more friendly.* **6** *spoken* used to encourage someone to do something: *Go on, have some more cake.*
go out *phr v* [I] **1** to leave your house, especially in order to do something you enjoy: *Are you going out tonight?* | **go out for dinner/lunch etc** *We went out for brunch on Sunday.* **2** to have a romantic relationship with someone: *How long have you two been going out?* | **go out with sb** *Lisa used to go out with my brother.*

in ¹ / ɪn / *prep* **1** used with the name of a container, place, or area to show where something is: *The paper is in the top drawer.* | *He lived in Spain for 15 years.* | *We swam in the sea.* ► see colour picture on page 474 **2** used with the names of months, years, seasons etc to say when something happened: *I was born in May 1969.* | *In the winter, we use a wood stove.* **3** during or at the end of a period of time: *We finished the whole project in a week.* | *Gerry should be home in an hour.* **4** included as part of something: *One of the people in the story is a young doctor.* | *In the first part of the speech, he talked about the environment.* **5** used to describe the condition or attitude of something or someone: *The company was in trouble.* | *She looked up in surprise.* **6** wearing something: *men in grey suits* **7** using a particular way of speaking or writing: *"I'm afraid," said Violet in a quiet voice.* | *I wrote to him in Italian.* **8** involved with a particular kind of job: *She's in advertising.* | *new developments in medicine* **9** arranged in a particular way: *We stood in a line.* | *Put the words in alphabetical order* **10 in all** used to say what the total amount of something is: *There were 25 of us in all.*

Unit 7, Speaking Exercise 2, page 57

QUIZ INTERPRETATIONS

Mainly 'A' answers

You are generally a calm person. You get excited when your favourite band is in town, or when you are going out dancing with your friends. You hate it when the summer is over. People tend to think you are reliable and trustworthy. You like art.

Mainly 'B' answers

You are a passionate person. For you, life is a roller coaster, full of ups and downs. You have had to deal with some difficult situations and relationships. But you are finding ways to make the good times better. You love sports and taking chances.

Mainly 'C' answers

You care a great deal about your image. People's opinions are very important to you. You like art, and some poetry. You can throw a party, or help a friend to organise one. Most people like you, and respect your opinions. Your friends mean everything to you.

Mainly 'D' answers

You are an individualist. You believe in doing things your way. You like to be different from other people, and you don't follow fashions or trends. You are an active person and prefer going out to staying at home and watching television.

Unit 15, Reading Exercise 5, page 127

Here's what colour experts say about your choices and your personality:

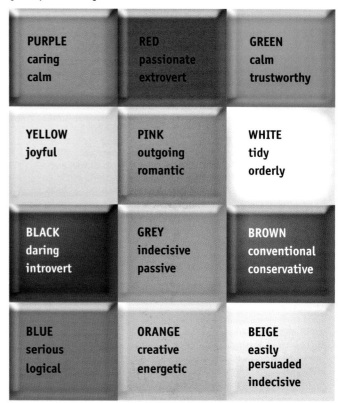

PURPLE caring calm	RED passionate extrovert	GREEN calm trustworthy
YELLOW joyful	PINK outgoing romantic	WHITE tidy orderly
BLACK daring introvert	GREY indecisive passive	BROWN conventional conservative
BLUE serious logical	ORANGE creative energetic	BEIGE easily persuaded indecisive

Unit 12, Listening Exercise 4, page 104

And who knows what new technological wizardries are waiting just around the corner to astonish us?

… some really important inventions began to change the everyday lives of ordinary people. They included new forms of transport and entertainment, as well as new machines and gadgets for use in the home.

Then an American called Henry Ford began to mass-produce cars in his factory in the USA.

In a huge country like the USA, cars made a real difference because, unlike the horses and carts which they replaced, they didn't get tired and they didn't need feeding when you weren't using them!

The first movie with sound, a musical called 'The Jazz Singer' was produced in 1922 – and it revolutionised the industry.

Unit 16, Speaking Exercise 2, page 133

QUIZ INTERPRETATIONS

 If you ticked mainly red buttons …

Oh, dear! You're not a Super Saver at all – yet! Just stop to think how much pollution you're creating to supply your energy needs. Start NOW! Help stop dangerous climate change.

If you ticked mainly yellow buttons …

Hmmm, you know all about the problems of wasting energy, but there's still room for improvement. With just a little more effort, you could really be a Super Saver and help cut pollution. Together we can make a difference.

 If you ticked mainly green buttons …

You are a dedicated Super Saver, that's for sure! You're keen to save energy at every opportunity. Keep up the good work, and tell your friends about what you do!

Grammar file

File 1: Articles (a/the/zero)

1 Indefinite article: *a/an* + singular, countable nouns

- speaking in general
*I want **a** pizza.*

- first mention of someone/something
*I've got **a** new bike!*

- jobs
*She's **a** model. He's **an** actor.*

! ~~I am student.~~ > I am a student.

2 Definite article: *the*

- only one of something
The sun is shining.

- somebody/something mentioned before
*The magician showed us a card. Then he hid **the** card.*

- names of cinemas, theatres, etc.
The National Theatre, **The** Times

- rivers, oceans, deserts, etc.
The Mediterranean, **The** Sahara, **The** Himalayas

- areas
the north/**the** west

- some countries and nationalities
the USA, **the** British

- musical instruments
*I can play **the** guitar.*

3 No article

- plural, countable nouns
I love rock bands.

- uncountable nouns in a general sense
I hate homework.

- most streets, roads, cities, etc.
Smith Street, Athens, America

- institutions, e.g. school, university, college, hospital, etc.
I go to school every day. My sister's ill in hospital.

- certain expressions
*My Dad's **at work/home**.*
*Paul's not **in class**. He's ill **in bed**.*
*Do you want to **go home** now?*
*We went **by car/bus/plane/boat**, etc.*
*We went home **on foot**.*
*What's **for dinner/breakfast/lunch**?*

! Use the article when referring to an actual building:
I went to the hospital to see a patient.

File 2: Countable/uncountable nouns and determiners

1 Countable nouns

- can be singular or plural
one student/two students
one child/four children

2 Uncountable nouns

- no plural form

- common uncountable nouns:
accommodation, advice, equipment, experience, furniture, health, homework, information, knowledge, luck, luggage, money, music, news, progress, rubbish, traffic, travel, trouble, weather, work

! Never use *a/an* with uncountable nouns:
*I need ~~an~~ **some** advice, please.*

3 Countable or uncountable

Some nouns can be countable or uncountable, depending on the meaning.

Countable	Uncountable
That was **a** really frightening **experience**!	I'd like a holiday job but I haven't got **much experience**.
We sang the song **three times**.	We haven't got **much time** left.
She found **a hair** in her drink.	My grandad hasn't got **much hair** left.
I'd like **two glasses** of lemonade.	The door was made of **glass**.
I need **an iron** to press my jeans.	**Iron** and steel are metals.
They heard **a noise** outside.	Don't make so **much noise**!
I bought **a paper** to read the news.	I need **some writing paper**.
There's **a space** on the form where you can write your name.	There isn't **much space** in my flat.
There are **six rooms** in our flat.	There isn't **much room** on the coach for luggage.
There's **a wood** with tall trees behind our house.	The fence is made of **wood**.

4 Quantifiers

• **some** + countable/uncountable nouns for positive statements
*There were **some people** in the room.*

• **any** + countable/uncountable nouns for negatives/questions
*He didn't buy **any CDs**.*
*Have you got **any cheese**?*

• **lots/a lot of** with plural countable and uncountable nouns
*They bought **lots of** souvenirs.*
*I've got **lots of** news to tell you.*

• **much** + uncountable nouns for negatives/questions
*He doesn't earn **much money**.*
*How **much time** is there?*

• **many** + countable nouns for negatives/questions
*There aren't **many posters** on the walls.*
*Has he got **many girlfriends**?*

• **a few/few** + plural, countable nouns
*There were **a few people** on the beach. (=some)*
***Few tourists** come to this area. (= hardly any)*

• **a little/little** + uncountable nouns
*We've got **a little time** to spare. (= some)*
*There's **very little butter** left. (= hardly any)*

• **all (of)/none (of)/no** + countable/uncountable nouns
***All passengers** must go to the check-in desk.*
***No passengers** can travel without tickets.*
***All of/None of the children** went on the trip.*

• **each (of)/every** + countable nouns
*I gave **each of my friends** a present.*
*We go to school **every day**.*

File 3: Adjectives and adverbs

1 Comparative and superlative: adjectives

• add **-er/-est** to most one-syllable adjectives
*Your flat is **larger/bigger** than mine.*
*Elvis was the **greatest**!*
*Anna's **the laziest** girl in the class.*

• add **more** and **the most** to adjectives of two or more syllables
*A computer is **more expensive than** a video.*
*London is **the most exciting** city I've ever been to.*

> **!** Some two-syllable adjectives, such as *clever, narrow, gentle, tired, pleasant* can form the comparative and superlative in both ways:
>
> *gentle – gentler – the gentlest*
> **or** *gentle – more gentle – the most gentle*

Irregular adjectives

good	better than	the best
bad	worse than	the worst
far	farther/further	the farthest/furthest

Irregular quantifiers

little	less	least
much/many	more	most
few	fewer/less	fewest/least

2 Comparative and superlative: adverbs

• with regular adverbs, use **more** and **the most**
quickly – more quickly – the most quickly
slowly – more slowly – the most slowly
*You'll get to the USA **more quickly** if you fly.*

• add **-er/-est** to most one-syllable adverbs that have the same form as adjectives
hard – harder – the hardest
fast – faster – the fastest
loud – louder – the loudest
late – later – the latest

Irregular adverbs

well	better	(the) best
badly	worse	(the) worst
little	less	(the) least
much	more	(the) most

3 (not) as ... as

• to compare similar things
*I am/am not **as tall as** my brother.*

4 less and the least

• to make negative comparisons
*My bike cost **less than** my friend's.*
*Sue's bike cost **the least**.*

5 the + comparative ... the + comparative

• for linking two actions
***The sooner** we go, **the better**.*
***The harder** you work, **the more** you will earn.*

6 Position of adverbs
Adverbs of frequency

least often ⟶ most often
never, rarely, hardly ever, occasionally, sometimes, often, usually, always

• after auxiliary/modal verbs
*I **have never** been to China.*

• before the main verb
*I **often meet** my friends after school.*

Adverbs of certainty

probably, certainly, definitely, etc.

• <u>after</u> auxiliary/modal verbs, <u>before</u> the main verb in positive sentences
*Alice **is probably** at the beach.*
*I'll **probably** go to the cinema tonight.*

• <u>before</u> auxiliary/ modal verbs in negative sentences
*I **probably won't** be in school tomorrow.*

Adverbs of manner, adverbs/adverbial phrases of time

• at the end of a sentence
*He sings very **well**.*
*We arrived late **yesterday**.*
*I play tennis **once a week, on Saturday mornings**.*

7 Intensifiers

• to qualify comparatives
*My sister is **a bit/a lot** older than me.*
*A computer is **far/a great deal** more expensive than a video.*

8 Gradable/ungradable adjectives and adverbs

• with gradable adjectives such as *good, bad, short, funny, sorry:*
rather, quite, fairly, very, extremely, really, terribly
*The film was **extremely good**.*

• with ungradable adjectives such as *fabulous, wonderful, incredible, stunning:*
quite, absolutely, totally
*The holiday was **absolutely** (NOT ~~extremely~~) **fabulous**.*

File 4: Present Tenses

1 Present simple

• regular actions and routines especially with frequency adverbs
***Do you go** to school by car **every day**?*
*I **don't often** watch TV.*

• permanent situations
*Pierre **comes** from France.*

• general truths
*Snow **melts** in the sun.*

• time clauses with a future meaning, after: *when, after, as soon as, until*
*I'll ring you **when** I **get** home.*

• fixed timetables
*Our plane **goes** at midday.*

• 'state' verbs which are not usually used in the continuous
*I **love** rock music!*
*I **don't understand** what he's saying.*

State verbs

be, have
feel, hear, see, taste, smell, sound
like, dislike, love, hate
know, realise, understand, think, imagine, recognise, remember
appear, look, seem
need, want, wish, prefer
agree, disagree, believe, doubt, suppose, deny impress,
    mean, promise
belong to, own

> **!** Some state verbs can be used in the continuous but with a change of meaning.

*You **look** happy!* (= appearance)	*I'm **looking** at you!* (= action)
*My girlfriend **has** blue eyes.* (= possession)	*We're **having** a party.* (= giving/organising)

Similar verbs: *appear, be, feel, forget, remember, see, smell, taste, think, try, weigh*

2 Present continuous: *be + verb + -ing*

• actions happening now
*Look! It's **snowing**!*

• actions happening around the time of speaking
*The world's climate **is changing**.*

• temporary situations
*My uncle's **visiting** the USA but he'll be back tomorrow.*

• plans and arrangements in the future
*I'm **meeting** Jane tonight.*

• with *always*, to describe annoying or surprising habits
*You're **always losing** things!*

3 *keep + -ing*

• to describe habitual actions which may be irritating
*My uncle **keeps making** silly jokes.*

File 5: Present perfect

1 Present perfect simple: *have/has + past participle*

• events that began in the past and are still continuing
*I've **been** here for ten minutes.*

• events that started in a time period that is not finished
*The phone **has rung** ten times today.*

• past actions/situations that have a connection to the present
*Look at this cheque. I've **won** first prize!*

• past actions, when the time is not known
*They've **made** a new Star Wars film.*

• with *just*, for actions that happened very recently
*I've **just got** home.*

• with time expressions like *How long ...?*, *for* and *since*
How long have you **been** here?

• with time expressions that mean 'up to the present time', e.g. *ever, never, already, yet, recently, so far*
Have you **ever been** to Paris?

• after superlatives
It's the **best** book I**'ve ever read**.

• after phrases like *It's the first/last time ...*
It's **the first time** I**'ve ever been** abroad.

2 Present perfect continuous: *have/has + been + -ing*

• actions that started in the past and are still continuing
I**'ve been living** in this flat since 2000.

• to emphasise how long something has been going on
I**'ve been waiting** for ages!

• recent continuous activities, when we can see the result
I'm hot! I**'ve been running**.

File 6: Past tenses

1 Past simple

• events that happened at a definite past time or are clearly finished
I **saw** John last week.
Agatha Christie **wrote** detective stories.

• a sequence of completed past events
I **got up, had** breakfast and **went** to school.

2 Past continuous: *was/were + -ing*

• interrupted actions
I **was (still) having** dinner when my friend called.

• two actions that were happening at the same time in the past
I **was reading** a book while my brother **was playing** his guitar.

3 Past perfect: *had + past participle/had + been + -ing*

• for events that finished <u>before</u> other past events or times
My brothers **had (already) gone** to bed by the time I got home.
By midnight, all the guests **had left**.

• the past perfect continuous focuses on the duration of an action
We were tired because we **had been playing** volleyball all morning.

File 7: *used to/would*

1 *used to/would*

• past actions and habits
I **used to** bite my nails but I've stopped now.
Did you ~~used to~~ use to suck your thumb when you were a baby?
My brother and I **would often play** in the woods when we were kids.

! Use *would* to describe past actions but not past states.
My best friend ~~would be~~ used to be very thin, but he's not now.
Would is not as common as *used to*. Do not use *would* in questions or negatives.

2 *used to*

• actions that didn't happen in the past but do now
I **didn't** ~~used to~~ use to play football, but I do now.
We **didn't** ~~used to~~ use to have mobile phones but we do now.

! *Used to* is only used in the past.
In questions and negatives, the *-d* is dropped:
I didn't use to .../Did you use to ...?

File 8: Future tenses

1 Future simple: *will/shall + infinitive*

• future facts and predictions with no present evidence
People **will live** on the moon one day.

• decisions made at the time of speaking
Are you having a party? I**'ll come**!

• offers, promises, threats, hopes, fears, requests, warnings
I**'ll ring** you tonight if you want.
I**'ll be** really angry if you're late again!

! Put *probably* after *will* but before *won't*.
It **will probably** rain tomorrow.
I **probably won't** see him tomorrow.

! *Shall* is usually only used in offers or suggestions.
Shall I get lunch?
It can be used instead of *will* in first person sentences, but is much less common.
I **shall** be here at 8 o'clock.

2 *Going to* + infinitive

• plans and intentions and things that are already decided
*I've decided what to get Tom for his birthday. **I'm going to buy** him a CD.*

• predictions with present evidence
*Listen to the thunder! There's **going to be** a storm.*

3 Present continuous

• definite future arrangements
*I ~~will meet~~ **am meeting** my girlfriend tonight.* (= it's all arranged).

4 Present simple

• timetables and scheduled events
*The bus **leaves** at 8 a.m.*

• after *as soon as, before, until, when, while*
*I'll meet you **as soon as** the class **finishes**.*

5 Future continuous: *will/may/might* + *be* + *-ing*

• actions in progress at a future time
*I'll **be lying** on a beach this time tomorrow.*

• predicted trends
*In 50 years' time, people **will be living** on the moon.*

6 Future perfect: *will/may/might* + *have* + past participle / *will/may/might* + *have been* + *-ing*

• actions completed before a time in the future
*I **will have finished** my homework by 6 o'clock.*

• the continuous focuses on the duration of the action
*By the time our plane arrives, we **will have been waiting** for exactly five hours!*

> ! Use present simple, not *will*, to refer to the future after time indicators like *when, before, after*.
>
> *I'll get a job when I **leave** school.*

File 9: -ing forms and infinitives

1 *-ing* forms

• after certain verbs
*I **enjoy** going on holiday.*
Similar verbs: *admit, avoid, can't help, consider, delay, deny, (dis)like, enjoy, fancy, finish, hate, involve, keep* (= continue), *mind, miss, risk, suggest*

• after all prepositions and phrasal verbs
*You can't learn the guitar **without practising** every day.*
*I'm good **at cooking**.*
*I've **given up** ~~to do~~ doing judo.*

2 Infinitives

verb + *to* + infinitive

• after certain verbs and phrases
*I **want to** study medicine.*
*We're **hoping to go** to Canada next year.*
Similar verbs: *afford, agree, arrange, begin, decide, expect, forget*, hope, intend, learn, manage, offer, need, plan, pretend, promise, propose, refuse, regret*, remember*, refuse, seem, start, threaten, try*, want, would like/love, would prefer.*
*forget, regret, remember and *try* can also be followed by an -*ing* form, but with a change in meaning. See section 3.

verb + object + *to* + infinitive

• after certain verbs
*My friend **asked me to go** on holiday with her.*
*I **persuaded Dad to buy** me some new trainers.*
Similar verbs: *allow, ask, command, encourage, expect, forbid, force, get, hate, help, invite, order, permit, persuade, prefer, remind, teach, tell, want, warn, would like*

3 *-ing* form or infinitive

• after verbs like *start, begin, continue* (no change in meaning)
*I started **to learn/learning** the piano five years ago.*

• after verbs like *like, love, hate, prefer* (small change in meaning)
*I love **swimming**.* (in general)
*I like **to swim** every day when I'm on holiday.* (specific situation)

• after verbs like *forget, go on, mean, regret, remember, stop* and *try* (complete change in meaning)
Compare:

1 *I'll never **forget meeting** Leonardo DiCaprio!* (I'll always remember it.)

2 *I **forgot to post** Mum's card!* (I should have done it but I haven't.)

1 *Do you **remember learning** to read?* (Can you remember that past time?)

2 *I must **remember to buy** my grandmother a present.* (I mustn't forget to do it.)

1 *I must **stop biting** my nails.* (give up)

2 *We **stopped to have** a coffee on the way home.* (stopped one thing in order to do another)

1 *If you can't find the information in a book, **try looking** on the Internet.* (I advise this.)

2 *I **tried to** repair my bike but I couldn't.* (I attempted it and failed.)

1 *I didn't **mean to break** the window.* (that wasn't my intention)

2 *Learning a language well **means** studying hard.* (involves)

1 *I **regret to inform** you that you've failed the test.* (I'm sorry to tell you this.)

2 *My sister **regrets leaving** school.* (She's sorry she did it.)

File 10: Other uses of *-ing* forms and infinitives

1 *-ing* forms

• after certain expressions
It's **not worth buying** that CD – it's useless!
I **can't stand watching** football on TV.

Similar phrases: *There's no point ...,*
It's useless/hopeless/pointless ..., It's a waste of time ...,
I can't bear ..., I'm fed up with ..., It's no use ...

• as the subject or the object/complement of a sentence
I love **swimming**.
Dancing is my favourite hobby.

• as the second part of a compound adjective
He's very **good-looking**.
She was wearing a **tight-fitting** sweater.

• to talk about the effect someone or something has on us or our feelings
It was a very ~~excited~~ **exciting** film.
The film was rather ~~bored~~ **boring**.

2 Infinitive

• with *to*, after certain adjectives
The homework was **easy to do**.
I was **happy to do** it.

Similar adjectives: *amazed, certain, difficult, disappointed, free, glad, hard, likely, pleased, possible, simple, sure, surprised*

• with *to*, after certain nouns
It was a real **surprise to hear** we'd won the prize.

• without *to*, in certain phrases
I **would rather go** to a disco than stay at home.

File 11: Conditionals

1 Zero conditional: *If* + present + present simple/present continuous/modal/imperative

• general truths, instructions
If you **heat** ice, it **melts**.
If it's **raining**, **take** an umbrella.
If he **looks** embarrassed, he **may be** lying.

2 First conditional: *If/Unless* + present simple + will/may/might/can

• things that are really likely to happen in the present/future
If I ~~will win~~ **win** the lottery, I**'ll buy** a yacht.
We'll miss the plane **unless the taxi** ~~will get~~ **gets** here soon.

• promises and threats
I**'ll buy** you a present **if you lend** me your guitar.

3 Second conditional: *If* + past simple + would/could/may/might

• unreal/hypothetical situations in the present/future
What **would** you do if you **were** a millionaire?
If I **had** my own bedroom, I **could** decorate it myself.

• advice
If I were you, I**'d go** home now.

> **!** Conditional sentences can be written in two ways with no change in meaning:
>
> 1 with the *if* clause at the beginning of the sentence
> **If you lend me some money,** I'll buy you a present.
>
> 2 with the *if* clause at the end of the sentence
> I'll buy you a present **if you lend me some money.**
>
> Note that the *if* clause is followed by a comma only when it comes at the start of a sentence.

4 Third conditional: *if* + past perfect + would/could/may/might have + past participle

• speculating about situations in the past which didn't actually happen
We **would have finished** the tennis match **if it hadn't rained**.
If you'd bought a ticket, you **might have won** a prize.

• something that was a possibility in the past but didn't happen
You **could have broken** your arm if you'd fallen out of the tree.

File 12: Wishes

1 *wish* + past simple/past continuous/*could*

• to express regrets about a present situation which we can't change
My sister wishes she **were** prettier.

• use *if only* to make a wish stronger
If only my dad **didn't snore**!

> **!** You can't say *I wish I/we would.*
> *I wish I* ~~would be lying~~ **were lying** on the beach now!

2 *wish/if only* + *would*

• when you want something to happen in the future but it is outside your control
I wish my parents **would buy** me a Mercedes!

• complaints
If only my brother **would stop** ordering me around!

3 wish/hope

• use *wish* when you imagine situations are different from reality
*I **wish** it would stop raining.*

• use *hope*, not *wish*, for things that are likely to happen in reality
*I **hope** it stops raining soon.*

4 wish + past perfect

• regrets about the past
*I wish I **hadn't eaten** so much last night!*

File 13: Reported speech

Reporting statements

• after reporting verbs in the present, there is no change
He says he loves her.

• After reporting verbs in the past, tenses go one step back in time. Pronouns and place/time words may also need to change.
He said he loved her.

Original statement	Reported statement
*'It's snowing in **my** country.'*	*He said **it was snowing** in his country.*
'I was dreaming,' he told me.	*He told me that **he had been dreaming**.*
'You've won first prize,' the man announced.	*The man announced that **they had won** first prize.*
'I've been watching TV,' he explained.	*He explained that **he had been watching** TV.*
'I'll buy you a present,' Dad promised.	*Dad promised that **he would buy me** a present.*

• modals *would, could, might, ought to* or *should* do not change in reported speech
*'I **might** be late.'*   *She said she **might** be late.*

• *must* changes to *had to*
*'I **must** go.'*   *She said she **had to** go.*

> ! Use *tell* not *say* before an object pronoun.
> *He **said (that)** he was lost.*
> *He ~~said me~~ **told me** that he was lost.*

• Changes in time/place indicators

Original statement	Reported statement
here	there
now	then
this/that/these/those	the
today	that day
tomorrow	the next day/the following day
yesterday	the day before/the previous day
last week	the week before
next week	the following week
ago	before

File 14: Indirect questions

1 Reporting questions

• Make the same changes as reported statements. Change the word order so that the question becomes the same as a statement.

Original question	Reported question
'Are you okay?'	*My friend asked me ~~was I okay~~ **if I was okay**.*
'Where do you live?'	*He wanted to know where ~~did I live~~ **I lived**.*

• *if* or *whether* for *yes/no* questions
'Are you a student?'   *He asked me **if/whether I was** a student.*

> ! Remember not to use a question mark for a reported question.

2 Reporting polite requests, advice or warnings: ask/tell/advise/warn + object + infinitive

'Listen, please!'   *The teacher **asked/told us to listen**.*

'Be careful!'   *He **advised/warned us to be** careful.*

3 Indirect questions

• with polite introductory phrases such as *I wonder if you could tell me ...?, I'd like to know..., Could you tell me ...?*
'Where's the box office?'   *'Could you tell me ~~where is the box office~~ where the box office is?'*

• asking for instructions: *Could you tell me where/how/when + to + infinitive*
***Could you tell me how to get** to the post office?*

File 15: Structures after reporting verbs

1 verb + *that* clause

The boys **admitted that** they had lost the money.

Similar verbs: *complain, explain, promise, realise, remember, reply, say, think*

> ! After most verbs you can drop *that*.
> They admitted (that) they had lost it.
> You cannot drop *that* after *reply*.
> He replied that he had lost it.

2 verb + object + *that* clause

The guide **warned us that** the castle was haunted.

Similar verbs: *tell, remind*

3 verb + *that* + should

Mum **suggested that I (should)** go to the cinema.

Similar verbs: *agree, demand, insist, recommend*

4 verb + *to* + infinitive

I **promised to wash up**.

Similar verbs: *agree, decide, offer, refuse, threaten*

> ! Some verbs can be followed by *to* + infinitive or a
> *that* clause. When there is a change of subject, you
> must use a *that* clause.
> 'We'll go with you!'   My friends **agreed to go** with me.
> 'You can go with us!'   My friends agreed ~~me to go with them~~ **that I should go** with them.

5 verb + object + *to* + infinitive

Dad **encouraged my brother to go** abroad.

Similar verbs: *advise, ask, beg, encourage, invite, order, persuade, tell, remind, warn*

6 verb + *-ing*

I **suggested going** to the disco.

Similar verbs: *admit, deny, recommend, suggest*

> ! Some verbs can be followed by an *-ing* form or a *that*
> clause. When there is a change of subject, you must
> use a *that* clause.
> 'Let's go to the cinema!'   Dad **suggested going** to the cinema.
> 'Why don't you go to the cinema?'   Dad **suggested that I go** to the cinema.

7 verb + preposition + *-ing*

My uncle **insists on visiting** us very late in the evening.

Similar verbs: *accuse sb (of), apologise (for), blame sb (for), congratulate sb (on), discourage sb (from)*

File 16: The passive

1 Use

• with most transitive verbs (verb + object), when the action is more important than the agent
That new car **was designed** in the UK.

• when the agent (the person or thing who did the action) is unknown
~~Someone invented television~~ Television **was invented** in the last century.

2 Form

Tense	Subject	to be/ modal + be	Past participle
present simple	Dollars	are	accepted (here).
present continuous	A new road	is being	built.
past simple	The President	was	assassinated.
present perfect	The manager	has been	dismissed.
past continuous	The car	was being	followed.
past perfect	The party	had been	cancelled.
future	The winner	will be	given a cheque.
	Her story	is going to be	published.
modals	Tickets	must/can/ should be	ordered (in advance.)

• only include the agent (*by* ...) when that information is important
The film was directed **by Steven Spielberg**.
Do not use the words *by someone/something*.

> ! When we have two possible subjects for a passive
> verb, a person and a thing, the person becomes the
> subject of the passive sentence.
> I was given a prize. ✓
> A prize was given to me. ✗

3 *let/make* + object + bare infinitive

My brother wouldn't **let me borrow** his guitar.
Dad **made me clean** the car yesterday.

> ! We use *to* after *make* in the passive.
> My friend **was made to pay** for the window he broke.

4 Impersonal statements

Use

When we do not know if information is true or do not want to state where the information came from.

Present situations

• *said/believed/known/thought + that clause OR + to + infinitive*
It is said that Italians are very passionate.
Italians are said to be very passionate.

Past situations

• *said/believed/known/thought + that clause OR + to + past infinitive (have + past participle)*
It is believed that the ship sank.
The ship is believed to have sunk.

File 17: The causative

• activities we arrange for other people to do for us
I had my hair coloured.
Dad's going to have his car serviced.
I get my hair cut at Tony's salon.

! Get is more common in the imperative form.
Get your hair cut!

File 18: Modal verbs 1

1 Ability

• *can* for present/future ability
Can you swim?

• *could/was able to* for past ability
I could play the guitar when I was five years old.

2 Permission

• *can* and *may* for requesting permission
May I go out tonight?

• *can't, may not, not allowed to* for lack of permission
I can't/I'm not allowed to drive a car. I'm only 14.

! May is very formal. In questions, it is polite and is used quite frequently.
May I help you?
In negatives, *may not* is rarely used as it sounds very formal.

3 Advice/criticism

• **should, ought to** for advice
You should/ought to see a doctor.

• **shouldn't/oughtn't to** for criticism of a past action
You shouldn't have done that

! Should and ought to have the same meaning, but should is used more frequently.

4 Obligation

• *must* for strong obligation or necessity imposed by the speaker
Policeman: *You must come to the police station.*

• *mustn't* for strong prohibition imposed by the speaker
You mustn't drink and drive.

• *have to, have got to, need to* for reporting/asking about rules/regulations/obligations
Do we need to/have to get visas to go to the USA?

• *had to* for past obligation
I had to tidy my room yesterday.

5 Lack of obligation

• *don't have to, don't need to* and *needn't* for lack of obligation in the present/future
We don't have to be home until midnight!

• *didn't need to* for actions that were not necessary
We didn't need to wait for the plane as it took off immediately.

• *needn't have* + past participle for actions which were done unnecessarily
You needn't have worried. I was quite safe.

File 19: Modal verbs 2

1 Possibility

• *may/could/might* + bare infinitive for something that is possibly true but we don't know
Susan's not in. She may/could/might be next door.

• *may have/could have/might have* + past participle for something that has possibly happened
I'm not sure where she is. She may/could/might have gone to the cinema.

• *may/could/might* + be + -ing for something that is possibly happening now
She could be watching a video.

! There is no evidence for any of these assumptions.

2 Deductions

• *must* + bare infinitive for deductions in the present
He must be a doctor. He has a stethoscope!

• *must have* + past participle for deductions in the past
The police arrested the man. He must have committed a crime.

• *must have* + been + -ing for the continuous past
They couldn't find him. He must have been hiding.

! There is usually some evidence for these deductions, e.g. the doctor's stethoscope.

• **can't + bare infinitive** for assumptions in the present
*She **can't** be a nurse. She isn't wearing a uniform.*

• **can't have/couldn't have + past participle** for things we are sure did not happen
*He **can't have passed** his driving test. He looks upset.*

• **can't have/couldn't have + been + -ing** for the continuous past
*He crashed. He **can't have been driving** carefully.*

File 20: Relative clauses

1 Defining clauses

• are essential to the sentence; cannot be omitted; have no commas
*I know the man **who starred in that film**!*
*That's the seat **where I left my wallet**.*

• relative pronouns can be omitted if they are the object of the verb
*The girl **(who) I met yesterday** was really nice.*
*The film **(which) we saw** was very exciting.*

• prepositions normally go at the end of the relative clause
*The boy **(who) I spoke to** was English.*

Relative pronouns

who	people
which	things
that	people/things
whose	possession
when	time
where	place
why	reason

2 Non-defining clauses

• give extra information that can be omitted; the information goes between commas.
*Martha, **who is Spanish**, is coming to stay in our house.*

• can refer to the whole previous clause
*We went to see the latest Star Wars film, **which was fabulous**.*

! In non-defining clauses, the relative pronoun can never be omitted.

File 21: Cause and result clauses

1 *so much/many, so little/few (that)*

• **so many, so few (that)** with countable nouns
*I've got **so many CD's that** I don't know where to put them!*

• **so much/so little (that)** with uncountable nouns
*We **spent so much time** in the theme park that we missed our coach.*

2 *so/such (that)*

• **so ... (that)** with adjectives and adverbs
*I'm **so glad (that)** I passed my exam!*
*He spoke **so quietly (that)** I couldn't hear him.*

• **such a ...** with singular, countable nouns
*I had **such a fabulous day (that)** I didn't want to go home.*

• **such ... (that)** with plural, countable nouns and with uncountable nouns
*They gave us **such large pizzas (that)** we couldn't finish them!*
*It was **such good news (that)** we couldn't believe it!*

3 *too/enough*

• gives a negative idea – something is not wanted or desired
too + quantifier (+ noun)
*I've eaten **too much (food)**. I feel sick!*

too + adjective/adverb
*My coffee's **too hot**. I can't drink it.*
*He runs **too fast**. I can't keep up.*

enough + noun
*I've had **enough food**.*

adjective/adverb + enough
*It was **cold enough** to snow.*

! *Enough* goes after the adjective/adverb while *too* goes before.

too + adjective/adverb (+ *for* + sb) + infinitive with *to*
• things that are difficult, and therefore impossible to do
*The film was **too scary for my sister** ~~to watch it~~ to watch.*
*We were **too tired to stay** awake.*

! Do not repeat the subject of the verb but remember to include prepositions where necessary.
The sun was too strong to look ~~at it~~ at.

Compare:
1 *The exercise was **too difficult**.* (= I couldn't do it.)
2 *The exercise was **very difficult**.* (= difficult but not impossible)

4 *not + adjective/adverb + enough(+ for + sb) + infinitive with *to**

• when a person or thing is insufficient in some way
*You're **not old enough to drive**. You're only 14.*
Compare:
1 *The sea was **too cold for us to swim in**.*
2 *The sea **wasn't warm enough for us to swim in**.*

File 22: Useful linking words

1 Addition
also, besides, furthermore, in addition, moreover, what's more

2 Listing points in an argument
First (of all), To start with, In the first place, Next, Secondly, Finally, Last but not least, In conclusion, To sum up

3 Time sequencers
at the beginning, at first, as soon as, afterwards, by that time, later, in the end, at last

4 Condition
as long as, if, unless

5 Cause and result
as, because, since, so that, that's why

6 Contrast
although, but, however, in spite of/despite, nevertheless, on the other hand

7 Example/illustration
for example, for instance, such as

File 23: Spelling rules

1 Doubling final consonants
• One-syllable words. If you add an ending to a word that ends in a vowel + consonant, the final consonant is doubled.
shop – shopping
fat – fatter – fattest

• Two syllable words. If you add an ending to a word that ends in a vowel + consonant, and the last syllable is stressed, the final consonant is doubled.
forget – forgetting
permit – permitting

2 Words ending in -e
• silent -e after a consonant is often dropped before a vowel
drive – driving
arrive – arrival

• silent -e is kept before a consonant
announce – announcement

3 Words ending in -y
• after a consonant, -y changes to -ie when you add -s
city – cities
cry – cries

• words ending in a final vowel + -y don't change
journey – journeys
say – says

4 Exceptions
• verbs ending in a vowel + -y form the past participle by changing -y to -i and adding -d, not -ed
say – said
lay – laid

File 24: Punctuation rules

1 Capital letters
• at the beginning of a sentence
• for names of people and places

2 Full stops
• at the end of sentences

3 Commas
• in lists of three or more items
I need paper, a pencil, a pen and a dictionary.

• with adverbial phrases
In the end, he managed to escape.

• after adverbial clauses
If I were you, I'd phone your parents.

• around non-defining relative clauses
My boyfriend, who is very ambitious, has just got a really good job.

4 Quotation marks
• around direct speech
'Help!' he shouted. 'I'm stuck.'

5 Apostrophes
• to indicate possession
Clare's jacket.

• to indicate omission
That's my wallet. (= That is)

> **!** When *its* is a possessive pronoun, we do not use an apostrophe.
> *The dog wagged ~~it's~~ its tail.*

Vocabulary file

1 Adjectives from verbs and nouns

We add these suffixes to verbs and nouns to form adjectives. Notice any spelling changes.

-able	-al	-ant	-ful	-ible	-ive	-ous
-(t)ic	-y	-ed	-ing			

-able afford – affordable, believe – believable, depend – dependable, drink – drinkable, enjoy – enjoyable

-al critic – critical, culture – cultural, environment – environmental, fiction – fictional, influence – influential, inspiration – inspirational, intellect – intellectual, music – musical, nation – national, practice – practical, profession – professional

-ant please – pleasant

-ful care – careful, cheer – cheerful, harm – harmful, hope – hopeful, success – successful, thought – thoughtful

-ible collapse – collapsible, horror – horrible, sense – sensible

-ive action – active, destruction – destructive, imagination – imaginative, sense – sensitive

-ous ambition – ambitious, courage – courageous, danger – dangerous, fame – famous, glamour – glamorous

-(t)ic artist – artistic, energy – energetic, optimism – optimistic, romance – romantic

-y fun – funny, mood – moody, scare – scary

-ed amuse – amused, amaze – amazed, annoy – annoyed, bore – bored, frighten – frightened, interest – interested, tire – tired

-ing amuse – amusing, amaze – amazing, annoy – annoying, bore – boring, entertain – entertaining, interest – interesting, frighten – frightening, tire – tiring

2 Nouns from adjectives

We add these suffixes to adjectives to form nouns. Notice any spelling changes.

-(an)ce	-(at)ion	-cy	-(en)ce	-(il)ity
-ness	-th	-ty	-y	

-(an)ce brilliant – brilliance, important – importance, tolerant – tolerance

-(at)ion aggressive – aggression, determined – determination

-cy accurate – accuracy, fluent – fluency, private – privacy

-(en)ce confident – confidence, different – difference, independent – independence, intelligent – intelligence, obedient – obedience, patient – patience, violent – violence

-(il)ity able – ability, creative – creativity, equal – equality, formal – formality, generous – generosity, popular – popularity, possible – possibility, opportune – opportunity, responsible – responsibility

-ness firm – firmness, fit – fitness, happy – happiness, lonely – loneliness, sad – sadness

-th broad – breadth, dead – death, deep – depth, long – length, strong – strength, true – truth, warm – warmth, young – youth

-ty cruel – cruelty, loyal – loyalty, safe – safety

-y brave – bravery, difficult – difficulty, honest – honesty, jealous – jealousy

We can change adjectives into nouns in other ways too.

beautiful – beauty, courageous – courage, dangerous – danger, high – height, hunger – hungry, mysterious – mystery, optimistic – optimism, pleased – pleasure, poor – poverty, proud – pride

3 Nouns from verbs

We add these suffixes to verbs to form nouns. Notice any spelling changes.

-al	-ance	-(a)tion	-ence	-ment	-ness
-nt	-sion	-ty	-ure	-y	

-al arrive – arrival, survive – survival

-ance annoy – annoyance, appear – appearance, disappear – disappearance, perform – performance, tolerate – tolerance

-(at)ion attract – attraction, celebrate – celebration, conserve – conservation, contribute – contribution, determine – determination, discuss – discussion, educate – education, explain – explanation, inspire – inspiration, invent – invention, motivate – motivation, organise – organisation, participate – participation, pollute – pollution

-ence obey – obedience, persist – persistence

-ment amaze – amazement, amuse – amusement, arrange – arrangement, astonish – astonishment, develop – development, disappoint – disappointment, embarrass – embarrassment, encourage – encouragement, entertain – entertainment, improve – improvement, treat – treatment

-ness forgive – forgiveness

-nt participate – participant

-sion decide – decision

-ty save – safety, vary – variety

-ure please – pleasure

-y discover – discovery

We can change verbs into nouns in other ways too.

behave – behaviour, believe – belief, choose – choice, destroy – destruction, die – death, fly – flight, laugh – laughter, live – life, marry – marriage, prove – proof, succeed – success,

4 Verbs from adjectives

We add -en to certain adjectives to form verbs.

-en broad – broaden, deep – deepen, long – lengthen, strong – strengthen, wide – widen

5 Making words negative

We use these prefixes to make words negative.

| dis- | il- | im- | in- | ir- | mis- | un- |

dis- agree – disagree, appear – disappear, approve – disapprove, like – dislike, obedient – disobedient, obey – disobey, organised – disorganised, pleasure – displeasure

il- legal – illegal, legible – illegible, logical – illogical

im- mature – immature, patient – impatient, possible – impossible, practical – impractical

in- dependent – independent, flexible – inflexible, formal – informal, visible – invisible

ir- regular – irregular, responsible – irresponsible

mis- behave – misbehave, behaviour – misbehaviour

un- able – unable, comfortable – uncomfortable, fit – unfit, happy – unhappy, imaginative – unimaginative, lucky – unlucky, reliable – unreliable, usual – unusual

We use the suffix -less to make nouns negative.

-less care – careless, harm – harmless, hope – hopeless, fear – fearless, sense – senseless

6 Compound nouns

We form compound nouns in three different ways. These combinations may be written as one word, two words or with a hyphen.

1 noun + noun

• one word

headphones, screwdriver, songwriter, soundtrack

• two words

CD player, compact disc, concert hall, disc jockey, fridge freezer, jazz band, lead singer, microwave oven, mobile phone, record producer, rock concert, solo artist, song writer, sound track, table tennis, tumble dryer, vacuum cleaner, video recorder

• hyphenated

tin-opener

2 noun + verb -ing

iceskating, sightseeing, scuba diving, weightlifting

3 verb -ing + noun

recording studio, running shoes, shopping centre, swimming pool

7 Compound adjectives

Compound adjectives contain two words, usually joined by a hyphen. The second part is often a present or past participle.

1 past participle (-ed)

bad-tempered, big-headed, grey-haired, left-handed, middle-aged, old-fashioned, short-sighted

2 present participle (-ing)

easy-going, good-looking, hard-working